FAMILY TREES

A Novel of the Northwest

LINDA CREW

For my family
Past and future
And especially for the ones
Here with me now

And for the community
of
Benton County, Oregon
My lifelong home

The best time to plant a tree was twenty years ago.
The second best time is today.

Chinese Proverb

CHAPTER 1

He had to get out of here. Out to the woods. Or at least far enough away from town and the campus to be driving one of the twisty Coast Range roads where he could rest his eyes on a green, sweeping slope of young Doug fir.

He pulled the truck into his own driveway just long enough to check his watch. Three minutes—that's all it took from his son's freshman dorm to the house.

Some launch.

He backed the truck out, cranked the wheel and headed west.

Scary, never knowing what the blindsiding trigger would be. Sheets, for God's sake. The roommate's mom wincing at the heap of fresh-washed ones he and Gar had brought from home and tossed onto the bare mattress. The intimacy of her chiding. Didn't he know they were supposed to buy new, extra long dorm sheets? She seriously doubted these would fit.

Sorry, mouthed the other dad.

But Will didn't mind the guy's wife. He only minded—felt wounded—that it wasn't his *own* wife here to point out how he'd blown it. Suddenly shaky, he'd lowered himself to the edge of the bed, catching Gar's distress from the corner of his eye. Easier, he sometimes thought, if he and Shelley had produced your standard-issue, oblivious teenager for a firstborn. But no, they got Garland

William Trask, a son to watch him with nervous concern, understanding that of course it wasn't about the sheets.

"I'm good, Dad," Gar'd had the presence to say, a clap to Will's shoulder. "You can go."

And unlike the other parents lingering in the hallways, reluctant to leave, Will instantly seized this reprieve, jumped up and beat it the hell out of there, heart pounding.

But then, in the parking lot, he ran into Bridget Garland, delivering her daughter, Gar's cousin Charlotte. Hey, it was *Bridget*, for cryin' out loud, his fellow Garland in-law. No way could he not offer to help. And no, he wasn't going to embarrass her by bringing up the obvious, like why wasn't her useless husband here to do the honors for his only child?

Doubling back into the dorm with these two, it was the strangest thing how, when the elevator doors opened onto the girls' floor, the fruity scents of whatever they were all shampooing into their flowing hair made him feel he'd been exported to some exotic land. Surrounded by twittering young female energy, he became a different guy. Nothing on this wing to be sad about, nobody missing. His brawn was appreciated, and an assigned job calmed his heart-rate. All he had to do was cheerfully muscle up to McNary's fifth floor the appalling amount of stuff Charlotte seemed to think she needed.

Wait. Was he supposed to be getting Gar a mini-fridge?

Boy, had it ever dragged him back, being on the Oregon State campus. To think his boy was now at the very point in his life Will had been when he'd first seen Gar's future mother walking across the quad. From that moment he'd been a goner, searching every crowd for her strawberry blond hair, that shy, flashing smile. He took to placing himself along her usual routes, much like stalking a deer, and if a guy admitted to doing that these days, he *would* get called a stalker, but back then it felt perfectly innocent. Hey, *he* was the victim. Just the sound of her sweet, flutey voice rendered him dumb and helpless.

One day in the Memorial Union he pointed her out to his roommate, who just laughed. "Don't you know that's Shelley Garland? As in Garland Forests? As in, rich daddy?"

"Oh, shit." As in the Garland Grant which was paying Will's full tuition to OSU, thanks to him graduating from Eden Mills High. He knew all about this wealthy family setting up funds to help the children of folks employed in the timber industry. Fine. Real nice of them. But the thought of their opinion on the son of a logger falling for their pretty daughter…whew.

Well, too late. He was like a big old cutthroat trout, already hooked, wildly flipping on the line. Not a damned thing he could do about it.

Heritage Realty occupied a large lot out on the highway where Corvallis ran into Eden Mills, pretty much marking the place where the beginning-to-fade Obama bumper stickers became the half-peeled–off endorsements for McCain.

Today, Will blew right by the office he kept at Heritage and, at the end of the business strip, took the left fork out the Alsea Highway, passing that wedding venue they were now calling Castle Glen, the one he'd sold. How many brides standing there under the trees along Hopestill Creek knew there was a rusting mound of old logging equipment piled up behind the nearby fence?

Into the hills, he floored it. Pathetic, he sometimes thought, how easily he found excuses to hit the road for the solace of Coast Range green. Didn't at least one of his management clients need some forest tract checked? Whenever he drove, he kept an eye on the growth of all the different timber stands, scanning the western sky for incoming weather, the open meadows for wildlife. He could spot a coyote trotting across a grassy stretch while taking a tight curve at forty-five miles an hour. He noted every orange LOG TRUCK warning sign parked along the shoulder. He'd usually have a pretty good guess as to where the loaded trucks were heading, and how much per board foot those mills were currently paying out as well.

Today he made the turnoff for Mary's Peak before the guilt got him and he stopped the truck. Sat there a minute, turned it around. Yeah, he wanted to keep driving forever. Just…away. But, come on, he couldn't avoid his own place indefinitely. He did still have another kid under that roof.

The house seemed even emptier than usual. Funny. It's not like Gar and Cody hung around much these days anyway. He'd been suspecting they had friends with homes more welcoming, mothers around baking cookies or something, although Gar once tried to set him straight on this. "Everything isn't about Mom not being here, Dad. People just like Nick's because the basement has an outside entrance and we don't have to see his parents at all."

Nice. These were the kids who'd clamored for his attention when they were little, boys who loved nothing better than doing a backyard building project with him, or being taken on a fishing trip. Oh, sure, he'd heard the rumors—teenagers don't like to spend time with their parents. But that wasn't supposed to apply to him. Not after what the three of them had been through together since Shelley's death.

He opened a beer and sprawled on the sofa opposite the empty fireplace, the painting hanging over it: *Castle Rock* by Manuel Valencia, 1886.

Four years ago, he'd known nothing about art except that Loren Caldwell, one of his wealthy clients, had, at the urging of his son's gay partner, invested in an abstract painting. When Will came in with an offer on one of his timber tracts, the man hit the ceiling. "A lousy million two?" He thrust a finger at the framed canvas of dribbles over his desk. "That's less than I paid for that damned thing hanging there!" Will wasn't sure what this proved, except that the world of art was a mysterious place, with methods for measuring value nothing like the cut and dried specifications for determining the value of a load of logs at a given point in time.

He stumbled into collecting after the accident. Unable to sleep, he'd sit in the cold glow of the computer screen, aimlessly searching. For what? He didn't know. He looked at real estate listings for timbered acreages. He figured out the program that sent him flying over the rivers and hills, checking out the topography of every wilderness area he'd hiked, every river he'd fished, every ravine he'd inched up, dragging his crossbow. The grids and lines left him feeling hollow, though. Nothing in those engineered renderings gave the *feeling* of anything.

One night he Googled "Castle Rock," the famous monolith on the Columbia, remembering the trip he and Shelley had taken up to The Gorge spring break their junior year when everybody else was heading down for that drunken orgy of a house boat float at Lake Shasta. It was on this trip that somehow, it had seemed clear to both of them that they were in love and now, before them, lay only their bright future. They were sitting on a picnic table bench, leaning back against the table itself, taking in the view of the rock on the north side of the river, and Will had his arm around her.

"Let's get married," he said.

In the next beat of silence he berated himself. Idiot. Should have done his homework, had the ring in his pocket. His roommate warned him girls expected you to make it special. Now he'd probably gone and blown it. And he just didn't want to have to *do* this. Try to figure women out, learn the right way to propose. He wanted to declare the hunt over. Turn in his tags on this girl and get on with it.

But then she said of course she'd marry him, and few moments in his life had ever felt so clear, so sure as this one, as they agreed they would, as Will thought of it, tackle life together.

So this guy—this Manuel Valencia—must have propped his easel right there where they'd been sitting. Will squinted at the screen, scrolled down to find that this particular painting, a perfect encapsulation of one of his life's best moments, was for up for auction at a place called Lincoln Galleries. Well, he just had to go up to Portland and claim it, that's all, and so began his little addiction. Over the next months, Shelley's rose-patterned walls disappeared under this haphazardly hung collection of 19th Century paintings: Mt. Hood, Crater Lake, Three Sisters—the iconic scenes of Oregon. And every damned one of them looked better, Will thought, than Loren Caldwell's, which always reminded him of his father's garage floor after a couple decades of slap-dash drift boat maintenance jobs. And Will wasn't paying any ridiculous million dollars, either.

He'd find the artists' biographies on the internet. Such losers in life, some of them. Stories of desperate poverty and how nobody would buy their paintings while they were living. In finding value in them now, Will felt he was sticking up for the poor guys. He'd even bid on the flawed works if he liked the scene and the artist's story—the ones with a little tear in the canvas somebody'd inexpertly tried to patch. It felt right: damaged art on the walls of a damaged guy.

He wasn't eager to let anybody see his collection, not after that time his best fishing buddy Doug Hudson walked in and hooted, "What the hell? You goin' fruity on me?" And he still couldn't forget his mother's sniffy remark the last time he'd mentioned going to an art auction: "Like you *need* another painting."

Only Shelley's mother had been nice about it, making a point of coming over to admire each new painting as he brought them home one by one. She even knew about the artists, having minored in Art History at that California women's college of hers.

Will had come to realize long before Alice died last spring, though, that it hadn't been the paintings alone that kept her coming over. He and his mother-in-law were the two who just couldn't seem to let Shelley go, and they took comfort in some unspoken pact that neither would ever start telling the other it was time they should.

It was Gar who pointed it out, that when Alice went into hospice, Will stopped going to the art auctions.

Now he fetched and opened a second beer, went back to the sofa to stare morosely at the Valencia. People talked about weddings—well, women did, anyway—how that was supposed to be the best day of your life. Or graduation day or whatever. Bunk. The best moments were when you got the good news.

She loves you. She said so. For the very first time. She's letting you into her bed.

Yes, she'll marry you. Even though you're the son of a logger while *her* family actually owns the forest.

She's got big news: she's pregnant with your kid.

That's what he remembered anyway. Not the official commemoration of a milestone, the moment the camera shutter clicked.

And now, what a goddamned bummer, knowing there wouldn't be anything else like that for the rest of his sorry life. No more golden moments. Shelley was supposed to be his wife, but she was gone. That was the bleak, bitter sum of it. Anybody who thought he ought to just get over it could go to hell.

CHAPTER 2

Everyone in Corvallis swore by Bridget Garland.

Everyone except her mother-in-law, that is.

Vaguely embarrassed by the career path chosen by her son's wife, Ardis Garland did not thrill with family pride to be assured her daughter-in-law was revered throughout Benton County for her wise and bossy manner of delivering physical therapy, nor was Ardis amused to hear Bridget affectionately referred to as "The Good Witch."

On the corner by the Birkenstock store downtown, a woman sympathizing with a story of back pain would pull an old Da Vinci Days flyer from her bag and write Bridget's name on it. "You'll love her," was the promise. "She's so smart. She knows how to put her hands on you and find the right place to press and it just…makes the pain go away. It's amazing."

Bridget was happy to give an explanation of the method she used, neuromuscular dysfunction as the basis of joint disorders, but most people, relieved to feel better, were quite satisfied to simply consider her hands pure magic, write her a check for seventy-five dollars, and let it go at that.

As for knowing this daughter-in-law of the Garland clan personally, well, nobody really did. Nobody could claim Bridget Garland as a friend. But everyone imagined that certainly there were lots of other lucky people who could.

She wondered if maybe people even figured she was happy.

So, wow, when the shit hit the fan, as it was about to now—what a surprise.

Bridget walked into her house, headed straight for the fridge and poured herself a glass of wine.

Seriously, she'd had no idea today would finally be the day.

Incredibly stressful, trying to stay nice while Charlotte couldn't bother to hide how much she wanted her mother to finish up at the dorm already and make herself scarce. Yes, Bridget knew her daughter wasn't excited about OSU and needed some slack cut, but the whole Yale debacle wasn't Bridget's fault. Her advice to apply to more colleges, after all, had been not just ignored but disdained.

The hardest part to take was Charlotte acting like move-in day was a particularly appropriate time to draw preventative lines. Bridget should remember, please, this was *her* life. *Her* start at college. As if the mere fact of being eighteen were enviable by definition.

Honey, you can have it, Bridget thought, driving home to the big house she'd always despised. She wanted to just get on Highway 20 and head for the coast. Or whirl the wheel for points east, and lose herself somewhere beyond the mountains. Even head for PDX and escape to Hawaii.

She didn't envy her daughter's life, okay? But she was thoroughly fed up with her own.

And running into Will...no way that didn't have an effect on her.

Charlotte and Gar were actually second cousins, but they knew their respective parents as uncle and aunt. So here's good old Uncle Will, insisting on re-parking his truck after getting Gar squared away, coming back to help her and Charlotte schlep her stuff up to the room. Just so...decent. Why couldn't John be like that? John couldn't even be there.

God. That Will. Even on a crappy day like this Bridget couldn't think about the guy without smiling. He was just so cute. And dumb! But in a sweet way. He never seemed to have any idea how bad he always made her husband look.

It had already been a couple of weeks since she'd confronted John about Labor Day weekend. She and Charlotte had been at Bed, Bath & Beyond, filling shopping carts with dorm room trappings, when they ran into Charlotte's friend Alix and her mother.

"Just who I wanted to talk to," Deb said as the girls distanced themselves. "Dave and I've been thinking about investing in a house up at Black Butte. You guys have a place there, right?"

"Well, my in-laws do," Bridget admitted. "A family retreat type thing. They let Garland Forests employees take turns. Actually John and I don't even get up there much."

"Oh. Well, we rented a condo there over Labor Day and when I ran into John getting a newspaper on Sunday morning at the little store…"

Bridget's stomach lurched. Deb kept talking, but Bridget heard nothing beyond those first incriminating words. John had been at Black Butte on Sunday morning? John was east in the Cascades when he'd claimed a three-day golfing weekend with friends down at Bandon Dunes on the coast?

Her guts were doing all the usual tricks, her eyes drifting from Deb's to scan above the aisles for the restroom sign.

As Deb rattled on, Bridget was imagining John's opening arguments. She'd misheard him! He never said Bandon Dunes. He said Black Butte. Didn't she remember? Big Meadow one day, Glaze Meadow the next. He would go on the attack. Couldn't she ever stop being so suspicious? How on earth would they ever hold their marriage together if she refused to trust him?

"I feel bad I forgot to ask you, honey," she said that night at home, having to force the *honey*. "How'd your golf go last weekend? Weather okay?"

"Aw, well, actually, it was great on the course, but you know how the fog can be down there. The beach was completely socked in. You wouldn't have been a happy camper."

Gotcha. At least she wouldn't have to defend her own sanity. But right: she was not a happy camper.

Now, half the glass of pinot gris downed, she took the kitchen phone off the hook and stood at the living room windows where she could focus on the Cascades across the valley as she mentally rehearsed, one last time, the speech she'd known for years she would eventually need to give. Finally she hit speed dial and sat down on the arm of the sofa, shaking. As soon as her mother-in-law answered, though, she stood back up. A fighting stance.

"Ardis," she said, "I need to talk to you."

A brief silence. Bridget pictured Ardis flipping open a note pad, motioning for Pete to pick up the extension. Every phone call was a chance to practice her organizational skills. She always took notes.

"Yes, Bridget, what is it?"

Bridget took a breath. "I wanted to tell you this before John talked to you. I know how convincing he can be, and if there's the slightest chance you were to believe even a little bit of my side of it, I figured I should get to you first."

"You're side of what, dear? No, now wait, let me get Pete on the other line." Okay, so she hadn't done this already. "You sound so serious. Maybe he ought to be hearing this too."

Bridget took another sip of wine and looked at the ghastly popcorn ceiling. Probably asbestos, but Ardis advised it best not to find out. Ugh, this house. A wedding gift from her and Pete. Bridget's stomach was churning. So many times she'd threatened to leave John, so many times he'd talked her out of it. Now she was finally standing up to Pete and Ardis Garland, the bosses of their lives.

"All right," Ardis said. "Pete's on too. Go ahead."

"Well," Bridget said, "I know this'll be upsetting to you two, but I'm leaving John."

"What?" Pete said.

"I've tried really hard all these years, and we never wanted to worry you, but John's cheated on me so many times I can't even count."

"Oh, for God's sake," Pete said.

"I'm sorry," Bridget said, "but it's true."

"In the Garland family," Pete said. "We do not divorce."

"I've noticed that." The only way to get out of the Garland family, apparently, was to die. "I really hate the idea myself, Pete."

"Now you listen here, Bridget, when you became a part of this family, when you accepted that house…"

Accepted that house! A burst of adrenalin shot through her. "I'm from a family too, you know. This isn't feudal China. Nobody's ever divorced on my side of the family either." With a sudden pang she missed her own father. He would have been outraged on her behalf to hear that Pete Garland, Mr. Big Timber, was bullying her like this when it was his own son who'd ruined everything.

"Ardis, I can't listen to this," Pete said. "You talk some sense into her." He banged down his receiver.

"Now Bridget," Ardis said. "Certainly this isn't something to be hasty about. Where's John now?"

"You're asking me? I don't know. I can tell you why he said he couldn't help with Charlotte's move over to the dorm today, but it's not like that would necessarily be the truth."

"Well, have you discussed this with him? That you want to leave?"

"Uh, actually, I've been telling him I want to leave since his first affair. But if you mean specifically this time, now, today, no. How could I? I just decided."

"Oh, Bridget, whoever said men were easy? Do you think Pete's been easy?"

No, Bridget certainly did not think that. Especially when Ardis herself didn't even know what-all she was dealing with regarding her husband and certain things that had happened in the Garland family past.

"I'm thinking of something my mother told me," Ardis went on, "something I've always believed myself. She said when a marriage is in trouble, it's up to the wife to hold it together. Look around. When a man strays, there's usually a reason for it. It's not going to happen if he's happy at home."

Oh, right.

"And surely you're aware of the financial ramifications. Of course we would always take care of Charlotte…"

Obviously. Their only grandchild.

"But as far as shares of Garland Forests, you know it all follows blood. That's how Pete's father set it up."

Wow. How fast it all went back to Garland Forests.

"Don't worry," Bridgett said, "John's been very careful to point that out to me every time I've threatened to leave. But I earn enough to take care of myself. And, I don't know, Ardis—this just isn't the life I was meant to be leading."

Her mother-in-law's deep sigh over the line made plain the inexcusable banality of this stance.

"Bridget," she said, "Seriously. Have you considered your daughter in this? I mean, aside from the financial aspects? Her feelings?"

"Ardis! If it weren't for her, I'd have left a long time ago. And what kind of example am I setting by staying? Isn't that just like telling her it doesn't matter how bad a man treats you, you have to stick around? Please, as a woman, can't you understand where I'm coming from on this?"

Another long pause. "He hasn't been physically abusive, has he?"

Oh, Lord. When did the bar for being a decent husband get set so appalling low? Anything goes as long as he doesn't punch you?

"He gave me gonorrhea once. Does that count?"

"Oh, *really*, Bridget!"

As if saying it out loud were worse than doing it, bringing this nasty dose home from, of all places, a philanthropy conference. Philanthropy/philandering. Did John know the difference? Maybe the upscale setting of that fancy California resort made it hard to separate the two. And then making her go to a doctor out of town for treatment—didn't they have a shared interest in this? Protecting from gossip the precious family name?

"Well, I'm sorry to hear about these past…incidents, but clearly the two of you worked through it. Are you sure you're not just imagining whatever it is now? Maybe you're being overly suspicious."

"Ardis, he booked the Black Butte house for Labor Day. He had some woman up there with him."

A silence. "Oh, dear. At *our* place?"

"Yes, that's what I'm saying."

This, at last, made Ardis shut up. Sexual infidelity exacerbated by venereal disease was one thing apparently, a scheduling deception and betrayal of the family vacation home quite another.

As soon as Bridget hung up, she went online to Craigslist. She would need a new place to live. Wasn't life amazing? When she'd got up this morning and started arguing with Charlotte about what would and would not fit into a dorm room, she'd had no idea that by evening, she'd be thinking about exactly how much would fit nicely into a small house of her own.

The best part? John Garland clearly would *not*.

CHAPTER 3

Dan Trask and his fishing buddy Ross Hendrix had driven the curvy mountain road in the dark to be on the Alsea in time for the morning rise. No place they'd rather be and, mid-morning now, sitting in the boat, it still hadn't begun to bother them in the least, the fact they were without the slightest evidence of any fish in their vicinity.

"Hey, I just remembered," Ross said. "My wife says she seen something in the paper. That kid a yours got hisself engaged to some girl from that big timber family? I told her maybe she got the name wrong but she says no. That article had *your* name on it. Said, like, 'His parents are Dan and Betty Trask of Eden Mills."

"'Fraid it's the truth." Dan cast his fly out over the pewter gray water and sat back down.

"You shittin' me?"

"Nope."

"So what *is* the deal with that family? The Garlands. 'Cause they're the ones had that hunting accident, remember? One a the brothers got shot?"

"Whoa. That's right. So long ago I'd forgot."

"They ever figure that out? Who shot him? 'Cause there was lots a talk. I mean, come on. Nobody out there but the family. Hadda be one of 'em."

"Yeah, you think of it."

"But them Garlands, say they pull together tighter'n a wad a bait worms. Now your boy's marrying into that bunch? Whoa."

"Yeah. Can't get used to it myself. I don't know, I should be happy for him. She's the prettiest thing you ever saw, Ross. That kinda shiny, reddy-blond hair, cute little figure. I guess Betty used to look like that, but you forget, you know."

"Go on! Betty never had no red hair."

"I meant the cute figure. The young part, I guess. The part that gets you crazy enough to go buy a ring. Get married and sign up for somebody piping up on whether or not you oughta go fishing every time you want to, for the rest of your life."

"Aw, come on now, Dan. Betty ain't that hard on you, is she?"

"Well, the damn thing is, if you told me ahead a time there'd be no way I'd be putting a single fish in my creel today, I'd still come out and be happy to sit here, right? I could get skunked and be fine with it, but with old Bet, I'll have to hear, 'Well, that was a wasted day, wadn't it?'"

"Yeah, but you know anybody got a woman who's halfway nice to him about fishing?"

Dan grunted. "Just Stan. But then you know how that turned out."

They shared a moment of silence in deference to Stan up on the Yaquina, bragging and showing off the nice lunch his wife packed him. Even bought his beer. Just when she'd become practically famous for the sweet, cheerful way she sent Stan off, it turned out she was spending his fishing days carrying on with that guy run the Texaco Station.

Ross gave Dan a sly smile. "So Will's little fee-on-say is a looker, huh?"

"Say so. Course, we're not supposed to be looking at the young gals, you know. But your son brings one home to dinner, says 'So, Dad, here's the girl I'm gonna marry.' You can't *not* look, right?"

"Nobody blaming you."

"And shoot, you know Betty's just scared of her, daughter a that family, coming over to our house. My God, I thought for awhile there just throwing that one little dinner was gonna put her under."

"Girl kinda snooty and all?"

"No, just Betty's *afraid* she'd be. Had to agree afterward she's a peach. Made Betty let her help with the dishes and all." Dan laughed. "Kinda funny really. I think Betty half wanted to bitch, you know, but this Shelley girl didn't give her a single thing to gripe about."

Dan watched his line in the river, the way the water ebbed around it. Couldn't help wishing he was back in that place again sometimes, so young and out-of-your-mind hot, like nothing else mattered.

Ross reeled in his line and recast. "My boy's got a cute little heifer from over to Cloverdale."

"Well, now see, that's probably better. One a them Tillamook County dairy princesses. But that Will, you try to warn him about stuff. Hell, he ain't listening. He's just dopey over this girl. I told him later, I said, 'Listen kid, your mother and I think she's nice and I'm sure she looks like the brass ring to you, but it's a tough job trying to keep a woman happy. If I haven't been able to give your mother half a what she wanted, how the hell you think you're gonna satisfy the Princess of Garland Fucking Forests?'"

"Whoa! You said that?"

"Most certainly did. Owed it to him. Figured he oughta think long and hard here, but he never heard a word of it."

Dan cranked his reel in, readying the line for another cast. Somehow he wasn't exactly proud to repeat it, how he'd also tossed off one of the worst insults one guy could give another. "Maybe it don't worry you," he'd said to his son, "because you're just figuring to sign up for the Garland Forests gravy train."

He stood and cast again. Sat down. Pinched the pole between his knees and lit a cigarette.

Still couldn't get over how Will'd walked off the job four years ago at the Bear Creek site. Thought he could do better than having his own dad for a log boss. Never actually said *go to hell, old man*, but that was sure as shit the gist of it. Just stomped off, hollering about college.

Then damned if the kid wasn't getting through just like he swore he would. Like he was some kid growed up on Country Club Hill over in Corvallis, for Christ's sake. Had his name right there in the newspaper Betty showed him. Dean's list or some such. Made straight A's. Well, classes about wildlife, for God sake. He oughtta. Still, he musta got some a Betty's brains, looked like. Sure, Dan wanted him to succeed. What kind of a father would actually root for his kid to fall on his face? But shit. Kid gets himself an education? A gorgeous girl to marry him and she's rich on top of it?

"They gonna have a big wedding and all?" Ross asked.

"Yeah, more's the pity. Some fancy church in Corvallis. Not until after they graduate next year, though. But they already warned me—I gotta wear one a them monkey suits."

Suddenly the tip of the pole bowed toward the water. *Hot damn,* a strike. Big old cutthroat trout. Dan tossed his cigarette overboard and cranked that reel.

CHAPTER 4

Couldn't stand it. Couldn't believe it when he got the call. His buddy Doug Hudson. Doug and his brother, Cal. Twenty-five years logging the woods, most dangerous job on earth, to go out fishing for the fun of it, get flung up on Nye Beach, drowned.

Will's cell had buzzed in the pocket of his Carhartts up on the Gooseneck Creek clear-cut, a job the Hudsons themselves had just wrapped up. Dead? Just like that? Both of them? Jesus Christ. Felt like a loose log choker'd flown down the line and slammed him in the chest. Had to drop to a stump and sit there, head between his knees for who knows how long, just trying to breathe right again.

Finally he looked at his hand braced on the rough, sap-oozing edge of the fresh-cut stump. Right here. Doug had been right here with his chainsaw just yesterday.

The Hudsons were more than just the first outfit Will called when he needed to set up a logging show. He'd grown up and gone to school with them. Skipped out with them, too. He and Doug still hunted and fished together, and when they spotted each other across some parking lot in Eden Mills, always took the time to shout a cheerful insult. Never too busy to be buds, never did that bit of faking not seeing each other just to keep moving. What with the lousy economy and not much logging going on lately, Doug had been dropping by Will's office almost daily to report where the likeliest elk herds were being spotted, or to get Will to go hit Taco Time for lunch.

And now, just like that, he was gone? Christ.

He'd be so glad to get this funeral over with. Double header, for cryin' out loud. Two good guys. And why was it, for God's sake, that the best people kept dying? Will could think of several people where he wouldn't mind one bit if they dropped dead this minute. But check it out: they never did. The universe just kept dishing it up, the decent people getting cut down. You had to wonder, sometimes, who the hell was calling the shots.

The church was only three blocks from Heritage Realty, but the thought of taking the sidewalk along the main drag never crossed his mind. He could have bushwhacked through five miles of thigh-high undergrowth more comfortably than walk three minutes open to public view wearing a sport coat and these dumb dress shoes.

He parked in the church's rapidly filling lot, went in and took a seat in the pew that ran around the back. Doug's program had mountains and an elk on the cover. Will opened it to a poem with the writer talking like he was Doug, a bunch of stuff about how he'd loved being alive and out there in the forests and everything else that was so beautiful.

The last line struck him: *I'm at peace, my life full and complete.*

Full and complete, at forty-two? Couldn't quite see Doug agreeing with that. Not as long as there were still steelhead in the Alsea. Who wrote this? Somebody young anyway. Somebody who thought guys in their forties had already put in a good run.

He looked around the huge sanctuary. Who made funerals happen, anyway? Who told all that stuff to the newspaper for the obituary? Who could think clear enough to say people should donate in Doug's memory to the Forestry Program at Eden Mills High? You knew Doug never wrote that down anywhere. Doug never made plans about dying.

Will watched a tall woman with a careless blond ponytail enter on his right. Just inside the door she paused, her placid gaze scanning the room. Not until her eyes met Will's and she started toward him did he recognized her: Robin

Garland, his sister-in-law. She folded her long legs to take a seat beside him on the pew. He'd have known her at a hundred yards in her usual pocketed vest and cargo pants, good old Mattie the Mutt at her side, but not disguised in a navy blue dress with a twist of fabric between her breasts, the sort of get-up he'd seen her in on only a handful of occasions over the years.

The two of them looked at their hands for a moment, then glanced at each other and sighed. Sad business, this.

People just kept coming in. Looked like all of Eden Mills. Place was packed. Older men had brushed off their rarely worn suits, but the younger guys who still worked the woods seemed to figure clean jeans and pressed plaid shirts was plenty dressed-up enough. With bow hunting season open, surprise somebody wasn't in camo, but it looked like the ones still hoping to hunt later on had kept their gear in their trucks out of respect for their dead buddies. When they took off later, though, that would be in their honor too. They'd be telling each other that's what Doug and Cal would have wanted…for them to get out there.

Heads turned as the wives of the two men came in, Doug's wife Donna supported by their two sons. She wore an otherworldly expression, almost as if she hadn't heard the bad news yet. Or had calmly chosen to not to believe it.

But she knew. At least every once in awhile the reality must have come stabbing through, because when Will had phoned her a couple of days after the accident she'd said, "Just put our place on the market, Will. I'm not staying out here alone."

Fifteen years in real estate had taught him to stall on going there with her at this point. You didn't want to be encouraging the newly bereaved to make hasty decisions.

"Are the boys looking after you?"

"Sure." A moment of static over the line. Or maybe it was her sniffling. "Well, they went fishing."

"Did they."

"They said Doug would have wanted them to." She laughed shortly. "I couldn't argue with that." Little gasping noises. "Oh, Will." Now she was full-out crying. "I just can't believe this."

Doug and Donna had chased each other around the muddy school playground since kindergarten, back when it was called Eden Mills and not Garland Elementary. Will had been pretty sweet on Donna himself, but even as a fourth-grader he'd seen it was those two who had that magic, meant-for-each-other spark. And with their families so tight in this same church, it seemed like a done deal, early on. They'd married right out of high school and, like that old song about kisses sweeter than wine, they hadn't hesitated. The babies came right away, grew up and started making babies themselves. Now, in her forties, with only a thread or two of gray in her long thick braid, Donna sure didn't fit any picture Will had of what a grandma would look like, but there you had it.

"Should have known," Robin whispered, directing Will's gaze to the aisle where her dad, his father-in-law, Ed Garland, was being escorted up front. "I told him I'd come for us." She shook her head. "Too soon for him to be putting himself through something like this."

But that wasn't Ed Garland. The Hudsons had worked for Garland Forests for years, logging tracts all over the Coast Range, shows Will himself had arranged. As co-owner of the family business, Ed would insist on coming today, paying his respects. You couldn't stop him from doing the right thing.

Robin craned to see the people up front. "Don't suppose you've seen Uncle Pete. Or John."

"Nope." Big surprise.

"Dad says Pete hates funerals."

"Yeah." Will stuck his finger in his collar. "Whereas some of us really like 'em." He tugged it away from his neck. Too hot. Around him, other guys did the same.

Finally a minister took his position up front. Will tried to tune out the religious stuff, but he couldn't ignore it when they started showing pictures on the two large media screens, images of the lost brothers smoothly fading one into the other, accompanied by a taped rendition of *"Amazing Grace."* A shot of Doug as a grinning kid holding up a rainbow trout reminded Will of fishing up at Rock Creek, Doug riding him home on the handlebars of his beat-up bicycle, Will precariously balancing their rods. He could almost smell the newly unfurled leaves of Spring, wished he could feel the cool dusk air rushing at his face instead of the close warmth of the church.

As the Hudson boys grew up before them on the double screens, the theme of trophies became clear: the fish they caught, the elk they shot, the trees they cut down. These were some of the best moments of their lives.

And then, just as the music switched from the hymn to the pop song, *"Stand By Me,"* there it was, the evidence of Will being part of some of those best moments. A shot of the two of them, camo and crossbows, ready to set off over the hills, Doug in his favorite baseball cap, Will his lucky floppy hat, grinning at each other, brothers in arms. Will tried to swallow. Couldn't. He ducked his head, pressed the side of his hand hard against his moustache. Don't cry. Don't cry. He shut his eyes against the screen, and only when Robin's gentle nudge gave the all-clear did he open them. He and Doug were gone.

He let out his breath.

Brother Cal had driven a log truck, and apparently made a point of posing beside each new one, each particularly fine-looking load. A sigh of admiration ran through those gathered as one slide of a handsome five-log load was given the extra time on the screen everyone knew it deserved. Didn't see many like that anymore. Was it possible Will even recognized those exact Doug firs? They'd been working on that Kitten Creek job, everybody daily marveling at the beautiful timber they'd been privileged to harvest from this site (None a them pencil loads guys they knew were stuck driving to the mill) and Will was asked to "loan" a load. Cal was booked to drive his shiny new blue truck in the Eden Mills Fourth of July parade, and five of these prime logs would be just the thing to show it off. Why not? So there was one bunch of logs that got to be famous in a patriotic detour on their way to the mill. Who knew they'd go on to further glory, commemorated in a big church funeral?

Now the sons of Doug and Cal took their turns speaking. Or rather, in Doug's son Wade's case, took his turn trying. Poor kid. Looked like it was hitting him all at once as he stood by the caskets, squeezing the mic, desperate to collect himself.

The gathered crowd remained silent, waiting. Patient.

Wade stared at his boots, his tiny silver hoop earring catching a glint of light through the stained glass.

Still, he said nothing.

And never had nothing said so much. Finally he managed to choke out one short line.

"It'll be hard to get over."

No shit.

Probably when a guy's dad dies, Will thought, it's bound to be a big mess of hurt whether that dad was a great guy or a total jerk, a man you'd been butting heads with for years.

Sitting there, miserable, Will wondered why he almost seemed to feel worse about Doug than he had about his own father or even—No. No, that couldn't be true. When Shelley died, he was so out of it, he couldn't remember half of what had gone down at the hospital the night of the accident or at the huge, overwhelming Episcopal Church memorial service. Hell, very little of the whole year after, if you asked anybody who'd been watching him in this shattered state of raw wretchedness, being alive while the only woman he'd ever loved was dead. Being without her.

But with Doug…well, it was like Doug was him. Same age and all. Suddenly: GAME OVER. Whole thing was just such a whap-up-the-side-of-the-head reminder: *Hey dummy, none of us is living forever.*

And damn. He'd tried so hard not to think about it. Pretend he didn't remember. But Doug had asked *him* to go over to the coast for this fishing trip.

Cal only wound up in the boat because Will did the white lie thing and claimed he had a property he had to show that day. But Doug would have made fun of the truth, called him a Touchy-Feely New-Age Dad for wanting to stick close to home these last weekends before Gar actually started classes. Yeah, Gar'd moved to the dorm, but what if he wanted to put in some time with Old Dad? Only when it was clear Gar's plans for that day did not include his father or younger brother had Will thought *What the hell* and got in the truck to go check out the Gooseneck Creek job.

If he'd gone with Doug, he'd be dead now, too.

Or…maybe not. Doug usually fished the coastal streams. It was Will who had experience with the ocean. Out in the fog, he might have heard the surf and realized they were treacherously close to shore, in danger of being caught and capsized. He'd have got them the hell out of there. Think about it. Maybe Doug didn't even hear the warning roar, half deaf like he was thanks to a cheerful scorn of earplugs. Even while running his chainsaw.

Sure, people said accidents were accidents, but any Will'd ever been close enough to consider always involved a lot of what-ifs. Choices people made. He'd made his choice when Doug invited him. Put his kid—or the idea of his kid—ahead of his buddy.

Doug and Cal had made their choices, too. Just nobody would ever know exactly what they'd been.

Now those two were up there laid out stone-cold dead in those flower-covered boxes.

And Will only wished he was.

Well, except for his boys. And what he owed the Garlands in shepherding them along now that they didn't have Shelley Garland as their mother.

The church's overhead screens once again lit up. At the fresh chord of taped music, Will cringed. Was it—? Oh, God, not that one. The cloying scent of the casket flowers filled his nostrils like some kind of dense, poisonous gas as

Garth Brooks started singing *"If Tomorrow Never Comes."* Will tried to pull in a breath, aware of Robin leaning toward him.

He had long ago learned to switch off the truck radio at those opening words—*Sometimes late at night...* First time he'd unwittingly listened to the song all the way through, driving along the Alsea Highway in the rain, he'd just about gone off the road in the sad, gray, regretful blur of the whole thing. Since then he'd knocked his lights out avoiding it, that and the Billie Joe Shaver thing, *"Hearts A'Bustin',"* about the guy missing his dead wife.

This time he couldn't turn the words off. Couldn't shut his ears. Had to watch all these images of the drowned brothers and their wives in their happiest times. A wedding shot of Cal as Doug's Best Man reminded him: Doug had been *his* Best Man. Jesus, he just wanted to laugh and cry at the same time, remembering, because Best Man at the wedding of a guy with a father like Will's had not turned out to be an easy job, his dad getting drunk and Doug having to haul him out when he started hollering crap about hoping to God Will would stick to fishing and never go hunting with any of those trigger-happy Garlands.

The slides kept coming as Garth sang about watching his sleeping wife and wondering—if he didn't wake up, would he have told her often enough how much he loved her? And then the warning to everybody to speak right up and be sure the people you loved knew you did.

Thanks, Garth. What about people like me where it's already just plain too late? Will couldn't bear to look around the sanctuary. You could hear the women crying, the men trying not to.

The finishing bit—and thank God it finally *was* going to finish—featured a five minute video clip, probably the first thing Doug's family thought worthy of filming back when everybody started buying video cameras. On the screen, Doug's kids watched in rapt admiration as he took a chainsaw to a fir tree three feet in diameter, executing the back cut. Then, to the exuberant and celebratory cheers of the little boys, now off-screen, that forest giant hit the duff with a deep, resonating thud.

"Hell of a thing," Ed Garland remarked as Will and Robin met up with him in the crowd outside in the hall afterward.

Will felt Robin's hand on his back. "Breathe, buddy."

He nodded. Tried.

"Hell of a thing," Ed repeated, and Will looked at him. Really something, the two of them. Couple of worn-out old widowers. Four years now Shelley'd been gone and what did Will have to say for himself? He'd taken good care of the boys, that was about it. Gar and Cody were his job and he was grateful to have it. But poor Ed. Nobody needed him in that same way anymore.

Robin gave her dad a sideways hug. Standing next to him, she was so clearly his daughter, both of them out of the same tall, lean mold. Shelley, Will always thought, took after Alice—shorter, rounder. Softer.

"I need to sign this book," Ed said. "Got steered right past it coming in."

While Ed scrawled his name and a remark of condolence, Will contemplated the accompanying flowers and an overflowing basket of cards also parked on the reception table. He hadn't brought a card. Was he supposed to? He'd thought calling Donna directly, right away, was the thing to do, but then, he wasn't sure. He'd always counted on Shelley for etiquette advice. And it's not like he could go by what people had done in the way of effective consolation when the tragedy had been his. Cards? Calls? Whatever it had been, no matter how well intentioned, it apparently hadn't helped much if he couldn't even remember any of it.

Ed turned from the book and the three of them made their way to the exit, nodding at loggers they recognized from having employed them on one job or another.

Robin shook hands with a few, just like a guy, and Will could see it threw some of them to see her in the dress and sandals. They knew Robin Garland in a hardhat and boots, giving them marching orders on some section of Garland land to be logged. She was an imposing presence, whatever she wore, with a handsome face, a woman to be respected. Everybody knew she was Ed Garland's daughter and Spark Garland's granddaughter. None of these guys would dream of messing with her.

Outside, Robin said her truck was parked on the other side of the church. "You up for a walk with Mattie after dinner, Dad? Woods Creek?"

"Oh, I don't think so."

"Why not? Come on."

He hesitated. "Well, okay."

She gave each man's shoulder a tender punch and strode off as if she were wearing boots and not sandals.

"She worries about me," Ed said.

"Yeah. So, should she? You doing okay?"

"Oh, sure, sure."

Ed Garland would never complain. Didn't believe in it. But the man had aged considerably in the year since Alice's initial cancer diagnosis and then, at the beginning of the summer, just days after their fiftieth anniversary, her death. His decline surprised nobody—not Robin or her brother in Seattle or the cousins. They'd all been watching Ed Garland in a certain state of suspense, having always figured their parents had the kind of marriage where, as soon as one went, the other would inevitably be not far behind. They'd pictured that happening when Ed and Alice were in their nineties or something, though. Not now.

"Still got that lady coming to clean?" Will asked Ed.

"Oh, yeah. She looks after everything."

"Doesn't cook, though, right?"

"No, but, you know, my freezer's still so full of all the casseroles these women keep bringing over."

Will laughed shortly. "Nice of 'em, I guess."

"Well, yeah, I appreciate it, but sometimes…Well, the other day this gal from church called and wanted to bring something over. Her husband died awhile back so I asked her, I said, 'So tell me, Shirley, does it get any better?'

And you know what she says? She says, 'No, Ed, not really.' Criminy! That's not what I wanted to hear!"

They had reached Ed's much dented Ford pick-up. All his employees were supplied with newer model vehicles neatly emblazoned with the Garland Forests logo, but Ed, like his father before him, did not see much need for clean or fancy when it came to his personal vehicle. Betraying a certain weary effort, he now climbed in.

Will was still stuck on his father-in-law's question: Does it get any better? Maybe only if you consider a thick fog better than deep darkness. He'd climbed up from the black pit he'd been thrown into the night of the accident, but nobody could call what he'd found at the top radiant light.

He stood at the open window of Ed's truck. "Thanks again for Gar's tuition."

Ed frowned, needing a moment, then remembered. "Oh, sure. He'll do fine. Say, think he'd like to have Alice's little Honda?"

"Ed! That's real nice of you. But don't you need it? For around town?"

Ed snorted. "Not going anywhere I can't go in this rig."

"Well, gee, if you're sure. He'll be thrilled."

Ed nodded, a ghost of a smile.

When was the last time either Will or his father-in-law had been thrilled by anything? These days their lives had been reduced to arranging and bearing wistful witness to the fresh "firsts" of the younger generation.

"I want to take it in and have it gone over, though," Ed said. "Put new tires on it. Make sure it's as safe as it can be."

Will nodded. That's all they could do, really. Check the fan belt wasn't about to break. Sign the kid up for an AAA card.

They didn't get to specify who'd be driving at him from the opposite direction around every curve in the road, or whether that person was even fit to get behind the wheel.

"Okay, well, take care." Will gave the door a light slap and backed up. "And thanks again."

Ed just sat there. He wasn't turning the key.

Will loosened his tie. God. Was this awful black weight going to be sitting on his chest forever?

Hell of a thing.

CHAPTER 5

"**A**nd now Spark's going to share with us the secret," Pete Garland said, "for making it through sixty years of marriage." He handed a mic to his father up front. The Gables' largest private room had been cordoned off for the clan's anniversary celebration and, along with a handful of close friends, every last family member was present and seated at the linen-draped tables.

The family patriarch squinted, thinking a moment. Then he lifted the mic. "Three rules: Marry young. Live long. Don't divorce." Spark grinned at the chuckles this got him, including one from his wife. Shelley's Grammie Charlotte was cute as hell, Will thought, always smiling, showing off that little space between her front teeth. Proud of it by now, she told Shelley. Proved they were real and her own, not dentures. When Spark started to sit down, she poked him back to standing. "And marry a good woman," he added, "who'll keep you in line!"

"Got mine," Will whispered under the fresh burst of laughter, winking at Shelley, a knowing nod for Bridget. Bouncing two-year-old Gar on his knee, he looked around at the size of the group gathered. Shelley's older brother Greg had even driven down from Seattle with his wife, Susan, and their little girl, Kit. Will shook his head, marveling. "Got every last person here, didn't they?"

Which seemed to puzzle Shelley. Agreed, her expression said. But what's the alternative?

Will, though, couldn't take any of this for granted. He regarded her relatives with warm satisfaction, proud to be part of it: a solid family capable of raising toasts to each other without worrying who'd get drunk and let loose with the opening insult, start spilling drinks, knocking over chairs. Shelley's confident expectation of the hundred percent attendance evidenced here was a luxury reserved for people with no notion of embarrassing absences or need for vaguely muttered explanations. She'd never had to gloss over an uncle in rehab. No young Garlands were ever in jail.

Will couldn't picture his family in a restaurant like this, and not just because they'd be too cash-strapped to pick up the tab. More that a gathering of what he thought of as the Black Sheep Branch of the Trask Family could not safely be confined to any actual room. Family parties had to be picnics, with plenty of paths into the woods where one aunt could run off in tears, the little cousins could torment each other unsupervised by parents, a brother-in-law could finally throw the inevitable fist.

His older sister had escaped (frying pan into the fire, Will thought) by marrying into a fundamentalist family and moving to Spokane. She expected Will to respect her new loyalties, but was so grateful he understood what a privilege it was, honestly, for him to be in a position to be able to take care of their parents. In other words, *You're on your own, buddy.*

Dan and Betty weren't divorced, but Will was usually wondering why not. Pretty much the same story with his aunts and uncles and Trask cousins, too.

But the Garlands all seemed to get along, and treasured every person on their family tree. Shelley had shown Will a huge genealogy scroll Grammie had researched and recorded by hand, the hard way, before computers. A surprise to learn that Shelley's dad, Ed, and her Uncle Pete had been the younger of three brothers. An older one, a John Garland, had been shot in a hunting accident. Shelley'd been quick to warn him that Garlands don't hunt and the kids learned early on they were never supposed to ask about their dead uncle.

When Will admitted he didn't know far back at all on his own family, Shelley said maybe she could trace his tree sometime and, given his dark hair and eyes, maybe he even had a Native American bloodline. Which would be cool, he thought. The only thing handed down he was proud of so far was his solid old Oregon name. The Trask River, he liked to point out, had a respectable run of salmon, steelhead, and sea run cutthroat trout.

Now Will stood Gar on his thighs and pointed to Spark. "That's your great-grampa up there, buddy."

"Gampa?" Gar frowned, swiveled and pointed at Shelley's father, Ed. "*Dat* Gampa!"

"Wow." Bridget's eyes widened. Apparently her little Charlotte—Grammie's namesake—wasn't popping up with this kind of stuff yet.

"That's right," Will explained to Gar, "but Grampa Spark is Mommy's grampa."

Shelley smiled fondly at their little boy, reaching to run a hand through his shock of dark red curls, resting the other on the swell indicating the imminent arrival of his brother or sister. Will knew she was hoping for a girl. Either way, she'd declared two was enough. Come on, wouldn't a whole tribe of little rug rats be kind of fun? He could've been happy with a girl and kept going. But she was doing all the work here. Not his place to argue.

Now, looking across the seated diners, old Spark pointed at little Gar and winked.

"Gampa Spark!" Gar crowed, straightening his knees hard and pointing right back, making a huge hit with the entire assemblage.

Will and Shelley smiled at each other, probably doing a lousy job at trying to hide the obvious: They were smug as hell! Will caught John taking this in, felt the vibe of rivalry. Well, well. Here was one Garland who maybe wasn't so thrilled to have a Trask branch sprouting from the family tree.

Will would never put this into words, even to Shelley, because he knew it was wrong somehow, but he couldn't help getting a charge out of them having produced Spark's first great-grandson. Charlotte—now sitting up on her grandmother Ardis's lap—had been born a few months ahead of Gar and, in theory, treated exactly the same. She hadn't lacked for the fussy attention of the women, anyway. And Greg and Susan's little girl Kit was four already, holding status as the first great-grandchild. But somehow you just knew the Garland men were looking for sons. Will's kids wouldn't carry on the Garland surname, true, but Will suspected in this family it wasn't so much about the name as it was about producing potential foresters to keep the business going, keep those trees growing.

Or maybe Gar being a boy had nothing to do with it. Babies weren't all the same, Will was starting to notice. Charlotte and Kit were perfectly fine kids. Charlotte in particular had the sort of sweet looks people seemed to like in little girls, blond curls that Bridget called Garland Gold. "She didn't get that angel hair from me," she always pointed out.

But Gar had this bigger-than-life personality. He looked at people, interacted with them. He was interested in everything, from the russet chrysanthemums on the table to the colorful curlicues of frosting on the big sheet cake.

Charlotte, by contrast, seemed a bit oblivious, and Kit, Shelley had quietly declared, was almost off-putting in the intensity of those steely blue eyes of hers and that dark cap of hair, a small, solemn judge in their presence. Of the three, no wonder Gar, at the moment, was the crowd pleaser.

After the dinner, Will was standing in the foyer, holding Gar to keep him from tearing around, waiting for Shelley, who always had the hardest time wrapping up a conversation with her mother.

Spark approached the cash register, all business, pulling out his wallet. He squinted at Will. "Your food good?"

"Oh, yeah. Great. Thanks for treating us."

Spark's worn leather wallet, Will noticed, was secured with a rubber band.

"Good, good." Spark tugged it off, started counting out hundred-dollar bills. "This whole thing's what the women said we should do, you know."

Will laughed and nodded. "Well, it was great. I think they were right."

"Yeah, I suppose they usually are, aren't they?" He executed a wink with a cluck for Gar. "Fine boy you've got there. I like thinking he's got some of my genes."

"Definitely, Spark. Shelley and I already think he takes after you."

"Maybe so. 'Bout a hundred years ago my hair was that red color."

"Really?" Will had never realized that. You wouldn't, from the black and white photos. "Well, what we noticed is, he likes to fish."

"Does he now?" Spark laughed. "Well, hot dog! 'Course he gets that from your side too."

"Well, sure," Will said, pleased and a bit surprised his own love of fishing had registered with the old guy. But he wasn't making it up about Gar. Kid had a cute trick of standing over any puddle, flinging a string tied to a stick, then pretending to reel up a whopper.

Now John appeared, Bridget struggling behind with their wriggling toddler. Bridget had worn her brown hair long and loose, the way it would look prettiest for the party, Will figured, but it wasn't working out too well, what with her little girl's fists clutching at the curly stuff. She made a goofy face at Will and he laughed in sympathy. They'd had a bond right from the start, he and Bridget, both being Garland out-laws, as they referred to themselves, neither of them opting to be on the family payroll.

She swung her baby to Will's, touched their heads as if in a kiss, and cooed, "Bye, cousin." Then she turned to join John.

In the next moments, as he waited for Shelley, Will couldn't help noticing he wasn't hearing quite the same enthusiasm in the old man's voice as he spoke to his namesake, John Garland, and to his great-granddaughter. He was not saying "Hot dog!"

What a jerk I am, Will thought happily. Children weren't supposed to be a contest. "Gar Trask," he whispered to his son as Shelley finally joined them. "You are such a little hot dog."

Shelley took in the whole scene, John and Bridget presenting Charlotte to Spark, Will giving them space. Then she did what Will thought of as that woman thing, where, just like that, she figured it all out. She smiled at Will as if she knew exactly the guilty, prideful thoughts he'd been thinking.

Knew, forgave, maybe even felt exactly the same way.

CHAPTER 6

If negotiations by phone weren't on tap, Will habitually left his office at Heritage Realty on the slightest excuse, a sunny day counting, to his mind, as one of the best. On such an afternoon not long after Doug's funeral, he was about to make his usual escape when fellow agent Kim Kelly popped out of her office between him and the top of the stairs.

"Hold on there, Will. I've got a property I need you to show."

Will sighed. The other half dozen agents quietly fought over new listings, but starting from the first time Will passed one to Kim, admitting how much he hated showing houses, they'd had a deal of helping each other out and, at this point, he owed her.

For him to happily show a residence, it would have to be something on a forested acreage, and admittedly he had blown more than one such sale by failing to give the potential buyers a chance to fall in love with the home in his rush to get them out into the trees.

True, there'd been the castle house that became the wedding venue. But that was a unique situation, the place needing a buyer with a solid business plan for the beautifully landscaped acreage. He'd mainly taken it on as a favor to the timber family who'd owned it. Cliff Howell had sent a lot of work his way over the years.

"Get that hang-dog look off your face," Kim said now. "This isn't a house. It's twenty acres clear up on Hopestill Creek, and I can*not* get there and back before my own open house at three. It's zoned for Forestry. That's good, right?"

"Twenty acres? Makes no sense at all."

"Well, I didn't write the zoning laws and, honestly, Will. Shouldn't you be thanking me? Here I'm handing you the listing *and* the potential buyer."

"Okay, okay."

"Sometimes I think you forget that showing properties is what real estate agents *do.*"

"Sorry." But the truth would sound mean—that he didn't think of himself as an agent like the rest of them. Yeah, he had the license. He had the official blazer (thanks, Shelley), although so far he'd managed never to be seen in it, the obvious excuse being that it wasn't exactly woods wear. Also, he wasn't *just* a real estate agent. He was…yeah, that word flung around by the engineer types from the Corvallis campus of Hewlett-Packard. He was a consultant, a title popping up with ever greater frequency now that the Corvallis division had let so many of them go, *in the current economy,* as everybody kept saying. Will had no idea what those poor guys got consulted about. How it felt to be unemployed?

As a timber consultant, what people wanted to know from Will was what to do with their timberland. Sell it? Thin it? Pre-commercial or commercial? Log it? Selective or clear-cut? Try to get somebody to pay them *not* to log it? (Look, we're sequestering carbon!) Try to push through some zoning change to sneak in a development? He avoided this one like poison oak—too damned many public hearings and tedious meetings with planners. Not to mentioned it just seemed wrong.

But whatever course of action he steered his clients toward, they needed him to line it all up—the logging, the replanting (Should we bet on global warming and try redwoods?), the road and bridge building. The permits for all of it. Hey, if they had to put in a well, he'd even be out there with his sticks witching the water.

Since nobody was building houses these days, nobody wanted lumber so nobody was logging. Who's going to pay to cut down trees when they're worth zip at the mill? This meant the big timber companies—Weyerhaeuser, Stimson, Hampton—were all looking to unload any awkward eighty-acre parcels, the sale of which would put money on their ledgers *now,* and not decades into the future as the timber matured.

That's when they called in Will Trask.

But these smaller parcels—well, times were definitely changing. He was seeing more of the sort of buyers interested in what they called "Heartstrings Investments," doctors from Corvallis, for instance, looking to sink their money somewhere while at the same time introducing their offspring to the idea of environmental stewardship. Will was always tempted to tell them if they just wanted their kid to plant a tree or two, it'd be a lot easier to just send them over to his in-laws' annual Tree Planting Day. Garland Forests would let them plant trees—free of charge!—and throw in a hot dog for lunch.

Management for these folks could be an incredible fiasco, too. He couldn't believe how long it took to get through that cardiologist's "landscape cut," what with his wife arguing over every last tree. And then when that one hemlock Doug Hudson had taken down turned out to be too big for any of the mills— well, wasn't *that* hell to pay? This woman wasn't having any of it, his suggestion that it made a nice landscaping addition, a nurse log lying there. No way! That tree had been cut and it broke her heart to have it wasted. Will explained how the mills had all re-tooled to handle smaller diameter trees and that's just the way it was. "Then you shouldn't have cut it," she kept saying. What, like he could stand it back up? He'd phoned all over the state trying to find a mill to take that one tree off his hands. Hull-Oakes still did the big stuff, but only Doug fir. He finally got Bald Knob Veneer in Creswell to take it once he put together a full load of hemlock, but that was crazily inefficient. Couldn't blame the doc's wife, how she felt, but it was no way for him to run a consulting business. And now Bald Knob had gone and burned down, so there went the last of the mills taking the big diameter white wood. He didn't want to wind up in that position again.

Still, at least Kim's listing would get him outside. And it wasn't like she was trying to send him over to show a condo in Corvallis or something.

"Okay," he said. "Let's see what you got."

She handed him the listing papers. "Here's the kicker." She tapped a checked-off box on the form. "Buildable."

"Well jeez, Kim. Why didn't you say so? How?"

"Grandfathered in. Lot of record."

"Okay, then," he conceded. Plenty of people interested in that, even if it wouldn't be his usual clients. But these days, with so many people flat-out afraid to do anything, he couldn't be turning his nose up at anybody with enough faith in the future to actually stick their neck out and lay down money for property.

And it was definitely what he liked to call real estate weather, the kind of mellow Fall day that made people—especially people from other places—forget what was going to happen in a couple of months here in Oregon. He scanned the specs. Looked good on paper. Nice picture of a flower-filled meadow.

Kim frowned. "I thought I had a better map on that. Lemme check." Turning away, she caught sight of someone in the lobby below, stopped and back-stepped to Will. *That's her,* she mouthed.

Will took a look over the railing. A blond woman in a gauzy Mexican blouse and hippie skirt stood swaying side to side as if to some distant drumbeat, a dreamy smile on her overly tanned face.

Kim tilted her head close. "Maybe I shouldn't be letting her get you out there alone."

Will played dumb. Sure, he got it, Kim's flirty shit, and you couldn't ignore her nice legs, the way she showed them off in short skirts and spiky heels, but after what happened with Liza Madison from Town & Country, it's hard to picture what sort of woman it'd take to tempt him to get involved like that again.

Kim went to forage in her office and from his he grabbed his truck keys and Filson vest, slipping into it as he nimbly took the stairs.

"Will Trask," he said to his new client, smiling broadly, sticking out his hand to shake. That was the safest, most businesslike—a handshake with everybody. They were all just potential buyers. "Kim says you want to check out the Hopestill Creek property."

The woman beamed and raised her eyebrows at Kim, who'd come down behind him—some kind of female signal he wasn't about to try interpreting.

Kim handed the map over his shoulder. Looking at it, he remembered. He knew this property.

As they headed west out of Eden Mills, Sierra Sunderland spun out a breathy tale of a search for a new life in Oregon, a longing to leave behind her tangled Bay Area past. Her voice was low, like a smoker who'd given it up. How old? Couldn't tell. Sounded like enough relationship drama in her life to fill several decades. (And why was she telling *him?*) She did have those crinkles around her eyes, but then, that could just be the California sun. He hoped she had some money to go along with this karma she claimed had brought her here. He'd long ago learned you could never really tell. You might miss a sale to somebody with a healthy trust fund if you didn't understand about people willingly paying good money for pre-ripped jeans, a concept he still couldn't grasp. The whole point of his Carhartts was that they *wouldn't* rip. You could push through blackberries without them immediately going to shreds.

By the time they turned onto Hopestill Creek Road, she had her bare feet up on his dashboard, a sparkling stone on a toe ring winking at him.

"I love that name—Hopestill Creek. Like—*still hope.*"

When she swayed his way, he caught a whiff of weed. Maybe her slow, throaty way of speaking, he thought, had less to do with a prior history of smoking and more with what she'd been smoking right before she showed up at Heritage Realty a half hour ago.

"Keep hoping," she said. "We have hope, still, you know?"

"Uh, yeah." On one hand, this seemed sadly obvious. On the other, he had to admit he hadn't ever actually thought of it himself.

"Words matter. The names of things are important to me. There was a property listed on a Shotpouch Creek Road. I wouldn't even look at it. I mean…" She shuddered. "That's about guns, right?"

"Yup," he confirmed. "But I think Hopestill was some pioneer lady. That suit you better?"

"Oh, yeah." She smiled at him, then craned back to look through the driver's side windows at sunlight sparkling on water. "So this is the creek, then?"

"Uh huh. The road follows right along it. They're doing a restoration project here, trying to get the fish back. They anchor logs in there to catch the woody debris. Helps keep it cool and make spawning places."

"Oooohhh," she said, as if he'd revealed something incredibly wise and mystical. "I *like* that concept."

They passed a sign at a piece of Garland Forests property. PLANTED 1978. Good PR, Will always thought, whoever came up with the idea of posting these on all the different tree farm properties. You'd hope people so upset over any kind of clear-cut would calm down a little when they saw how fast the new forest would grow. Those nuked-out areas didn't stay bare too long.

"Soooo," Sierra said, "the creek runs along this property we're going to see?"

"Well, the nice part about this piece is that the creek actually loops out through it, so the creek area's more private, you don't have people driving right by."

"*A River Runs Through It*," she said dreamily.

"Uh, well, a creek anyway."

It was this particular geographical configuration on the map that had reminded him of looking at it with Shelley almost twenty years ago. He remembered it being pretty special.

"So why are the owners putting it on the market?" Sierra asked. "And who are they, anyway?"

"Texas address. Don't know the story." Not that he'd be telling her much if he did. Heritage Realty was representing the seller here, not the buyer. Probably another project pulled from the file marked Dreams Deferred. People would buy a plot of land with the idea someday they'd build on it. Then life would take the turns it does and none of it would pan out. Divorce was a biggie. Marriages bust up + properties change hands = agents collect commissions.

"I have *such* a good feeling about this," Sierra said. "I was just down at Burning Man and—"

"At *what?*"

"The Burning Man Festival? Out in the desert? Nevada?"

His blank look seemed to floor her.

"You really haven't heard of it?"

"Nope. Should I?"

She grinned. "You're really something, you know that? Well, anyway, I was in a little hut thing with this guy. People were going crazy all around us outside. All of a sudden I just got this message: *Go up to Oregon.* Honestly, I don't know where that voice came from, but I stood right up, put on my clothes and walked out. They hadn't even torched the Man yet, but I didn't care. Just got in my car and drove. It's so weird I ended up in Corvallis. People mostly talk about the great vibe in Ashland and Eugene. But I missed the Ashland exit and when I came to that place where there's Eugene on one side of the freeway and Springfield's on the other, I couldn't even decide which exit to take. So I kept driving and then there was an exit for Corvallis, and I thought, okay, so let's try this. And then it was so beautiful, the farm fields, driving west. That mountain in the background. What do you call that?"

"Mary's Peak?"

"Yeah. And then coming over the bridge with that old courthouse tower sticking up. So I'm sitting at a sidewalk café table having my chai and somebody'd left the real estate section on the table and I saw the ad for this property. Like it was meant to be. Like I'm following this mystical path. When you get a message like that, you can't just ignore it, know what I mean?"

Will became aware she had stopped talking briefly, apparently awaiting his answer.

"Uh, sure."

"I mean, it was just such a strong gut feeling. And I'm really into trusting that, you know? Did you read that book about how we really ought to go with our first feelings about something? *Blink*, it's called."

"Musta missed that one." As if the miss might have been a near one. The truth? He didn't truck much with books except for one of Shelley's grease-stained old cookbooks and a well-thumbed copy of *Trees to Know in Oregon*. The last real book he'd read was Jon Krakauer's mountain climbing story, which Shelley'd packed for him to read in Hawaii. How could you live in Corvallis and not read *Into Thin Air*, she'd insisted, with everybody talking about it because Krakauer grew up here? He'd like it, she promised. And he had. Shelley always knew what he'd like.

Ha! He couldn't wait to tell her about this spacey woman—

Crap. Still forgetting. Was this going to keep happening forever? The thought would be gone before he finished it, but the fact that it was fleeting didn't mean he hadn't thought it.

"See, I'm not a religious person," Sierra confided, "but I'm very spiritual, and at this point in my life, one of my main goals is to be truly, genuinely honest with my inner spiritual self." She tilted her head back, looking at him through the blond hair whipping around her head. "You seem like a guy who'd under-stand what I mean."

He smiled. Nope. Not at all. Claiming to be spiritual, not religious? What, she wanted to make sure people understood she didn't go to church, but she still believed in angels or something? He especially couldn't think what it had to do with making decisions about real estate.

She rambled on and he was only half listening as he negotiated the curving road upwards. He knew most of the properties on this road, and his mind ran to the selling price on every piece he'd brokered the last time it had changed hands, which quarter section of trees would soon be ready for harvest, and whose heavily wooded yard needed some serious clearing work to keep the house and outbuildings defensible in case of fire.

"Here we go," he said, pulling in left at a white-washed wooden gate, double checking the address on his papers. Dubiously, he eyed Sierra's leather flip-flops and layered skirts. For Pete's sake—looked like little mirrors sewn in there. "Uh, do you want to drive in or walk?"

"Oh, I'm absolutely all about walking." She pushed up her sunglasses and squinted into the woods. "Is the road clear enough?"

"Kim said they'd cleaned it up." He got out, slammed the truck door and stuck the key in the gate's padlock. "Tell you what, if it's too bad I'll just come back and get the truck for you, okay?"

But, no problem. Once past the grassy verge the light at the road allowed, the canopy of firs kept the road to a carpet of needle duff with a mossy ridge in the center.

"Wow," Sierra said, looking up. "The famous old-growth trees of the Pacific Northwest."

"Not really. Nothing's really old-growth around here."

"Come on. You're just teasing a California girl, right?"

"Hey, you've got the redwoods. You know what big trees look like."

"Well, yeah," she conceded, "but…these really aren't old-growth?"

"Nope. Everything around here's been logged at least once or twice."

"Seriously?"

"That's right."

"But this tree here…" She laid her palm on the bark of a handsome Doug fir. "This has to be hundreds of years old."

"Nope. Not even close. Trees just get big fast here."

More complicated than that, but Will didn't feel like explaining. Sure, there'd always be individual trees the last loggers left as rejects. If you checked their tops, they'd probably have double crowns or some other defect. So, yeah, maybe some were older. But people who didn't know just looked at a big tree and had no idea the size of the true old-growth forests of the past. Also, they were clueless that a lot of the plantations in this area were actually *first-*growth. Aforestation. Before the white pioneers ever showed up, the natives had routinely burned the undergrowth to improve the hunting, so in lots of places there'd been no forest at all, just grassy hills studded with oak groves.

"Wow," Sierra kept saying as they moved down the road lined with these stately giants. "Oh, my God."

It *was* impressive. Will, too, gazed up in admiration. He took a deep breath. Something about this time of year, when the sun's warmth baked the smell of the fallen fir needles and over-ripe blackberries into what had to be the sweetest lungful of air on earth.

A ways on they came to the open meadow where the wildflowers and green grass of the spring listing photos had dried to gold.

"This must have been an old homestead," Will said, making his way to a cluster of gnarled apple trees. He picked one of the green and rose-washed fruits and took a bite. "Not bad. Gravenstein, I think." He picked a second, held it out. "Want to try one?"

She frowned at the offering. "Is it organic?"

Will laughed, spewing apple bits. "If the owners don't even come here, I seriously doubt they've got some kind of nasty spray program going."

"But you don't wash it?"

"What's to wash? It's just hanging here in the air."

Her skeptical expression faded as she caught sight of something beyond him. She squinted. "Is that a snow peak over there?"

He followed her gaze. "Yeah, that'd be Jeff. Mount Jefferson? Over in the Cascades."

"Well, it's far away. Not like a view of the Tetons or something, but still, it's cool you get a little glimpse of it." She stepped out into the meadow grass. "Oh, I *love* this place. Can't you just see a log cabin here?"

He could. In fact, that had been *his* thought too the first time he'd seen it. But it was a brief fantasy, even when a house for himself and Shelley was the big issue of the moment. She'd let him do his stint at commercial fishing, but now she was done with Pacific City and wanted to get back to Corvallis and her family. She'd only humored him, coming out here. She'd never liked log houses anyway, even if one had been sitting here, already built. She wanted flat interior walls for wallpapering. Will hadn't cared enough to fight about it. He'd already caved on the subject of living closer to her family; now he just wanted, like any normal guy, to be subjected to the least amount of disruption in terms of moving, remodeling, sorting, cleaning and such.

Actually, if Shelley'd had her way, they'd have been living in a big old Victorian with a spindle-railed porch and gingerbread trim tacked into every available right angle. Since there were only a handful like this in all of Corvallis and none on the market, their search had been a tedious waste of time. He'd been dragged through dozens of houses anyone could tell with a quick drive-by would never be right for her. What was the point of even going inside?

Their futile hunt had mercifully come to a halt with the serendipitous revelation that Shelley's grandfather's vintage Dutch Colonial on Western Boulevard had gone on the market. The current owners had bought it when Spark and Charlotte Garland finally had to move over to assisted living at Stoneybrook, and there'd been rumors of regret in the family ever since. Why'd they let it get away? A house built with all that clear-grained, old-growth fir? Never see the likes of it again. Now everybody, including Spark and Charlotte, were delighted to think of Shelley and Will living there. And since she'd already broken down his resistance to accepting parental help on the down payment, it certainly seemed easiest and only polite to settle on a house that meant so much to the family.

Why fight fate?

Shelley always gushed about the wonderful Christmases there, the games they'd played on the stairs and the huge apple tree and grape arbor out back. And the "Owl's Nest." From all the fond recollections he'd heard about this particular structure and the events it had hosted—the cookouts, the overnights—he was slightly underwhelmed at the screen-fronted shed with the stone fireplace. "Oh, look, Will," he remembered Shelley saying, "the lamps I was telling you about! It's faint but see the little owls and the moon on the glass?" The rusted lanterns looked kind of beat-up to him, but if she was happy, okay.

Sierra brought him back now, saying, "Two-seventy-nine seems so low for this."

"Uh…" Will fumbled with the listing papers, re-checking the price. "Yeah, I'm sure, compared to California."

"Something wrong with it? Like a buried meth lab?"

"Naw. Prices are just down. Three years ago it would have been different." He climbed up on a huge stump overgrown with salal. Thing must have been six feet across. "Okay, this is what was here. This is your old-growth. Or was."

"Oh. That must have looked amazing." She regarded it thoughtfully for a moment. "But it would have been really dark in here, right?"

"Yep. Trees do make shade. They say those pioneer women, first thing they wanted done was get the guy to chop back the big scary forest." They moved out into the meadow. "Okay, see?" He pointed. "The creek runs along the bottom of the meadow there. Through those alders."

She started down at a lope, exaggerating the left/right movement of her shoulders as she dragged her gauzy skirt through the grass.

Will looked up at the sky, scanned the tops of the encircling trees. The middle of the meadow seemed the obvious, logical house site…

"Hey," she called. "You coming?"

He started after her. Weird. Usually while a potential buyer looked at the trees and the lay of the land, he watched *them*, gauging their reaction to everything. Were they liking it? Maybe more than they wanted to let on? Trying to play it cool? Would they likely make an offer?

But this place…She was obviously in love with it, yet somehow he wasn't mentally running the commission percentage. He hadn't been estimating the standing timber's board footage.

In the middle of the meadow she did a slow, euphoric whirl. Julie Andrews and the Sound of California Money. Flushed and exuberant, she stopped and faced him, shouting back, "I think this is my place!"

Something buzzed through him. *The hell it is.*

She dragged back through the grass, happily breathless. "I don't just want it for myself, see. I want to make a place where people can be healed. And find peace. And do art. And write. Write poetry. Oh, this place *is* poetry. It would just be so inspiring for everybody! Like that thing over on Cascade Head? I came up and went to a pottery workshop there one time. I would so love to make something like that happen here."

Will shook his head with phony regret. "You'd have zoning issues. It's actually kind of unusual that you can even put a house on a piece this small."

"This small? What are you talking about?"

"Well, the zoning laws are to keep the big timber parcels from being chopped up into subdivisions. So if you've got your quarter section, your hundred and sixty acres, and that's your tree farm, they might let you put a house on it. But this is a freak deal here, this twenty acres, and I doubt you'd get away with a conference-center-type set-up."

"Oh." Her face fell. "That is *so* sad. Because we should be about sharing, shouldn't we? Doesn't it seem selfish for me to build a house out here for just myself and…" She flashed a wan little smile at him. "Me and whoever. See, my grandmother left me this money and I just feel so strongly that I need to be doing the moral thing with it."

Ah! So, Sierra the Heiress. How much money had Granny left her? Did she have any idea how much it would take for the sort of project she was talking about?

"This place deserves to be enjoyed by more people." She tenderly placed a hand over her heart. "Not just me."

Will knew that to sell this place, he should be aiming for all the empathy he could muster, but somehow, with this woman, he just felt like arguing.

"Thing is," he said, "places more people can enjoy…that's kind of what they have in mind with the parks. The state parks, the county parks. Okay, your national parks?"

She stuck out her sunburned lip in a little-girl pout, but it was brief. Momentarily a slow, satisfied smile again spread across her face. Apparently she liked the place too much to let it get her down, the annoying news that she wouldn't be allowed to share this glorious twenty acres with the masses yearning to breathe free. She turned and sashayed a step or two, and when she caught her skirt on a blackberry vine, just ripped it away and kept going, arms uplifted.

"The fresh air here…" She drew in a deep breath, closing her eyes in ecstasy. "And the sound of the creek. I mean, that's *water*. Water is the stuff of life itself, isn't it?"

"Yup."

"And that's its music."

Will followed her, wondering why she pissed him off so bad. Actually, he had to admit he thought of the sweet forest air like that himself, how it seemed like a couple of deep breaths of it could cure you of anything. And the mystery of the sound of flowing water being so soothing. Maybe he just didn't like having it said out loud in a lot of airy-fairy words. By a woman from California.

Oh, great. He saw, before she did, the fawn emerge from the shadows. He caught the moment she spotted it. She froze, her hands up and open in a posture of Walt Disney delight, then slowly turned and lifted her shoulders with the eager question. Had he seen it? He nodded. Yeah, yeah. These foothills were lousy with deer, but then, she wouldn't know that.

"Oh," she whispered, coming back toward him. "Wasn't that just magical?"

Oh, yeah. Now all he needed was for some damn bird to land on her shoulder and start chirping a cheerful little tune in her triple-pierced ear.

CHAPTER 7

"I hate this!" her little sister Shelley cried, holding up wet yellow tree-planting mittens. "My hands are frozen."

Robin flipped her blond braid back and looked across the muddy slope. Other kids seemed to be edging down to the bus. "Just stick it out a little longer. Then you're done for a whole year."

"Huh. What I want to know is, if Tree Planting Day is once a year and so's Christmas, why does Tree Planting Day always come around so much faster? And those other kids only have to do this field trip one day in their whole life, not every stupid year."

Robin shrugged. "They're not Garlands." She always felt proud that this was *her* family's tree farming business and *her* dad showing everybody how to dig the hole, slip the tree in and tamp the dirt firmly down around the roots. She even got a thrill the first time she realized the Garland kids had all been issued the proper tool, a hoe-dad, while the kids who signed up with their Boy or Girl Scout troops had to bring their own shovels. Her father said they were planting the Forests of the Future, and she always found herself standing up a little straighter when he gave that speech at the doughnuts-and-hot-chocolate morning kick-off.

"You actually like this, Robin. I can tell. So I think you're a little weird."

Robin shrugged. Maybe she was. Or the cold and rain just didn't bother her as much. True, this vast hillside of mud up off Hopestill Creek Road just couldn't have been uglier or more dismal on this foggy February day, with the thick, rain-laden clouds pressing low enough to obscure the forested ridge tops. But she was thinking how it would look in the future. The bleakness was a problem they were solving. They'd plant these trees and then pretty soon this acreage would match the lush green forest surrounding it.

"I'm going to tell Mom I don't want to do this anymore," Shelley said. "I bet she won't make me."

Probably not. It was just so obvious Shelley was Mom's favorite. She could get babied all she wanted. Well, who cared? Robin had Dad.

"At least I'm going to ask if I can stay in the shelter next year," Shelley said, "and just hand out the snacks to the other kids. Then I wouldn't get wet."

Funny. Robin had been thinking that *her* plan for staying dryer next year would involve lobbying for a set of official rain-proof tree-planter's pants. Dad would probably agree, if the suppliers made them small enough.

"If everybody sat under the tarp staying dry," Robin pointed out, "how would the trees get planted?"

"The boys should do it! I just don't think it's nice to make a girl be so cold."

"Oh, Shelley. You are such a little princess." *Crybaby*, she wanted to say, but Mom and Dad didn't approve of name calling.

"Well, I'd rather be a princess than a crazy person who thinks it's fun to be wet and miserable. You know that thing about 'soaked to the skin?' That's what happening." And then, indignantly, "Even my underpants are wet!"

"Well, Shelley—"

"And don't tell me how much the trees like being planted in the rain. I know and I don't care!" She flung down a seedling and threw herself to the ground, flat on her back, arms and legs spread wide. A mud angel. "I'm done! I'm dead. We ought to tell the police or somebody. They shouldn't be making little kids do all the hard work."

"Oh, come *on*." Sometimes her sister seemed way younger than just two years. Part of it, sure, was probably that Robin was already so tall. But also, frankly, what a wimp! Shelley knew perfectly well Tree Planting Day was not about forcing free labor from children.

As soon as they could hold a hoe-dad they'd each been led out to symboli-cally plant their first tree, mothers poised with cameras to document the historic moment. It had all been explained to them, how Tree Planting Day was started so kids—and not just Garland kids—would be able to come back and take pride in seeing trees they'd planted grown up tall. They were Oregonians; they should understand what it meant to live in one of the states that grew such a huge proportion of the nation's trees. The world's trees. And as for the Garland kids themselves, it was Grampa Spark Garland who wanted to make sure they all knew just how hard that tree-planting work was. They were re-foresting only the tiniest fraction of Garland Forests' lands. It took lots of crews of tough people with strong backs working awfully hard out there to keep all those logged over sites planted. He didn't want the Garland kids ever to take that for granted.

"Go away," Robin heard Shelley say, and turned to see their cousin John standing over her.

"You leave me alone," Shelley told him.

"Fine." He pivoted, his rubber boots sucking mud as he passed Robin, who eyed his empty bag, the minimal grime on his gloves. Something wasn't right. He grinned. "You don't have to work so hard, you silly gooses. Just ditch your trees behind a stump. They'll never know."

Robin's mouth fell open. She couldn't have been more shocked if her cousin had advised stealing money from her own father's wallet.

"They will *too* know! When they find the bare spot. Or a whole pile of trees grows up in the same place." Because even carelessly thrown, the roots might wriggle in and take hold. The young trees would compete for light and air and water. They would twist themselves and fight each other to grow.

John flashed that smile of his and shrugged. "They won't know it was me, though. And you won't tell 'em. That's what so great about you, Robin. You're such a goody-goody you'd do anything they tell you to. And then you're even too good to be a tattletale."

With a jaunty jerk of his chin, he turned and let the force of gravity help careen him down the slope, slipping and sliding, dragging his empty bag.

"I hate him," Shelley said, turning her head toward Robin. "He tried to kiss me at Christmas out in the Owl's Nest."

"What!"

"He said Kissing Cousins was a big tradition, but not to tell the grownups."

"Shelley! Did you let him?"

"No! What do you think?" She sat up. "Did he try to kiss *you*?"

"No." Ugh, what a thought.

Everybody always thought John was so great just because he knew how to look grownups in the eye and stick out his hand to shake like he was already an adult himself. "Nice to meet you," he'd tell some person Uncle Pete introduced him to. Since he got the name John Garland, which was Grampa Spark's real name, it seemed like it had already been decided he was first in line to be the next boss of the tree farms.

Robin's older brother Greg never got quite the attention John did when the whole family was together. So what if he wasn't quite as handsome in that golden-haired way John was, or as quick with his talking? At least he wasn't a sneak. Up the slope, Robin could see Greg doggedly sticking in his trees. He didn't have Robin's intense interest in the whole project, but he always did his share without complaint.

Robin gave Shelley a hand up, sat the soggy little girl on a stump, went back to planting.

A dozen seedlings later their father, Ed Garland, made his way toward them in his orange vest.

"Shelley's really tired, Dad." As if this weren't clear. "Maybe you should let her quit."

"Sure. Okay. But how about you?"

"I'm okay."

"Good for another bag?"

"Sure." She fished the last two seedlings out of her bag, trading the empty for the full one he'd apparently felt confident enough to haul up to her.

"That's my girl."

Magic words. She smiled and slung the new load over her shoulder. Actually, by now she was pretty wet and worn out herself. But somehow her father always made her want to keep plugging away.

"Okay, Shelley," Dad said, pulling the bedraggled child up by the hand. "Let's head down. Grampa Spark just got here to check on us and I'm sure he'd like to see you."

Shelley turned back wide-eyes at Robin. She liked to claim she found Grampa Spark scary, but really she just liked Grammie better. Robin understood he was simply a serious guy, not some sort of jolly Santa Claus grampa. Being a serious sort of person herself, she never found this a problem.

She bent back to the earth, spreading the tangle of tree roots over a mound of dirt in the hole. She liked the stories they told about Grampa, how he got his nickname the summer during college when he sat up in a forest fire lookout, his mail arriving by donkey pack. Somehow his letters just started coming addressed to Spark Garland, because that's what he was supposed to be watching out for up in that wooden tower. And maybe, too, it had to do with his spark-red hair.

He had helped his own father build the lumber mill and then, during the Depression, when people couldn't pay taxes on their cutover forest land, the Garlands bought it up and re-planted. When people mocked them for planting trees they'd never live to cut down, Spark Garland just shrugged and said, "Somebody better do it."

Robin's father always told them their great-grandfather was a man of character. He believed in putting his loggers and millworkers first and trying to keep them employed during hard times. And then of course Grampa Spark aimed to be as good a guy as everybody thought his dad had been, and make him proud by not only going to college, but becoming a Forestry professor.

Robin lifted her head, looked down to where they had the shelter set up. She could see Grampa Spark's mud-spattered truck parked there. He loved that truck so much, Dad said he absolutely refused to buy a new one, even though they had all been trying to convince him to for years.

Dad had Shelley under the shelter by now. As Robin watched, Dad looked up the hill and singled her out to Grampa, who turned around, following Dad's pointing arm. Grampa tilted his face up.

Robin straightened and executed a big bold arc like she was bringing in an important plane for landing. No wimpy Rose Festival Princess waves for her. Spark and her father seemed to be nodding at each other, then Grampa waved back.

Twelve-year-old Robin Garland gave herself a moment to enjoy this.

Then, okay, enough of that. They wouldn't want to watch her standing around. She reached into her bag for another tree. The Forests of the Future were counting on her.

CHAPTER 8

Doug's boys were getting pretty good at their chainsaw art, Will thought, slamming his pick-up door in the gravel turnaround at the Hudson place. Had a couple pieces flanking the steps up to the iron-hinged double doors of the massive timberframe house—a bear on hind feet clutching a salmon, another depicting an eagle in flight. Donna'd said they were selling the wooden statues over at some highway shop on the coast. Guys had to do what they could, timber business slowing down like it had.

Great spread Will had found them here, some five years ago. It showed to great advantage on a crisp October day like this, with the deep green forested ridges sharp against the bright blue sky. A hundred and sixty acres total, half in hazelnuts, half in mature timber running up the rise from the Luckiamute River. Seemed like the previous owners lost interest in the whole thing about five minutes after they moved in. Got caught up in a new dream, a notion of being happier somewhere else. They wanted their money out of the place. Now. All of it.

"Not so easy," Will'd had to school Brent Townsend. "You've got too much value locked in that timber up there. Not many buyers with pockets deep enough to buy it just to have a nice private forest in their backyard."

"Well, that's what *we* did."

"Yeah, and Brent? There aren't a whole lot of buyers out there like you, trust me. If I say, okay, who'd like a three-bedroom, two-bath house in a nice little college town like Corvallis, well, tons of people, right? But if I'm looking for a buyer for a big acreage out in the sticks with timber, a farming business, a huge house and the price tag to match, that makes the pool a little shallower. You've got a great house here, but the next guy with the money to spring for it'll have his own idea what a dream house ought to look like. Hey, remember when I sold you this place? How many other places did I show you that already had big fancy houses on them and you were like *nothin' doin'!*"

And Will went straight to Doug and Donna and told them he had a place with their name written all over it, an acreage just crying out for the Hudsons—loggers who could cut that timber in their own good time, when the price was right or they were short on other contract work. And if they could cut down trees, how tough would it be every Fall to pick up a few nuts?

In their early years together, Doug and Donna had been too busy working and taking care of babies to ever stop to think what a dream house of their own would look like, so when Will took them out to the Luckiamute spread, their only qualm was the embarrassingly huge size of the house. The Townsends, having heard the call of Costa Rica or Costa Mesa—Will could never remember which—were so impatient to move on that, for an amazingly reasonable price, they threw in all the furniture, the harvester, the sweeper, a practically brand new John Deere tractor with a sprayer, plus a self-propelled forklift. Hot damn! Doug had been so excited about all that equipment. Like shiny toys under the Christmas tree.

Donna just knew it was a good deal. She'd always been sharp as anything, the business brains behind their whole operation, right from the beginning. Will remembered her out on some job with baby Wade in a backpack, estimating a bid for building a bridge strong enough to support an eighty-thousand-pound log truck over a fish-bearing little crick that couldn't be driven straight through the way they did in the old days. Over the years, Will had steered her to all the various properties she and Doug had then bought up. They'd log the timber, replant, repair the houses, rent them out. Signing yet another set of escrow papers with her at Willamette Valley Title one time, Will said he hoped

Doug didn't feel he was out of line, egging her on too much in this land acquisition thing.

"Oh, come on! You know Doug. He's happy to leave all this to me. Anyway, I'm only doing like it says in the Bible. Right there in that part about what it takes to be a virtuous woman. She's above the price of rubies and all that? Proverbs 31:16. *She considereth a field, and buyeth it.*"

Will laughed. "Okay then, my virtuous woman," he said, "signeth here."

She'd pulled this off enough times that when the Luckiamute place came along and prices were still high in those years on the other properties, they were able to cash in three of them and swing the deal.

Now, hearing the hum of machinery out in the orchard, Will didn't bother going up the front steps, but followed the noise and the cloud of dust out to find Donna driving the sweeper.

"Don't want to keep you from your work," he shouted, which of course prompted her to shut off the engine and climb down.

"I could use a break," she said, swigging water from a canteen.

Will swiveled his gaze up and down the long row of neatly swept nuts between the trees. "Looks like you've about got this whipped."

"Yeah." She smiled, her teeth flashing clean and white from her dusty face. "Dirty work, but, you know, I kinda like it." Then she stopped, squinted at his chest and frowned. "Will Trask. You're the last guy I'd ever expect to see wearing a pink shirt."

He looked down. "Not pink. It's red."

Her mouth went sideways. "Maybe back when the first covered wagons rolled in."

"It *used* to be red," he said defensively. "Shelley always made me wear it in the woods."

"Duh. Didn't want you getting shot."

Yeah, yeah, and he had always cursed that nameless, long-ago yahoo who'd carelessly fired into the woods and killed Shelley's uncle, making her think Will's odds out there were way worse than they actually were. The whole point of hunting in camo was not letting your prey spot you, right? At the time her vigilance on his behalf had done nothing but annoy him; now he remembered her safety reminders with a certain sad fondness, evidence she cared. He only started wearing and washing the red shirt out to pink when she wasn't around to hassle him about it anymore.

"Well," he said to Donna now, "I thought I should stop by and follow up on what you said about putting the place on the market."

She pulled back, looking over her nose at him. "Who said anything about that?"

"Uh…" He hesitated. "Well, actually, Donna, you did, but…" He put up two blocking hands, like this could be the end of it right here. No need to argue.

"You know, I probably did. But for a couple of weeks there, I have no idea *what* I said. Wade's wife swears the day after the accident I was sitting there talking about signing up for a cake decorating class. Now you know that wadn't me talking!"

He laughed. "Okay."

"I think the kids are all just going to move in with me. They were hanging around at first just to, you know, make sure I didn't do anything stupid, I guess. But they all like it out here and of course I love having those babies around and—well, look at it—you know the house is ridiculously huge. Besides, I don't think Doug'd want to see me go bailing on the place just like that."

Will smiled. Amazing how well she seemed to be holding up. He'd actually stalled on this visit, to be honest, dreaded finding her in deep, dark mourning. A relief to see her looking pretty much like the old Donna he knew.

"Well, if you're not wanting to write up listing papers, I should let you get back to work."

"Yeah, but listen, I gotta tell you. That brother-in-law of yours was sniffing around out here."

"Brother-in-law?" No way she could mean Shelley's brother, Greg.

"Well, cousin-in-law or whatever he is. That John Garland guy."

"Oh, him. Bonnie Prince Johnnie."

She hooted at the nickname, then dropped her voice. "Will," she said, "he was wearing a suit."

Will grinned. "Yeah, doesn't that kill you?"

"But...why?"

"Gotta keep up appearances, I guess. Doesn't want anybody to forget he's actually a lawyer. Jeez, we all laugh about it 'cause he's the only one in the family like that. Musta got it from his mom's side or something. Sure didn't get it from old Spark Garland. That guy was famous for dressing like a bum." Will shook his head. "So what did our boy want?"

"Asked if I might be interested in selling my timber rights. You know, just go for the cash now and then Garland Forests would log it later."

"You don't want to do that, do you?"

"Don't I?"

"Not if you're okay without that money for the moment. Because you know it's not going to be top dollar, not with prices like they are now, and when the market goes back up, you won't be happy to have somebody else making a killing off it."

She nodded thoughtfully.

"So, what'd you tell him?"

She smiled. "That I'd need to talk to you about it."

Will burst out laughing and clapped her back. "Oh, Donna, I'll bet he loved that!"

"Now why'd I guess you guys don't get along? What's the story?"

"Ha! One that's too long to bore you with on such a pretty day. But let's just say if he coulda killed me without going to prison, he'd a shot me years ago."

"Will!"

"It's the truth. Hates my guts. Feeling's mutual."

"Hmm. And he's married, right?"

"Oh, yeah." Will thought of Bridget. Long-suffering Bridget.

"Well, this is going to sound so lame, Will. And maybe I'm just imagining it. I don't really trust my own brain these days, but, the thing is, I thought maybe he was kind of hitting on me."

"Aw, gee."

"Oh, that's stupid, isn't it? I was probably just imagining it."

"No, no, that's not what I meant. You *weren't* imagining it. He's a total jerk. Always has been. Shelley had this story of the Christmas she was ten and he tried to talk her into playing Kissing Cousins."

"Ten! That's sick!"

"Yeah, well, he was only twelve. But that just shows what an early start he got, chasing women. Shelley always kicked herself for telling me, because it made me so mad she was afraid I was gonna punch the guy out ever since. I still wouldn't mind taking him down." Will smiled. "Want me to?"

"Oh, no, no…"

"Well, what'd he do, anyway?"

"Oh, the usual sympathy, and sorry for your loss and all that. But then gets into stuff about how am I doing on my own, and it must be lonely, and if there's ever anything he can do for me. *Anything at all.*"

Will shook his head. "I'm so sorry, Donna."

"Not *your* fault." She clucked. "And boy, that poor wife a his. You know, if I ever thought Doug was running around acting like that on me…" She shook her head. "I don't know what I'd a done, but it wouldn't have been pretty!"

"Doug was totally loyal to you, Donna."

Her eyes pooled. "I know."

"Hey, I can't tell you how many times I watched Kim down at my office try to get a little something going with him. That guy just wasn't having any of it."

She nodded, smiling. "Wished I could've seen that."

"She liked to give him a hard time for tracking mud up the carpet steps to our offices, but then she was always telling him he ought to be on TV, that he was better looking than most of those pot-bellied jokers on *Ax Men*."

"Yeah? I bet he liked hearing that. It's the truth too."

They stood there, quiet, devoting a moment to goodlooking, mud-tracking, totally-faithful Doug.

"Well, hey," Will said. "I'll get out of your way. You're a workin' woman, here." He threw an arm around her and gave her shoulder a squeeze.

"Oh, Will." She curled toward him, slipped her dust-coated flannel sleeves around him.

Whoa. Guess she needed a hug. But you had to be so careful. He didn't want to be coming off like Bonnie Prince Johnnie.

CHAPTER 9

Cindy Stuckey imagined other mother/daughter duos chatting over coffee at one another's kitchen tables, or on the phone if they lived at a distance. With Ardis and herself? Not happening. Not with adjacent Garland Forests offices. Her mother had only to buzz if she had something to say, which today she apparently did.

Now Cindy stood, by command, in the doorway.

"Have a seat," Ardis said.

Oh. So, something serious. The hand-off of a file wouldn't warrant an invitation like this. Her mother actually pushed up from her padded swivel chair to close the door, a quivering of her jowls indicating that, obviously, Cindy should have thought to do this without her having to ask.

"I have some very bad news for our family," Ardis announced, retaking her seat.

Cindy's gut clenched. *Cancer.*

"Bridget's leaving John."

"What?" Cindy blinked, fear fading to surprise. "She is?"

Ardis nodded gravely. Then, referring to her notes, she proceeded to outline the telephone conversation she'd had with Bridget.

"And that's just it?" Cindy said after the summation. "She's filing for divorce without even trying a separation?"

"That's right," Ardis said, "and she's booked an attorney in Salem. According to John, one of the most ruthless divorce lawyers in the state. Of course your father and I have taken appropriate measures ourselves, put up a fire wall around his assets, so to speak. That girl will *not* be cleaning us out."

Well, although Cindy was never quick to leap to any defense of her sister-in-law, she couldn't picture the Bridget she knew cold-bloodedly trying to calculate how to come out the financial winner in something like this.

"Of course we wouldn't be in this position," Ardis continued, "if your father had taken my advice back when I was arguing for making John get a pre-nuptial agreement. Oh, no, he wouldn't consider it. Said he couldn't see planning for a divorce the minute a son comes home announcing his engagement. You can be sure he's sorry now."

Cindy considered this. "You two never had a pre-nup, did you?"

"Of course not! People like us didn't worry about that back then. We knew we'd never get divorced. Your father felt confident I wasn't a woman who'd ever think of running off."

"So, when I got engaged, did you try to talk Dad into making Phil sign one?"

"No, but that was different. Phil was the perfect addition to the family. We've always been so grateful that you gave us a Forestry grad all set to sign on with us. But Bridget...Your father and I could see from the very beginning she just wasn't the right choice for John. Honestly, right away talking about going off to grad school? She never had the sense of what her position would be, marrying into our family. The role in the community she ought to be taking on. Your father and I had even agreed if John didn't get over his infatuation with her we would step in at the appropriate time and speak up."

"Mom, really?"

"Yes, but the time never seemed right and suddenly they were getting married and I got all caught up booking the reception, arranging the wedding. Not that she was ever one bit grateful."

Cindy nodded, dazed, still unable to get her head around it—a divorce in the Garland family.

"Now really, Cindy, you know I understand about young women wanting to have their own careers, but honestly, in a family like ours? Where it just isn't necessary? Where we've got all sorts of jobs available for anybody who wants to be involved? It made no sense, Bridget dragging them both off to Seattle for physical therapy school. Remember us scrambling around to get him into law school up there? We certainly weren't going to let him go off and play house-husband. And then when she got pregnant with Charlotte, wouldn't you have thought she'd see it was time to forget the foolishness? I'm sure Charlotte's insecurities and issues go right back to Bridget insisting on pursuing this *career* of hers when she should have been home, mothering her full-time."

Over the years, Cindy had heard most of this, but today Ardis seemed to feel a need to sum up the case against her daughter-in-law once and for all, and as she soldiered on, Cindy tuned out, inching her chair around to stare dully out the windows overlooking the valley floor's grass-seed fields stretching to the south. Had there been more to her mother not lobbying for Phil to sign a pre-nup? Was she confident Cindy was such a catch, no husband would ever think of leaving her? Or—dark thought—had Ardis figured with her extra pounds and generally ordinary looks, Cindy couldn't qualify as a catch *without* the lure of the Garland fortune? Had her mother feared the first hint of a pre-nup might scare boyfriends away?

Cindy swiveled her chair back around. "So why's Bridget doing this? Did she say?"

Ardis made a sour face. "She informed me this isn't the life she was meant to lead."

Cindy returned the semblance of disgust her mother clearly required, but it took some effort to mask a twinge of empathy for Bridget's claim. Cindy wasn't leading the life she'd meant to, either. Her plan had been to contribute at least three new members to the Garland clan, proudly mothering them into responsible positions in the family, the business, and the charitable foundation.

She certainly never thought she'd have no children at all and merely be stuck helping keep the books.

"Of course it's not exactly a surprise Bridget's been unhappy," Ardis continued. "But then, I've always felt that people who think of themselves first can't possibly ever *be* happy."

Cindy pressed her lips together. Lots of people in town glad to testify they'd benefitted greatly from Bridget's "selfishness" in pursuing her career. More than once Cindy had been with her mother at church when someone had come up to them in the parish hall after services and instead of saying how impressive John was with his recent Rotary speech, they'd disappoint Ardis by wanting to rave in detail over the way Bridget had made their hip pain go away after four doctors and two other therapists had failed.

"And haven't we tried to instill it in you and John," Ardis said now, "how families sticking together and putting others first is the most important thing in life?"

Cindy nodded, wondering why always being hammered with this had never provided the least bit of comfort.

"I did think our views on divorce had been made plain enough," Ardis said. "So it came as quite a shock to have Bridget pick up the phone like that and just…make this announcement."

"Well, yeah."

"Did you ever get any hint of this? Did she ever say anything to you?"

"Not really. She always talked a lot more to Shelley. Which I always thought was a little strange. I'm the closer relative, right?"

"That's just it," Ardis pointed out. "She always knew anything she said to you would get right back to me."

Disturbing, her mother's confidence in this, especially since Cindy knew it was true. She hated this need to ingratiate herself with her mother, try to make points by being quick to confide or report. Lucky John. He never even had to try. She crossed a leg over her knee and tucked her hands into opposite armpits.

He'd always been the favorite. If he'd been born first, with his Y chromosome, good looks and charm, would they even have bothered to have her? Maybe one male heir apparent was all they needed.

Cindy had put in several years of counseling sessions down in Eugene, ostensibly trying to get a grip on the fact that she would not be experiencing motherhood in any form. Far too often, though, she found herself complaining to the psychologist about her brother, recounting the latest ways in which Pete and Ardis had shown their favoritism. At each new infraction, she always managed to work up the same level of shock and outrage as she had over the last one until finally the counselor called her on it.

"My question," the counselor said, "is why on earth does this keep surprising you?"

Now, sitting here in her mother's orderly, drab office, Cindy was experiencing the strangest tangle of emotions over these revelations. It bothered her more than she cared to admit, this business about Bridget and Shelley being so buddy-buddy. They had babies and she didn't, yes, but there was more to it than that. She'd imagined with Shelley gone, maybe Bridget would become more of a friend to her, but clearly that wasn't happening. She also felt distressed: poor Charlotte. And concerned: this wouldn't do the blood pressures of either Pete or Ardis any good.

Somehow, though, in this knotty, confusing weave of feelings, one little thread did provide an undeniable hint of pleasure. A divorce was embarrassing, unpleasant business for the whole family. Her parents were obviously devastated. So wasn't it nice to know that no matter whose fault the divorce, it was the marriage of their fair-haired boy that was crumbling, not hers?

Returning to her own office, Cindy realized that strangely, though, the foremost emotion engulfing her was plain old envy. Bridget was actually going to get away with this?

Because Garlands weren't *allowed* to divorce. Everybody knew that. Certainly no one suggested it to Cindy as a solution when she saw how it was going to be with Phil. Bridget boldly making a break on her own behalf just brought it all up again, what Cindy had worked so hard to put in the past. As if anyone got over the heartbreak of a miscarriage. But maybe it was more the aftermath that had done her in—finally figuring out Phil had a major problem in the form of a pathetic sperm count, not to mention the ones he did manage weren't looking too lively. Her doctor had privately hinted he could hardly believe Phil had even been responsible for that first pregnancy, given his subsequent lab results. The doctor almost seemed to be inviting her, in a sympathetic way, to confess that she'd "made alternative arrangements."

What? Did he imagine she'd had a quick affair with ulterior motives? Or loaded some guy's stuff in a turkey baster and taken care of herself? She hadn't, of course, but the odd part in recalling this was always the undeniable thrill of realizing her doctor apparently thought her even capable of such a thing. That she, Cynthia Charlotte Garland Stuckey, would consider coloring anywhere outside the lines of the playbook of pre-approved behavior.

It did get her thinking, though, and when the doctor suggested formally arranging for donor semen, she brought it up to Phil.

Please. The way the very idea horrified him, you'd have thought she'd suggested murdering a full-term pregnant woman for her fetus.

"The doctor says people do it all the time," she'd pleaded, but Phil said he didn't care what other people did. He could never feel comfortable having his wife carry a baby that wasn't his.

When she explained about in vitro, he indignantly refused to "mess with that stuff."

So what about adoption?

No way. Who knows what kind of start the kid got?

The final blow came when he admitted he now realized he really didn't want children at all. In spite of what he may have said to the contrary before they were married, he had soured on the idea, and all this trouble just seemed like God's way of saying it wasn't meant to be. Cindy would need to start accepting that.

Well, had anyone suggested divorce at that point? Had anyone sympathized and agreed she had a right to feel tricked, a right to—just this once—put her own needs at the top of the list? Because if Phil had been upfront in the beginning about his feelings regarding children (she couldn't believe he had only recently changed his mind), she was sure that would have been a deal breaker before she'd ever brought him home for her parents' approval. And at the time when it became clear there'd be no more efforts toward parenthood, she'd been young enough that she could have divorced him, and if a cooperating second husband hadn't shown up in short order, had a baby on her own, booking herself a likely donor through OHSU.

But, oh no, that wouldn't do for a daughter of the Garland clan. No encouragement along those lines for *her*.

"Guess who's getting divorced?" she said when she climbed into Phil's clean white Garland Forests logoed truck at the end of the workday. He'd been over at the mill as usual, although what he found to keep busy there with it temporarily shut down she had no idea. Probably just left on any excuse rather than sit in his office next to hers at their corporate headquarters. Fine. She felt the same. Except—unfortunately—no escape hatch for her.

"Divorce?" Phil kept his eyes on the long driveway leading out to the highway. "Who, us?"

So not funny. So excruciatingly not funny. "Bridget's leaving John."

Now he did turn toward her. "You're kidding."

"No. Mom called me in her office to tell me."

"Really?" Her husband adjusted his bulk behind the steering wheel. He pushed his hat back and scratched his head. "But why? Because you know your parents'll make sure she comes out of it just as poor as possible."

Cindy regarded him coolly. So sadly plain, wasn't it, that his own thoughts might have trotted down this same path a time or two?

Phil's doughy face looked particularly unattractive in his befuddlement. "So why would she do a dumb thing like that?"

Cindy turned away, looking out the opposite window as the trees and fields flashed past. "Maybe," she said, "maybe she wants to be happy."

CHAPTER 10

I can't believe how much this must be costing them," Will said in the backseat of the taxi van that was taking them from the Kona airport up to their resort.

"Yes," Shelley whispered, terse. "You've mentioned that. Ten or eleven times now." She clearly didn't want to be arguing in the driver's hearing.

"Well, if each little grass shack is a thousand dollars a day, and your parents are forking out for four…And Pete and Ardis are doing the same for theirs…"

"Will! Can't you ever stop running the numbers? I never should have shown you that brochure."

"Well, yeah, you shouldn't have. Because it just makes me feel…nervous or something."

"Oh, for heaven sakes. I hope you're not going to be walking around talking like this the whole week. You've got to relax and stop worrying about it."

"But it's just so much money, that's all."

"Well, so what? Nobody's asking *you* to pay." She glanced behind to their two belted-in boys. Shouldn't be arguing in front of them, either. "I told you Dad said Spark even wrote this trip into his will, right? If getting everybody together here for their fortieth anniversaries means so much to them, why can't you just have the good grace to be grateful and shut up?"

Will blew out a weary sigh and sank sideways against the window, flinging his left arm over the seat back and twisting to Gar and Cody.

"Are we having fun yet?"

They returned wan, uncertain smiles. This probably weirded them out as much as it did him.

"Dad," Cody said, "is it still January here?"

Yeah, what was this bright sunshine? This warmth? The five-hour flight into an alien climate had done a job on all of them.

The van stopped at the resort's gatehouse where a Hawaiian guy with a clipboard checked off their names. He was picking up the phone as they passed through the gate. Another long stretch of driveway led through high banks of bougainvillea blooming deep pink.

Wow, what would his parents think of all this? He'd been as vague as possible in telling them about the trip, but even without knowing how expensive Kona Village was, it didn't take a genius to figure that bringing this many people to Hawaii would cost a pretty penny.

"Hell," his father had said. "Your mom and me couldn't pull that off putting people in pup tents. Even if we all rowed over in drift boats."

"Don't worry about it, Dad."

"How many years we got, Bet?"

"Thirty-six."

"Huh. Well, see now nobody told me I was supposed to be saving up for big fancy anniversary trips. I thought, we stayed married, you kids threw *us* a party."

"Well, yeah, Dad, really. That's more how it's supposed to go. They just want to do this. It's really kind of stupid when you think about it. Probably won't be any fun."

"That's the spirit! Say, they got any fishing there?"

"Shelley says you're supposed to just swim around under water looking at 'em."

"You shittin' me? Well, damn, you have a good time, kid!"

Will ached, remembering the exchange, knowing how he'd made his dad feel.

"That's the fitness center," Shelley said now, nodding at a Polynesian-style building they were passing.

"Huh. Okay." If things got too boring, he could always go over and lift weights.

At the far side of the circular drive, a man in an aloha shirt and a woman in a muumuu stood holding a couple of leis.

Will tensed. "They're not going to hug us, are they?"

"No, but they *are* going to put one of those leis over your head, so could you just brace yourself and try to be polite?"

"Okay, okay. Hey guys, look. It's Grandma and Grampa."

Ed and Alice, who'd apparently been awaiting their arrival, now stood from a teak bench and came to the edge of the finely graveled drive.

Will slid open the van door, not waiting for the cabbie, and he and Shelley extricated the boys. As Will paid the driver, Shelley received her lei and melted into her mother's arms.

"I can't believe we're finally here."

"Rough trip?" Ed asked.

"Oh, you know. With the kids…" Shelley's sweeping glance seemed to include Will in this, and he noticed her turning from the sight of him getting his lei. Hey, he was trying. Had he made a bad face?

"Where's the TV?" Gar said the minute they'd been left to settle in by the shuttle cart driver.

Shelley switched on the ceiling fan. "There aren't any."

"None at all? Not in any of our little huts?"

"They're called hales in Hawaiian," Shelley informed him, "and no, none of them have TVs."

"That's a rip-off," Cody said.

"No, that's good," Shelley said. "You'll see, honey. There's lots more fun things to do here. You wouldn't want to waste your time sitting in front of a TV."

Gar shrugged out of his backpack. "It's not fancy at all, is it?"

"No, and that's what everybody loves about this place. It's like summer camp."

"So, did you come here when you were little?"

"Yes, but it's been a long time. Grampa and Grandma come almost every year, though, they like it so much. And now they're just so happy you guys are going to be here with them and the whole family can all be together."

"Yeah, that's cool," Gar said. "When's Kit coming?"

"Tomorrow, I think. Or maybe the next day."

Greg and Susan had a bit more trouble trying to cut loose for vacation days in January, both being academics in Seattle and not their own bosses.

"This is mine," Cody said, hurling himself in a twist onto one of the twin sofa beds in the front room.

"That's right. You guys can be out here and Daddy and I'll sleep in back."

Will followed her into the bedroom and swung his satchel onto the bed.

"So what exactly *is* the plan here in terms of this anniversary thing?" An actual recommitment ceremony had apparently been ruled out, neither Ed nor Pete having it in himself to allow a request for the setting up of tiki torches on the beach and whatever other attention-grabbing theatrics would inevitably go along with such an event. *Hey, look at us! Look at our family!* Oh, no, none of that falderal for the Garland boys. Shelley promised Will that after forty years of being married to them and understanding this, Alice and Ardis had not wasted more than a brief moment wistfully picturing themselves in white Hawaiian gowns and flower wreaths, lovely as that might have been.

"If they're not having a celebration," Will persisted, "what's it even got to do with their anniversary? It's not even the date, right?"

"Well, duh! Why would anybody leave heaven-on-earth in Oregon in June to come to Hawaii?" Shelley had her back to him, putting clothes in the dresser. "We're just all going to be together. That's what they want. That's the celebration."

"But I still don't get what we're supposed to do for a whole week. Just hang out with your cousins?"

"Will?" Shelley hunched her shoulders, then let them drop, turning to him. "Do you have any idea what a grouch you're being?"

He blinked. "Sorry. It's just that I haven't got a clue how a guy's supposed to act in a place like this."

"Honey, trust me." She put her hands on his arms and squeezed. "It's going to be fine. You just need to unwind a little bit. Here." She picked up the glass containing what was left of the rum punch he'd been given at the welcome desk and handed it to him. "Take this out on the lanai."

"Lanai?"

"The porch, okay? Get out of those boots. Just sit there and look at the ocean for a little while and breathe deep. I'll unpack your stuff. Then we can walk down and get some dinner."

"Okay," he said, leaving her to it. "Sorry for being a jerk."

From a table in the front room he picked up a coconut shell painted with red and blue designs.

"What the hell is this?" he asked, going back to the bedroom, holding the mystery object aloft.

"Oh, *that.*" She smiled. "I think you'll be wanting to refer to that particular Kona tradition with a little more respect."

"Yeah?"

"That," Shelley said, "is for privacy. You set it on your front steps when you want to let everybody know you're...not in the mood for company."

"Oooh." He felt his spirits lifting. "I can go with that." But wait. Was he guilty of wishful thinking? Maybe she meant the coconut could be a sick-headache warning? He checked her face. Ah, good. No. He'd hoped right. Because that was the blush she had when they talked about sex. Well, when they didn't actually talk about sex but that's what they meant. Okay! So! Things were looking up. Maybe they knew what they were doing around here. He'd have to give Kona Village a chance.

He took his drink out onto the lanai. This place *was* pretty amazing. Framed by the roof's fringe of palm fronds and the peeled-pole porch supports, their hale afforded a perfect view of the ocean. The sun was lowering to the left, and to the right, he could see the resort's sandy cove. He sat on the edge of the chaise and unwound the laces of his Gore-Tex boots. Shelley'd urged him to make the trip in tennis shoes, but he hadn't listened. It had been thirty-three degrees and sleeting in Portland this morning; he'd have felt like an ass, going around the airport in sneakers. And he sure couldn't have pictured being anywhere this balmy in a matter of mere hours.

"Hey, Dad!" Gar's red head popped up from a hammock slung between two exotic trees down on the beach. "There's a big old turtle down here. Come see!"

"Be right there, buddy." Will finished his drink and started barefoot down the sandy wood steps. Jeez, the temperature was perfect. The air felt so soft. You could walk around naked here and it would be just right.

Maybe this wasn't going to be so bad after all.

Will adjusted to paradise with a speed that amazed him.

Down at the Talk Story Bar, the men of the family gathered in the late afternoons and had a drink together. *So this is what they do,* Will thought on the first day, and by the fifth day he was thinking, *This is what we do.*

Ed always raised a toast to Spark, echoed among them as the glasses clinked. "We wouldn't be here if it weren't for him. In more ways than one."

Legend had it that Grammie'd had a heckuva of time convincing her husband to give Kona Village a try, for never had a guy been more resistant to trying new things—at least on the social/vacation front. And then, once here, Spark, like Will, had been almost instantly won over by the beauty, the relaxing effects of the climate, the friendliness of the staff and the utter lack of pretentiousness. Garland men did not care for the presence of those cabana boys they had at other resorts, young men running around, setting up beach chairs, hand ever outstretched for a tip. Garland men liked to think they themselves were capable of spreading a towel on a chaise. "I'm happy to pay more for it to look like less," Spark had reportedly declared, and that was the line family members had quietly quoted to each other forever after. Spark and Charlotte had joined the ranks of loyal patrons who showed up the same week every year.

The Garlands always came at the end of January, the time of year a bunch of tree farmers would most want to get out of Oregon. And the place was packed with Northwesterners. Ed and Pete seemed to know a lot of people. "Those are the Olsons," Pete would say. "Olson Timber up out of Olympia. Said at breakfast this is their twenty-second visit." And there were the folks from the San Juans, and the two couples in their eighties from Seattle who showed up every year to play tennis in the morning, a round of poolside bridge in the afternoon. Plenty of folks from the Bay Area too.

Ed enjoyed telling the story of the convenience store franchisees who'd one year been sent here as a perk and wound up feeling totally ripped off by the lack of TVs. Out on the terrace at dinner they were heard boorishly complaining. Pete and Ed laughed, mocking these clueless Midwesterners, congratulating themselves on knowing how to appreciate the place.

Ed leaned toward Will, sotto voice. "Eat, read, and have sex. That's what we do here."

"Got it covered, Ed." Even the reading. Shelley would have packed him a book.

On what was probably the third evening—they all blended together in Will's memory—they'd been set up with frosty Mai Tais and Margaritas, except for Cindy's husband Phil, who was nursing a beer. *Loosen up, boy,* Will found himself thinking. *You're in paradise.* And then caught himself. As if he'd been doing this forever and was an expert in how to relax into the good life.

"Well, Phil," he said instead, "Shelley just told me congratulations are in order for you."

Phil dropped his head a little sheepishly and nodded as his father-in-law, previously informed, gave him a confirming slap on the back.

Will addressed Greg, newly arrived that afternoon, who wore a blank look. "Cindy's pregnant."

"Ah! Terrific, Phil!" Greg lifted his glass and the others joined him.

Will scanned the women stretched out on towel-covered lounges on the beach. Cindy didn't look that far along, but her muumuu made it hard to tell. They'd been trying for quite awhile, Shelley had confided, so this was great. And nice timing: a wonderful anniversary gift to Pete and Ardis.

Only John seemed uninterested in his sister's pregnancy. "Nice shirt," he said to Will, mocking.

Will looked down at his chest. "You know, these aloha shirts aren't too bad." The very first morning, Shelley had strolled down to the gift shop and bought him a couple. He'd never have thought in a million years he'd be wearing a shirt with flowers on it, but if this was as dressed up as anybody had to get around here, he wasn't going to gripe. And if John wanted to stick to his shirts with the little polo guy on it, what did he care?

So there they all sat at the bar, facing out to sea and the gentle trade winds.

With no news from home (by order) and little news from the outside world at all, there wasn't much to talk about in the Talk Story Bar. The men's idle chat betrayed their agricultural roots. Where were they getting the blueberries served at breakfast? The waiter said California, but the Garlands felt they knew better. Chile more likely.

They discussed Kona Village's business model. Remarkable how they'd managed to keep this much real estate from going high-rise, and certainly the Garlands hoped it wouldn't change.

"You know what I like best?" Ed said, leaning toward Will. "We don't own it. All we have to do is show up and enjoy it."

And pay, Will thought. But clearly it had been years since Ed worried about that. And maybe that was the whole deal about this place. You had to have enough money that you could space out and pretend the rest of the world didn't exist for a little while. Lock your wallet in your room safe and forget it. Choose your meal from a menu with no prices, sign for your drinks with your hale number.

Damn, I'm one lucky dog, Will thought as the bartender set his second drink in front of him. He admired the sight of his wife on the chaise in her orchid-print bikini, engrossed in her current book—*Tuesdays With Morrie.*

Gar and Cody played in the ocean with their cousins, Kit and Charlotte. Poor Susan was marking up a sheaf of papers, apparently unable to completely disengage from work.

Will's sister-in-law Robin and her partner Jane were in the ocean wrestling with surf boards, providing a bit of a show for the family at the bar. As the men watched, Robin suffered a dramatic wipe-out—well, as dramatic as was possible in this tame surf—provoking groans and laughter from her audience. But Robin bobbed up and yanked the board back to climb on again.

"You watch," Ed said. "She'll get the hang of it. When that girl gets going on some kind of challenge like that, she's not giving up."

"Remember the climbing thing, Dad?" Greg said.

"Oh, yeah." Ed sipped his drink and addressed the others. "When she was about fourteen, she saw the Forestry kids at Eden Mills High learning to climb that tree pole, and darned if she wasn't going to learn to do it too. Wouldn't let up pestering until I took her out with Mike O'Connell and had him get her rigged up with spurs and all. She caught on just like that. Scooted right up that tree. And rappelling back down in one whoosh—that was her favorite part. Course Alice doesn't know a thing about it. To this day! She'd have a fit."

"What about you?" Phil asked Greg. "You do that too?"

Greg looked askance. "You kidding? I can't stand heights. No interest whatsoever."

Phil turned to Will. "You?"

"Oh, sure," Will said. "But then see, at Eden Mills it was more like who *hadn't* tried it."

John sneered. "The macho men of Eden Mills."

Will leveled a look at him. "The girls did it too."

"Okay, then, the macho women of Eden Mills."

Get bent, Will thought.

"So when did she come out to you and Alice?" Pete asked Ed. "Isn't that what they call it when they admit they're gay?"

Uh-oh. Will had heard Pete hadn't been that pleased that Jane, a prof at OSU's vet school, was being brought along on the anniversary trip as a family member.

Ed took a drink, set down his glass. "Don't much care for the word 'admit,' Pete. Not in this situation. And why would she have to make some kind of formal announcement anyway? She's our daughter. We know her."

"But come on," Pete said, "if a kid's gonna pull this, they at least owe you an explanation, right?"

"What's to explain? She doesn't like guys. Not in that way. Alice noticed it from the very first."

Cindy's husband Phil looked completely befuddled, like he'd never heard of people being gay, or couldn't believe the presence of such a person was being pointed out right in the heart of the Garland family. What, Will thought. Did he imagine Robin and Jane, sharing a hale, were just good buds? Like Robin, Jane wore no makeup and had her brown hair cut short and no-nonsense. They were out there in swimsuits cut for comfort in action, not designed to draw the attentions of men. Their set-up had always seemed obvious to Will. They were getting a puppy together, for crying out loud.

"You suspected she was homosexual," Pete persisted, "and you didn't *do* anything about it?"

Greg rolled his eyes. Uncle Pete had already drunk way too much to be getting into a discussion like this.

"Seems like something you'd want to nip in the bud."

"O-kay," Greg said, getting up. "I'm outta here." Nobody thought more highly of Robin than her big brother, who'd once told Will how indebted he'd always feel to her. In spite of what Ed and Alice always said about their three kids being able to do what they wanted with their lives, Greg wasn't sure he could have made quite the clean, guilt-free getaway he'd managed if Robin hadn't stepped up. So obviously he couldn't sit here and listen to this. But he wouldn't want to argue either. Not with a member of the older generation. The paying generation. "Thanks for the drink, Dad."

Ed waved him off and turned back to Pete. "Robin's been who she is from the word go. She's fine with it and so are we."

"Oh, come on." His brother gave him a look of the gravest skepticism. "Even if you don't think about—Well, didn't you want to walk your little girl down the aisle in a white dress?"

Ed took his time. "Robin being who she is, that's just not a picture I ever had in my mind, Pete. So it's not like something was stolen from me. I did get to walk Shelley up the aisle to Will here. Wasn't that a regular wedding gown?"

"Oh, yeah," Will said. "A big-deal wedding gown." Actually, for a while there he'd feared the wedding was more about that damned dress than it was about marrying him.

"No," Ed said. "I've got no gripes."

"Boy howdy." Pete took another drink. "Gotta admire how calm you're taking it. Ardis wouldn't sit still for it, one of our kids came and told her this."

Will felt himself ready to blurt something, but Ed caught him with a quick, insistent shake of his head. Time to drop this.

Will sank back and, turning again to the ocean show, they watched as Robin muscled herself to standing on the surf board, slick as a seal, and rode a wave toward shore, hopping off in the shallows with a fist pump.

Ed gave Pete a look. *What'd I tell you?*

Now Will noticed that beyond the group on the beach, at John's waterfront hale, Bridget had come down the lanai steps in one of those filmy cloth things. Her hair hung down long.

"Looks like your wife's gone native," Will said.

John gave her the briefest glance and smirked.

Will watched the breeze lift the edge of that sarong. Intriguing, the way her thighs were backlit through the wispy fabric. He squinted. Was she wearing anything at all under it? Hastily averting his eyes, he slurped his Margarita. When he again looked up, it seemed this fellow out-law of his still wasn't finished messing with his brain. He blinked. She was just posed there, looking straight at them. Was this his over-sexed imagination a couple of drinks on? Because he could have sworn she looked...inviting. Or at least available.

"Uh," Will said, without taking his eyes off her, "I think maybe she's trying to get your attention, John."

"What? Oh, yeah, she's like that." John motioned for another drink and shrugged. "She's not going anywhere."

What the hell? Will watched Bridget climb the steps, momentarily turning her face their way one last time, hesitating just an instant before drifting back inside. He shifted his gaze back down to Shelley on the chaise. Damn, what was this pang he felt? He was pretty sure if his wife stood on the porch in a see-through dress and looked his way, he wouldn't be starting in on a fresh drink. He'd be knocking back whatever was left in his glass and beating it up to that hale.

At night the trade winds blew away the veil of volcano dust, revealing the wheeling stars spangled so much brighter than ever they shone above their overlit hometown. In the morning Will and Shelley woke to the cacophonous coo and twitter of exotic birds, and strolled the sandy garden road beneath the gracefully gnarled banyan trees as the boys scampered loops around them. A lovely breakfast awaited on the terrace overlooking the cove. Afternoons were lazed away on the sandy beach. At home in Oregon, whale watchers had to be content with the sighting of distant spouts and the knowledge that the great beasts were still out there. Here in Hawaii, the whales breeched playfully, extravagantly, closer to shore, hurling their entire bulk skyward above the waves. No book could compete with this dazzling spectacle, and the readers, even those engrossed in the latest best-selling thriller or political tell-all, would be compelled to look up, transfixed.

Will watched the local fisherman on the rocks, thinking of his father (There *was* fishing Dad, just not for us), and studied the way the Japanese gardeners scaled the palms and with machetes sent dead fronds dropping to the ground. By the last evening at Kona Village, he had relaxed so thoroughly and tanned so fast, Shelley said again how he must have Native American blood. The same for Cody, who turned just as dark, while a lobstery-looking Gar was constantly being chased by one female elder or another wielding a tube of heavy-duty sunscreen.

And now the Garlands gathered for one final dinner at the string of tables lined up especially for them on the dining terrace.

They raised the usual toast to Spark and then Ed called up to Robin, sitting with Jane at the far end. "How was it?"

For this last day, the couple had rented a four-wheel drive and gone down into the Waipi'o Valley.

"Amazing," Robin said, she and Jane gazing at each other with that tired but happy look of people who've been outside all day with someone they love. "That waterfall."

Susan winced at Greg. "We should have done that. What a waste, sitting on the beach grading papers."

"Next time," Greg said.

"Oh, yeah, for sure," Will said. "Next time we'll all go."

Shelley tilted against his shoulder, simpering sweetly up at him, a clue as to how he was sounding. Check it out: the guy who'd had to be dragged here kicking and screaming was ready to take full charge of the next trip.

Up by the bar, a fellow in an aloha shirt was playing a mellow slack-key guitar. Below, on the lawn, the four children chased each other, their hair gilded by the setting sun. Beyond them, the waves spun toward shore, pinweeling across the little bay, spraying plumes in a backlit froth of gold, a continual yearning of the water for the land.

I must be a little drunk, Will thought. Beside him, Shelley had never looked—or smelled—more alluring. She had started using a coconut lotion he found totally intoxicating, and she was wearing a long, peachy-colored dress, one of those styles he couldn't help thinking of as *easy access.* Her hair was loose and fluffy around her face and just above her breathtaking cleavage rested the little gold plumeria necklace he'd bought her at the tiny jewelry store the management kept on site. Under the table, he reached over and put his hand on her thigh.

"Will." Smiling and frowning simultaneously, a little flustered, she laid her own hand over his, as if fearing how far he might go. "Later," she whispered.

"Okay," he agreed happily. So he *was* drunk. He *did* need reining in. He looked up to see Bridget catching him, gave her a grin and shrugged. He couldn't help it. It was this place! It just had such an effect on everybody. Bridget had to understand. Look at her and her own husband—arriving fighting, as she'd confided to Shelley, and then by the end lining up a lei-making class for Charlotte and putting out that painted coconut.

Will took another sip of his Margarita and leaned back. Life was so beautiful. His beautiful wife, his beautiful boys, this whole beautiful family that was now *his* family. Alice, sitting next to Ed, was wearing a necklace similar to the one Will had bought for Shelley. She, too, looked particularly luminous tonight. Everyone did.

"Ed," Will said, lifting his glass again. "We've toasted Spark every single day. But I want to toast you and Alice."

"And Mom and Dad, you too," Cindy put in, also aglow in this long-hoped-for pregnancy.

"Right," Will said, winking at Cindy, turning back to the two older couples. "Congratulations on your fortieth. You're, like, the best role models ever and... and...well, just thanks. For everything."

Ed clapped him on the back. Uh-oh. Will's eyes filled, forcing an attempt to laugh it off. Glasses were clinked, agreement to these fine sentiments were expressed all along the teak table, and the waiters started bringing the salads.

Up the stone steps from the lawn the lovely new generation came clamoring.

CHAPTER 11

The grape arbor in the backyard of Will's house was laden with ripe Concords, a few already splatting the bricks beneath. From the Owl's Nest he dug out Shelley's old bushel baskets. Every year she used to do it: clip the clusters and turn them into dozens of quart jars of the sweet purple juice. That amazing smell filling the kitchen had always been a nice part of Fall.

He couldn't say what happened to the grape crop that first year right after she died. So much around the place had been handled by the female relatives who swooped in with the casseroles, taking over the household chores. It could have been Robin and Jane, or maybe it was Bridget. Cousin Cindy had been around too, seeing the boys got to school okay.

Whatever. One thing for sure—Shelley wouldn't have stood for these grapes to be wasted. Hadn't her own Grammie made Spark build this arbor and plant these vines? No choice but to harvest every year. Sentiment aside, you had to, really, or the terrace underneath would wind up a sticky mess.

When Will started doing it the second year, he found Bridget would gladly take the grapes to juice, and this had become his routine. Now, clippers in one hand and cell in the other, he called her.

"Ready to take delivery on your grapes?"

"Oh," was all she said, which seemed odd. Usually she'd get all excited.

"I can wait to bring them over if it's not a good time."

"No, see, it's just that…Well, have you talked to anybody? The family? Because, the thing is, I've left John, so I'm not at the house anymore."

"What!"

"Actually, I'm glad to take the grapes, but you'll have to bring them to my new house. The one I'm renting. You caught me short because I had to think what I'd done with my steamer and the jars."

"Bridge! When did this happen?"

"Uh…two, three weeks ago? Actually, right after you helped me with the dorm move-in thing. And now I've already filed the papers."

"Divorce?"

"That's what they call it."

"God, Bridge, I'm sorry."

"Why? I'm not."

"You're not?"

"Hell, no!"

He had to laugh.

"I feel like I've been reborn. Okay, wait. The storage unit. That's where the stuff's stashed. See, once I walked out of that house I didn't want to have to be going back."

"Bridget." He was picturing her doing all this on her own. "Why didn't you call me? I could have helped."

"Actually, that's the very first thing I did think, but I knew you'd say yes whether you really had time or not, and I didn't want to be a pest."

"Hey. You could never be a pest to me."

There was a silence on the other end. Then Bridget said, "Okay, you know what? Suddenly making grape juice just sounds like the perfect thing to be doing. So get those grapes over here and let's get going on this. Just give me an hour to get my jars, okay?"

No problem understanding why Bridget would want to ditch the guy, and no surprise to have the misery of their marriage exposed; Shelley'd been reporting the drama all along. But hadn't they found some sort of truce in recent years? Probably, Will now realized, he'd just been too wrapped up in his own problems to pay any attention, and it had been four and a half years since Shelley had been around to clue him in.

What amazed him now was Bridget finally getting up the nerve to use the D word to the Garlands. Because that would be flat-out scary.

He knew, because he'd been there once himself. It was early on, when he and Shelley had first moved into Spark Garland's old house. Will had gone hunting with Doug Hudson and a couple other Eden Mills buddies and brought home what they all agreed was the most impressive four-point stud of a buck any of them had ever seen. Will was so busy enjoying his triumph, he had no idea he was committing some atrocity in hanging the carcass in the Owl's Nest. The beer- swilling, butcher-and-package party was in full swing, everybody pitching in, when Shelley came home early from a Portland shopping trip with her mom and stumbled in on them. Went ballistic. Just completely lost it.

His buddies hit the road. She wasn't their wife. They didn't have to stick around for this. Sure wasn't worth a package or two of freezer meat.

None of Will's pointing out how thoughtful he'd been in laying down plastic over the wood plank flooring had done a bit of good in calming her titanic rage. His insensitivity was unbelievable! Forget the mess, forget that the Owl's Nest was practically a sacred sanctuary, a hallowed hall. Didn't he know perfectly well how her family felt about hunting? And this horrible thing hanging here, dripping blood. Made her want to throw up on the spot! Did he even *care*?

She wouldn't hear any of his attempts at explanation, and finally Will stopped trying. Just watched her have this tantrum, thinking: *Wow, this is how marriage is gonna be?* What had he signed on for? They'd only been together two years; there were no kids to consider. Maybe he should cut his losses. So what if she was beautiful? Shelley Garland Trask was clearly a mental case. The idea of directing her parents' attention to this sad fact, however, did memorably painful things to his guts.

And of course as it turned out, there *was* a child involved. Shelley had been newly, unknowingly pregnant with Gar. Okay, so, hormones. He thought they agreed on this, but the one time the story had come up subsequently, it was obvious neither of them had given an inch in retrospect. Clear to him she'd overreacted, hormones or not, and she just flat out couldn't ever forgive him for being such a barbarian.

Will never again brought home a carcass. If he bagged a deer or an elk, he either hung it at Doug's or dressed it in the field and packed it out.

They'd had their arguments after that, sure, some even quite bitter, but once the boys were on the scene, he never again gave a moment's thought to divorce. Now, for Bridget to have filed the honest to God papers…well, it really made him wonder exactly what had been going on over at the Witham Hill house all these years to bring it to this.

When he pulled up in front of Bridget's bungalow—yellow with a green door, like she said—he was thinking how Shelley always loved this neighborhood, one of the oldest in town. Bridget's house would have been too small for her, but any one of these other Victorians with the fancy porch posts would have suited her fine.

As he hoisted the first bushel of grapes out of the truck bed, Bridget came bounding down her front porch steps in her usual flannel shirt and jeans and took up the second bushel of grapes.

"Oh, Will, these are *so* beautiful."

"You say that every year."

"Well, it's *true* every year. There's just something about them. I *love* making grape juice. And you know what? This year I get to do it without John bad-vibing me, saying what a mess it makes. He always says the electricity costs more than just buying it, so it's stupid."

Will followed her in the front door. "Nice porch swing."

"Yeah, but I can't picture spending much time sitting there. The porch is like this little stage. And my landlady has a front-row seat right across the street. Luckily there's a back porch too." She led him through to the kitchen and set her bushel on the chipped tile counter next to the stove, nodding at the breakfast nook for him to take a seat. He had to, really, just to get out of the way.

He looked around. "They built these bungalows small, didn't they? Hard to picture a family crammed in here."

"Try a bunch of college kids. That's why my landlady thinks I'm the answer to her prayers. I'm *not* four frat-boy types like she had before." She started grabbing the grape clusters, swishing them under the faucet and piling them in the steamer. "Perfect timing. See? I've already got the water going underneath." She piled the grapes high and put the lid on. "There. That's what I love. The stove does all the work." She rinsed her hands and dried them on a dishtowel. "Are you hungry? I was just going to fix a little lunch."

"Yeah, great."

"Beer?"

"Sure. But not in the yard like frat boys, right?"

"Right." She winked, opened one for him, cocked her head as she held it out. "Why're you looking at me like that?"

"Uh…I'm just surprised. You seem so happy."

"I *am*," she whispered conspiratorially. "I just keep thinking of all these great things." As she laid out bread slices on the cutting board and spread mayonnaise, she kept talking to him over her shoulder. "I love how I won't have to go through with the twentieth anniversary party Ardis was planning. Ha ha! We won't make it." She cut dill pickles, tore leaves of dark lettuce from the head. "I won't have to fake being happy in front of her friends. I won't have to ruin a beautiful June evening."

"Well, I'm not big on parties myself," he said, watching her lay on the turkey slices, "but isn't divorce a pretty drastic solution for getting out of one?"

She laughed, topping the piled-up fixings with second piece of crusty bread. "That's the least of it. My life's been full of stuff like that." She halved each sandwich. "The point is, I'm determined to be doing something way better with myself by then."

"Oh. Well, okay."

"I'm telling you, Will, it's almost scary." She slid his plated sandwich in front of him. "I could have missed feeling like this if I hadn't finally made up my mind. God, what took me so long?"

"Well, what happened? You haven't said."

She set her own sandwich on the table and joined him. "Couldn't take it anymore."

He raised his eyebrows.

"Him cheating on me." When he didn't say anything, she tilted her head. "Come on. You knew, right? I'll bet everybody knew."

What could he say? "Shelley used to talk about it."

"Yeah."

They both concentrated on their sandwiches for a few minutes.

"That jerk," Will finally said. "I guess I just wanted to think things were going better for you lately."

She cast him a mournful glance. "Nope."

"Well, gee, I'm sorry about that. I never did think that guy appreciated you like he ought to." Then, disconcerted by what he'd just said, he hurried on. "So, this is it? You're going to live here—like, indefinitely?"

"Oh, no. I mean, it's fun being so close to downtown. And it suits me for now. I like the old cabinets. Original. One place I looked at seemed cute and vintage on the outside, but then the kitchen turned out to be redone in the sixties. Horrible. So this is definitely better, but the thing is, I'm going to be looking for a place to buy. A place with some land around it. You know, just an acre or two. For now this'll be my place to sit here and sort of plan out my new life. Figure out what I want."

She seemed so excited. She made getting a divorce and starting over sound so appealing, you kind of wanted to say, *Hey, can I come on this adventure, too?*

"Well," he said, "what do you want?"

"Hey, what a fun question. Nobody's asked me that in ages. Not seriously. Not unless it was like *What the hell do you want, anyway?*" She closed her eyes and sat back. "I want…" Her eyes popped open. "Chickens! I want chickens."

Will laughed. "Chickens."

"Yeah, for eggs, you know. And I want a compost pile. And a garden. And I want to hang my laundry out to dry on a line without some neighbor complaining about it."

"Gee, Bridge, looks like maybe you're just an old hippie at heart."

"Maybe I am. I'm looking forward to finding out. But don't worry, that's real turkey in your sandwich there. I'm not going all tofu on you."

He snorted. "Like you could fool me on something like that. Bridget, this sandwich is way too good to be anything but the real deal." He finished enjoying it as the sharply sweet smell of the steaming grapes began to fill the kitchen. Then he inhaled. Shut his eyes. "I'd kind of forgotten."

"What."

"How good the juice smells." Remembering Shelley in their kitchen, he had to press the side of his hand to his moustache. And Bridget—Jesus—instead of looking away like he wished she would, she was just watching him, puzzled, not getting it. He sure didn't want to try explaining and *really* choke up.

"Hey, wanna hear a good one?" she said.

You bet. If it changes the channel here.

"Ardis called me up and asked whether I'd thought of leaving town."

"You're kidding."

"No, she was dead serious. Well, as if Ardis has any other way of being. Anyway, she put it how I'd have so many more opportunities in Portland or Eugene or whatever. 'I'm thinking of *you,* dear,' she says. Is that bogus, or what? She just wants me out of here. I'll always be this awkward reminder of—oh, heavens—her son's scandal."

"Well, you're not thinking of doing it, are you? Leaving, I mean." It surprised him, how much her answer suddenly mattered.

"No way. The Garlands may own the forests, but they don't own this town. Corvallis is my town too, now. And the part of my life I've loved is right here. My practice. I don't want to sound conceited, but I think if I left, my patients would be pretty upset."

"Well, of course they would. And it's not conceited to say so, either."

The lid of the vat on the stove started tapping, letting puffs of steam escape. Bridget jumped up, grabbed a couple of pot holders and lifted the top section, peeking underneath into the juice pan.

"Now we're cooking."

As she siphoned the steaming juice into the jars, Will walked into the short hall off the dining room that connected the two bedrooms.

"You gonna make this bigger room in front your bedroom?"

"Nah. Not with that window to the porch. You know, the landlady thing. Even with shades it kind of creeps me out, that she could see if I was in there or not. That can be Charlotte's. Like a guest room."

"Not a bad little house, though," he called back to the kitchen. "Do you think your landlady might want to sell it?"

"I don't know," Bridget said, coming out and following him. "But my real dream was always a log house. I'm going up to the log home show in Portland next weekend."

"Oh, yeah?" He stuck his head in the back bedroom. "Bridge. You're sleeping on the floor? Come on, have a little self respect."

"But I do. Too much to ever sleep one more night in the bed I shared with John. And anyway, that's not the floor, you dope. Haven't you ever seen a futon?"

"Looks like a sleeping bag to me."

"Well, okay. Technically, a sleeping bag on a futon. But that's just temporary."

"And meanwhile he's still in a big old king-size or whatever you had."

"Hey. I don't want to be thinking about where he's sleeping and who's with him, okay? Anyway, I always wanted a brass bed. You know, like that song, '*Lay, Lady, Lay?*' But nothing doing, for him. Thinks he's such a big man, he's got to have a king-size bed. Be ashamed not to."

Will shook his head. He'd never had the slightest use for John Garland, and he could already see he wasn't going to mind one bit listening to Bridget vent.

"What's the point, anyway," Bridget said, "of two people sleeping in a bed so big they have to send out a search party to even find each other?"

Will grinned. "Yeah, we always thought a queen was big enough."

"Of course it is, and I found out you can put these adaptor railings on an antique double so it'll take a queen-size mattress."

"Well, I guess this means you'll just have to go brass bed hunting."

"Ha! Been there, done that! Found it in a shop in Albany. Not one of those femmy things with lots of curlicues and stuff. This thing is solid. Like it could have been the master bed at some guy's thousand-acre ranch, you know? It's got spindles that are good and thick with these massive finial balls on the corner posts. It's actually over there just waiting for me to bring it home."

He blinked. "So what are you waiting for?"

She gave him a slow, squint-eyed smile, crossed her arms over her chest and cocked her head appraisingly at him. "It is a truth universally acknowledged that a single man in possession of a good pick-up truck must be in want of…a woman for whom to do guy-type errands."

Say what? He just looked at her. Almost sounded like some foreign language. Except he did get the part about the pick-up.

"Well, hey. You need me to take you over and get it for you?"

"Will!" She looked so happy, like he'd been really smart to think of this. "That would be so great!" She screwed a canning jar cap tight. "As soon as we finish this up, we can go."

Then she turned around. "You've always been so nice to me." She reached up and laid her palm on his cheek. "You have no idea how much that means to me right now."

CHAPTER 12

"Dad," Gar said. "That lady, that Liza?"

"Yeah?" Will's eyes stayed on the TV screen. With both kids playing soccer, he'd been watching some games, trying to catch on. Growing up in Eden Mills had always been more about football and baseball.

"We need to talk to you about her."

Now he turned to his two sons standing there, Gar redheaded, pale and so clearly a Garland, Cody with the dark eyes and hair of the Trasks. What struck Will at the moment, though, was the suspicious emptiness of their hands. No cell phones. Something was up. Something requiring everybody's full attention. He clicked off the TV.

"Uh, well," Gar began, "we don't like her."

Not to be too blunt about it.

"Yeah? Why's that?"

The two boys cut their eyes at each other.

"Guys. I know I can't replace your mom. I'm not trying to." He stood up and threw his arms wide, drawing them into a football huddle. "But wouldn't it be kind of nice to have a woman around here again? Just to…well, I'm not much of a cook."

"You do okay, Dad," Cody said, awkwardly backing away. "We don't care what we eat."

Gar likewise shrugged off Will's pitiful attempt to force camaraderie. "If it's just about cooking, we could go to that place where you put together all these meals. They tell you how to do everything. Then you just shove the boxes in the freezer and you're set. That's what Nick's mom does."

Ouch. Will turned from them, retreating to the sofa. That his eldest had felt obliged to venture this far down the road toward checking out their dinner options…Shouldn't be any concern of a sixteen-year-old boy, Will felt, not one with a halfway competent parent in residence, anyway.

But get real. Dating Liza Madison hadn't really been about meal prep. He did okay with the barbecue, cooking out in the Owl's Nest all winter long last year, using the crane apparatus and swing-out grill somebody'd rigged up years ago.

In making excuses to his sons, though, the prospect of a steady lineup of decent dinners was the only G-rated reason he could think of for bringing a new woman into the house. How could he plead loneliness to his teenage sons? Start talking about how he was dying for another warm body in bed, bringing up the awkward specter of sex. Which, yes, he was probably supposed to be discussing with them. Damn, he missed the nudge Shelly would have given him when the time was right. He was just so…*weary* of every last thing around this place being entirely up to him.

But he couldn't get over the realization of one crucial fact, something people might think should lift his spirits, but instead only made him feel guilty. And the fact was this: widowers *could* re-marry. A man could get a new wife.

But you couldn't get a new mother. A second wife wasn't a step-wife. If he married again, he'd get a wife, they'd get a step-mom. Unless he found someone they liked, it did seem like a sketchy deal for them.

Cody crossed his arms over his chest. "She said I ought to cut my hair."

Awhile back, Will's fourteen-year-old had started parting his shiny dark hair in the middle and letting it grow. Now it was long enough for a leather-bound ponytail. Will thought his son, charging across the soccer field, looked like a clean-limbed young Indian, and he liked the effect of it flying out behind. Shelley might not have been as enthusiastic, though, had she still been around to voice her motherly opinion.

"So, do I have to? Cut it?"

"Not on my account."

Gar looked annoyed at his younger brother. "Didn't we agree we weren't going to bring up every little thing?"

"Not a little thing to me."

"Well, anyway," Gar said, turning back to Will, "we're worried about you, Dad."

Okay, so they'd even planned these lines. Like a freakin' intervention.

"*You're* worried about *me?*"

"Yeah. When you came home the other night after, you know, you went out with her. Well, Dad, I saw you, and you were pretty drunk."

"I was not!" He wouldn't do that. How could he when his most important remaining goal in life was simply to be a good dad to these boys? And a good dad wouldn't come home drunk. Except…He exhaled, backing down. Maybe that's what he really meant with his denial. Not that he hadn't been drinking, because—face it—he most certainly *had* overdone it at Liza's, but that he wasn't a bad dad.

Gar held his eyes downcast. "You're acting different, and…" He glanced at Cody. "We just don't have good feelings about her. I'm sorry, Dad. I guess you must like her but…"

"Well, Gar, don't you think it'd take some getting used to with anybody I brought home? Maybe you just need time to get to know her. She seems to like the two of you."

They glanced at each other. *Right.*

"And this haircut thing is no big deal. You know your mom probably would have been on your case about it, Cody."

Gar sighed deeply, as if everything Will said was exactly what they'd expected to hear, and none of it was going to wash. Still, these things had to be said. Said and got past.

"Dad? Well, I didn't want to tell you this, but you know when you made me go mow the lawn at that house she was getting ready to show the other day?"

"Hey, she took us out for a nice dinner, remember? And she was going to pay you just like the rest of your lawn people, right?"

"I didn't take her money, though."

"You didn't? Why not? What happened?" Now that he thought about it, Liza *had* made a cryptic comment coming out of the restaurant about Gar being "at that age."

Gar sighed. "Okay, so this is partly my fault because I wasn't real nice. I just want to admit that up front, okay?"

"Yeah," Will said, coaxing, "and...?"

"Well, she said I missed a spot. Told me to drag the mower back to that far corner again. She goes, 'Anything worth doing at all is worth doing well,' acting all cute about it and I said, 'yeah, I've heard that saying, but my dad says it's a waste of time and money to do a job better than it needs to be done.'"

"Gar!"

"She goes, 'Garland William Trask'—she called me that—'you better get back out there and finish the job up right.' And I said, 'No thanks, I'm not gonna. Waste of fossil fuel.'"

"Oh, jeez, Gar." Will put his head in his hands.

"Yeah, I know, I warned you, but here's the thing, this is the important part: she gets right up in my face and she goes, 'Tell you what, young man, you better start shaping up because you won't be talking to me that way once your dad marries me and I'm your step-mom!'"

Will rocked back. "She *said* that?" Arms flung wide, his hands gripped the back of the sofa. Then he leaned forward, elbows to knees, and ran his hands up his forehead into his hair. He glanced around the room. Where was the door out of this one?

"So," Gar said tentatively, "is it okay I told you?"

Will dropped his hands to dangle. "Uh, yeah. Okay."

Damn. For the first time in a year, his life these past weeks had been a shade better than totally shitty. He'd actually had a few days where he woke up and didn't think, the very first thing, *Oh, right—Shelley's dead.*

For a brief stretch, he stopped having the goddamned dream. The *Where's my wife?* dream.

And now this.

Could Gar have made it all up? Nah. He wished it weren't so easy to picture Liza talking like that. Talking like that to his son. Conniving little—

Scary? Jesus.

So, no more dating fellow real estate agents. No more dating anybody. Actually, the whole thing had been enough to put him off women and booze both, for…well, maybe forever.

At least that's what he thought right that minute, Gar and Cody standing there.

Turned out his skittishness about relationships was way more pronounced and long-lasting, though, than any adherence to the benefits of abstinence from alcohol.

As soon as the boys retreated to their rooms, he went to the kitchen for a beer.

CHAPTER 13

Back at the house where he'd lived every day of his pre-college life since birth, Gar had been lying on the sofa with his laptop. When his father appeared in the kitchen's arched doorway, he pulled the buds from his ears and sat up.

"Hope you don't mind." He nodded toward the thump of the dryer from the laundry room. "Turns out the dorm washing machines are way down in the basement."

"No problem."

"Well, I just…you know, I made such a big deal about wanting to move out and—"

"Oh, shut up. You know I'll always be happy to see your car in the driveway. So how's school going? Classes and stuff? Grandma's Honda working out for you okay?"

Gar nodded. "Yeah, it's all good."

Then they just waited, looking at each other expectantly, neither seeming to have anything else to say. At least not on the subject of his reappearance. It was so much easier, Gar had begun to think lately, when you had some women around, the way they would always just start talking about anything, fill up those awkward silences.

Better give it a shot.

"Did you hear that Uncle John and Aunt Bridget are getting divorced?"

"Yeah, I guess that's the story."

"Well, that sucks." Gar looked to his father. "I mean, doesn't it?"

"Well, I guess what they always say about marriage is that nobody really knows what's going on except the two people involved."

"Char says it's her mom's fault."

"Oh, she does."

"Yeah, she came ripping down to my dorm room, ranting about how could her mother do this to her and everything. Because I mean, she's the one who's filing. Bridget is."

"Well." His father looked away. "I wouldn't be too hard on Bridget. Probably got her reasons."

"Kind of embarrassing because wow, Char really freaked out my roommate. And course I couldn't say what I was thinking. People never get cheered up hearing how you have it worse."

"Nope."

"I wanted to say like, hey, at least neither of your parents are dead."

Silence. Instant. Stone-cold. Okay, was there ever going to be a point where Mom dying was…accepted? Could be mentioned without triggering this darkness in his dad? Seemed like Gar ought to be able to do some unloading himself, right? Wasn't he the kid here?

Oh, well. Next prepared conversational topic: Cousins Gone Wild, Part Two.

"You saw that thing in the paper about Kit didn't you?"

"Your *cousin* Kit?"

"Yeah. A picture right on the front page of *The Oregonian*. Don't you get still get that?"

"Get it, don't read it much." Will gestured to a pile of papers sliding down beside the fireplace.

Gar rose, went over and riffled through. His father was sure letting every-thing fall apart around here. "Okay." He tugged one out. "Here it is."

A big color picture showed a group of hippies being marched out of the woods near Ashland. A protest busted up. Everybody who'd been up on plat-forms, chained to the old-growth fir, now routed, dragged out, and hauled to jail where they'd be charged with this and that so the loggers could get on with it. A girl in front provided a striking image. Fiercely pretty, the way she held her chin tilted. They had her arms handcuffed behind her so her chest stuck out in a way that was both dramatic and undeniably provocative. With her short chopped hair, she looked like Saint Joan tied to the stake. Joan of the Forest.

"So I'm looking at this," Gar went on, "like, whoa, because, you know, she's kind of hot, and then I see the caption: Katherine Garland. And I'm like, hey, that's my cousin!"

"Oh, boy," Will said.

"Is that creepy of me, to think my cousin's hot?"

"Gar, for God's sake. You're more worried she's looking hot than she got arrested? I wonder what Ed thought. He musta seen this."

"Think he'll be mad?"

"Oh, no, not really. Alice had such a soft spot for her, I can't see your grampa wanting to come down that hard."

"But Uncle Pete'll be mad, right?"

"Yeah, probably. Who cares? How far into the future does he think he's going to be able to boss people?"

They stood there a moment admiring beautiful, righteously angry Kit.

"Well, how's that gonna work?" Gar said finally. "I mean, is it really okay if we don't want to major in Forestry?"

"You kids can do whatever you want, far as I'm concerned."

"Yeah? Hey, remember when Grampa took me over for a tour of the mill? Man, I hated it. The logs slamming around and saws screeching. I thought he'd be mad when I said I didn't think I'd want to work there, but he was like, 'Good! What do you think I'm bringing you here for?'"

"Oh yeah. Spark actually made Ed put in a summer there. Always said it was the best incentive for wanting to learn whatever it was you needed to know to *not* be working in the mill."

"Nice trick." Gar grinned. "Worked on me."

"I thought maybe you wanted to get into this whole video-making business. That ad you did for me was pretty impressive."

"Oh, come on, Dad. That's not a serious thing. That's just for fun. I was thinking...I don't know, maybe like get into climate science? I want to do something that'll actually *help*. Help the earth, I mean."

"Uh, does it surprise you to hear we like to think that's what we're doing growing trees?"

"Hey, I know it's a good thing, Dad. I'm just saying studying climate science might be a better contribution than making advertising videos, that's all."

"Well, you could do that, Gar. You've got the brains."

Gar shrugged. Of course he did. That wasn't his worry. More like maybe everybody expected him to use those brains for the benefit of the family and Garland Forests.

"So what *did* happen with the video I made you? The Cape Lookout Lodge."

Will started laughing. He'd paid Gar to make an promotional video to sell this huge mountain top place on the coast. Gar had a slick computer program where he could pan still shots, zooming in and out, very professional. He'd strung together pictures of the lodge plus the usual scenery stuff—sunsets, seagulls, boats on Netarts Bay, people out there clamming on the sand flats, and of course the forested ridges, layers of them into the distance.

"What's so funny?" Gar said. "Weren't the owners happy with it?"

"Oh, buddy, they loved it. The way you used that music and all. Romantic as hell. Made 'em fall in love with their place all over again. Took it off the market."

"You're kidding."

"No, it just reminded them why they thought a house on the coast of Oregon was such a great idea in the first place. I guess they'll just let it sit there. Give their grandkids a few more years to see if maybe they might want to fly out from New York and see what they own."

"Well, crap, Dad. Sorry about that."

"No, it's fine." Will was still laughing. "You did what I asked."

"Well, lemme know if you want me to do any more."

"Yeah, for sure. If I ever want somebody to take their property off the market, I'll know who to come to. Hey, are you hungry?" Will turned back for the kitchen. Gar heard the fridge opening. "I might have something in here."

"No, that's okay." Gar was meeting Hannah, but mentioning that he'd already found the most amazing girlfriend seemed kind of cruel. "I'm...meeting some guys back at the dorm."

"Sure, sure."

Was his dad disappointed? Must wind up eating dinner alone a lot. Did he have any buds at all now that Doug was gone?

Will reappeared with a beer.

"Ever think about going on Facebook, Dad?"

"Facebook. What for?"

"To meet people."

"Who says I want to meet people?"

Fair enough. But did his father realize what a big favor he'd be doing everybody if he'd get a life? Were he and Cody going to have to worry about him forever?

"Dad? Remember that lady you were dating and we didn't like her?"

"Liza Madison?"

"Yeah. We still feel bad about that. Cody says maybe we were selfish. You know, when we said we didn't want you to be with her."

"Oh, no. Pretty sure you guys helped me dodge a bullet there."

"Really?"

"Oh, yeah."

"But we didn't mean like, that you could *never* have a girlfriend."

"I know, I know." His father waved him off, apparently annoyed to be reminded of the whole thing.

The dryer dinged and Gar went through the kitchen to the laundry room, piled the load in his basket, and brought it back to the living room. Sure was weird to be home. It'd only been a few weeks, but now he was looking at stuff like it was the first time.

"Dad?" he ventured. "Have you ever thought about losing the roses?"

"The what?"

"The wallpaper."

"Oh." His father turned to study the swirl of pink blossoms still revealing themselves around the edges of his paintings.

"Think something plainer might look better?"

"Huh." His father turned away, took a swig of beer. "What do you care?"

"Well, I don't. Not for me, but—"

"If you're not even here anymore, I don't know why you'd give a rip."

"I don't. I'm just saying."

"Hey, I'm not coming over to tell you what to put up in your dorm, am I?"

Gar scrunched his mouth tight. Touchy, touchy. And so fast. One minute his dad could be laughing his head off, the next all nasty. Obviously he was still as ticked off at life as ever.

"Dad, I know the wallpaper was Mom's idea."

"It's got nothing to do with your mother!"

Like hell. And even though it made his stupid heart thump to keep pushing this, he did. "Then why do I remember you fighting about it?"

Instead of getting madder, though, his dad backed down. "Were we?"

"Yeah, actually, you were."

"Well, it was probably just that I never liked having everything all torn up."

Gar hung his head. Actually, all three of them had acted pretty pissy about having to dodge Shelley's re-decorating projects. He wished he could have a do-over on some of the sulky stuff he'd pitched at her himself, but when you're fourteen, you think it's important to be testing the limits. You've got no idea any given snarky remark might be the last thing your mother ever hears out of you.

"Okay, so say it's not about Mom. I just thought, don't you think your paintings would look better on a nice plain wall? Tan or something?"

"I guess."

"I mean, no offense, but you're kinda living in an old-lady gift shop here."

Will walked over and picked at a seam of the offending paper. "How would you ever get this stuff off?"

"Hmm. Hey, I know. Ask Aunt Bridget. She knows about all that. Remember, after Mom, when she came over and finished painting my room?"

"Did she?" His dad looked distressed. Maybe not so much that she'd done it, Gar thought, but because he didn't seem to remember.

"Yeah. Mom was in the middle of it when, you know…."

"Oh, yeah."

"That was kind of nice, I remember, having Bridget around. But now that I think about it, it's just kinda…"

His dad waited. Then, "Just kinda what?"

"Well, when Mom started the job I was being cranky at her. Then I was nice to Bridget. Wish I'd been nicer to Mom."

"You were nice to her, Gar."

"No, I wasn't. Well, I could have been nicer."

"Yeah. Well, that's the problem, isn't it?"

"That we aren't nicer?"

"No, that we don't know what we've got 'til it's gone. It's in all the songs, right?"

"Yeah. And now we don't have Bridget anymore."

"What do you mean?"

"Well, if she's not gonna be part of the family anymore, I kinda doubt she'll be hanging around much."

"Hey, if I wanna ask Bridget about my wallpaper, I'll just get her over here for a goddamned consult. I'm sure not gonna let whatever shit that idiot John Garland pulled stop me!"

Huh. O-kaaay.

Hard to say why, but somehow this made Gar happy. Maybe it sounded like a little flicker of hope. Like maybe his dad wasn't ready to lie down and die himself quite yet. And if he had to go around mad, might as well be mad at the right person.

Uncle John was a jerk. Always had been. Gar remembered one time when he was little and John got to tickling him down in their rec room. Oh, sure, all in good fun, ha ha, but it was *not* fun and he wouldn't stop, even when Gar, in tears, begged him. At the time it seemed wimpy to complain. Weren't you supposed to be grateful for attention from grown-ups? But tickling, he read later, could actually be considered sadistic behavior. So, yeah, John was a bully all right. Smart on Aunt Bridget's part to escape.

His cousin Charlotte wouldn't want to hear his analysis on this, though.

Better keep his mouth shut.

CHAPTER 14

It wasn't enough to be mired in grief. Oh no, the whole world had to nag you, too. *You should get out more, Ed.* And going over to his office at Garland Forests didn't seem to count. Well, besides that, where was he supposed to go? Until she got cancer—or, more accurately, until they lost Shelley—Alice had always arranged everything and informed him of their social schedule. His part in it, he'd always felt, was to exhibit sufficient reluctance about every engagement to ensure she wouldn't get carried away filling up the calendar. Now he felt at loose ends, having lost this gentle tug-o-war, what with nobody holding the other end of the rope.

True, Good Samaritan Episcopal still held the same Sunday services as ever, but wouldn't that just be a whole bunch of people aiming at him that look he couldn't stand? Bad enough one face at time down at the bank or the barber's or the gym. Pity and Concern. That's the name he gave it. And he knew all too well what it meant, that he was walking around looking—for criminy sakes—like he was in dire need of it, pity and concern, which only made him that much crankier.

He'd grown so accustomed to the tender deference everyone dished up to him, it caught him off guard when some woman from the Greenbelt Land Trust phoned his office early in October and *didn't* say anything about being sorry for his loss. For just an instant he thought, *Hey, lady. Don't you know my wife just died?* But then—wait a minute—hadn't he been wishing people would quit dwelling on it?

The call was nothing to do with Alice. They were scheduling tours of some of the new land on which they'd acquired conservation easements. They just wondered, would he care to come out and take a hike around the Henry Bennett acreage along the Little Willamette?

So maybe this *did* have to do with Alice dying. They probably knew all about it and figured he wouldn't be far behind. They probably wanted to weasel their way into his will. They wanted his money. They wanted his land.

Well, what the hell. Somehow, on the day that call came, this straightforward proposition didn't sound that bad. And honestly? People currying your favor made a guy feel a whole lot better than being the object of pity.

"All right then," he told the woman, "you can put me down for it."

If nothing else, maybe it'd shut his kids up, give him an answer for Robin next time she dragged him out for a hike with Mattie on one of the forest tracts, wanting to know if he'd been anywhere since their last outing. Helluva deal, getting babysat by your own daughter.

The day of the hike brought the sort of changeable weather that, while ominous, was never considered grounds for cancelling such events in the Pacific Northwest, and Ed prepared for potential rain, rubbing a fresh coat of mink oil into his boots and digging out his old yellow tree-planting slicker. Kind of dirty. Didn't Alice used to put these through the washer once in awhile? Maybe he should do that.

Driving east out over the river, Ed thought about the Greenbelt Land Trust's agenda. Like every other bunch, they probably wanted to make sure they were being considered for inclusion in his will. Yes, he knew he wasn't going to live forever, and you were supposed to plan for this, but that didn't mean he enjoyed it, knowing he'd hit the numbers on some actuarial table that had triggered a flood of slick brochures. This had already been going on for a few years, of course, but when you've got no plans to die, they're not as bothersome as when your wife suddenly gets cancer and does die and you have to face it, the fact you need to get things set up to pass on. And the charitable issues were nothing compared to trying to figure out the best way to hand down Garland Forests.

He remembered Spark working it over for a decade or two, trying to make sure Garland Forests would remain the thriving, family-run business he'd built it up to be. Even though Pete and Ed had been running things for years, Spark had the last say, and as long as he'd been alive, a delicate balance between the two brothers had been maintained. Once he was gone, things got difficult. John had immediately started lobbying for a grandiose new office building. Said they'd already stuck it out way longer than they should have crammed into that shack Spark always insisted was good enough. They had twenty employees who needed and deserved actual offices of their own. Ed hadn't really disagreed; he just didn't like always having to debate everything with his brother. And his pompous nephew.

Their fundamental differences went way back. Pete and Ardis had been shocked when Ed and Alice produced the first Garland grandchild and named him Gregory for Alice's father. In conferring Spark's given name—John—on *their* son, Ardis had implied to Alice they were pleased to be rectifying an unfortunate mistake.

As if a name could fix it all, God help them. Bring back their oldest brother, John Garland. Ed always wondered if Pete had ever told Ardis about the accident. Would he, himself, if he'd been the one to mistake their brother for a deer? He'd confessed it all to Alice, but only in trying to help her make sense of Pete and the burden he'd been shouldering ever after, feeling he'd let the family down unforgivably and could never do enough in his fierceness to hold them all together.

It didn't help much with softening up Alice. How did Pete's guilt give him the right to decide all the kids had damned well better get on board with tree farming? She'd told Ed right at the start she was delighted to marry into such a fine family, but she wouldn't be having children for the purposes of providing employees for Garland Forests. If their kids were interested when they grew up, great. If not, they'd be entitled to do their own thing. They'd agreed that the way it had turned out, one out of three, was perfectly fine, especially when the one was Robin, just as loyal to the business as she'd been since the day, as a child, she'd been helped to plant her first Doug fir in the hillside mud.

And Gods knows Ed appreciated the way he could always count on this one child of his. So dependable, there when he needed her, always doing the right thing. He never had to worry about her, even if Alice thought he ought to. She'd been after him for years to get the succession of the business better organized, pointing out how unfair it was that, if he dropped dead, Robin would have to contend with Pete and John. Every time he thought about restructuring, though, he pictured the inevitable arguments with his brother, and found a way to put it off. Figured planning for death was bad enough without having to sit around arguing about it too.

Having declined the offer of a carpool ride from the Greenbelt office, Ed turned out to be the only one arriving alone in the Bennetts' farmyard. He didn't recognize any of the other people standing in clusters, but several came over and shook his hand like they were expecting him, which of course they were.

Then a final SUV pulled in and disgorged a half dozen passengers, including an older blond woman who flashed a big smile at Ed and immediately headed his way. What the—? Like she knew him. Maybe aiming that smile at somebody else? He glanced over his shoulder. Nope.

"Hello, Ed," she said warmly, reaching out her hands and taking his.

He felt paralyzed. Who *was* this? Damn, he missed his wife. Alice always kept him clued in with strategic whispers on people's identities, especially somebody approaching. She'd never have left him standing here like an idiot. But then, not exactly an unhappy idiot, because he couldn't feel sorry this attractive person seemed so glad to see him.

The pretty woman laughed. "I guess you don't recognize me. Julie Pomeroy?"

Julie Pomeroy? For land sakes.

"Oh, I'm sorry," she said. "This isn't fair at all. I must be totally out of context for you."

Out of context? Try out of the past, the distant past. Fifty years or more.

"For cryin' out loud," he stammered. "Julie Pomeroy."

Damned if tears weren't stinging. He'd heard that happened when you got old. You cried easier. Maybe so, and here she was again, adorable sweetheart of the big brother he'd worshipped. Here, vibrantly alive, was one of the few people on earth who'd known his brother John, carried memories of him. Somebody who'd suffered his loss right along with the whole Garland family.

"Because you're not out of context to me," she said. "I saw your name on the list of people who'd signed up today, so I expected to see you." Her smile turned startlingly intimate. "Actually, you're the reason I came. When I saw your name I thought *Oh, I hope he shows up.*"

"Oh. Well." When was the last time anybody'd been hoping his sad-sack self would show up anywhere? Especially somebody with such lovely blue eyes who wasn't making Pity and Concern her leading theme. Darn, wasn't she cute? A light blue turtleneck that matched her eyes peeking up from the collar of an ivory colored jacket. Suede! Lord. Didn't look like *she* was figuring on rain. But she *was* wearing jeans and sturdy little boots.

"Maybe you didn't even know I'd moved back to town," she said.

"No, I sure didn't. When was that?" Did anybody else know? Did Pete? Because suddenly it hit Ed that this was really going to throw his brother. So much never got put into words with the Garlands, which meant that what they did say tended to be remembered. Ed could hear it like it was yesterday, Pete lamenting Julie Pomeroy's presence at their brother John's funeral. He would never, he said, get over seeing her in that black dress, so beautiful, so sad.

And now, here she was, these many decades later, still beautiful, not sad at all.

"I moved up about three months ago," Julie said. "We'd been in the Bay Area and my kids had already come up to Oregon. My daughter and her family are in Eugene and my son's in Portland. When we lost Jim—that was three years now—of course everybody was saying I wasn't supposed to make big decisions right off, but I always knew I wanted to come back to Corvallis. I guess my family's had too many generations in Oregon for me to ever really feel like a Californian."

As the group was herded out onto the farm's muddy roads, the two of them fell in beside each other, and perhaps because they weren't quite up to the pace of the younger people, they found themselves bringing up the rear. Julie was quick to point out, however, that at least they were still making the hike under their own power. They were not among the truly elderly being driven in Henry Bennett's John Deere Gator. Also she said she'd rather hang back and talk to him than hear every last word of the educational, promotional, put-us-in-your-will pitch.

"I already know what they're saying anyway," she confided. "They were talking about it in the car coming out. See?" She nodded at Henry Bennett, who was addressing the group gathered around the Gator. "They're getting him to tell how his great-great grandfather or somebody was born in a covered wagon parked under that big old black walnut the very day they first laid eyes on the place."

"He was?" Ed said. "The very day they got here?"

Julie laughed. "See! That's just what they were saying. How people love a story. They'd much rather donate for a place with some intriguing history attached to it."

Pretty smart little cookie, Ed thought, following her.

"This is so beautiful, isn't it?" she said. "I thought this'd be perfectly flat floodplain out here. I'm surprised at all these little hills and dips."

"It could use a few more trees."

"Oh, you Forestry boys! Honestly, if you had your way there wouldn't be a clear spot for a duck to splash down anywhere from here to Portland."

He laughed. "Naw. It's nice. Guess every piece of land can't be a Site One Forest parcel. And this good valley loam *is* what everybody came out here and claimed first. Guess I've just got it bred-in-the-bone to favor north facing slopes way up out of the floodplain. Our family ended up with the land people had to take when they couldn't get in on any of this river bottom stuff."

"The way you put that." Julie tsked. "*Our family ended up with…*as if your father and grandfather weren't the smart old coots they were and knew exactly what they were doing."

"Well, there's that, too." He took a deep breath. It was oddly pleasant to be walking on land that wasn't his own, a freedom in being able to just appreciate it without having to think what he ought to be *doing* with it. Probably a good idea these land trust kids had, setting this aside from development. Give the ducks a break.

Shafts of sun darted from behind the blackest of clouds to gild the last of the leaves along the waterways, and the dramatic play of light on the land was truly spectacular. Ed wasn't accustomed to this faraway view of the town's landmark, Mary's Peak. All the Garland Forests properties were snugged up closer to it, in the foothills, and a view of it from there might include only the top of the mountain, rising above a ridge line. The complete Mary's Peak silhouette seen from the valley floor was the iconic image people put on Sierra Club T-shirts or printed on their Chamber of Commerce calendars.

"I still choke up every time I've been away and catch that first sight of Mary's Peak," Julie said. "Especially out a plane window. To me it still says *home.*"

They stood there a moment, watching the clouds edging in puffs around the mountain. A V of geese went honking overhead. Interesting, Ed thought. The world was still out here. He just hadn't really looked at it in such a long time.

"I've told my daughter about Mary's Peak," Julie said, "that she can scatter my ashes up there."

Ed halted in his tracks. Ashes. Good Lord.

"Oh, dear, I'm sorry. That wasn't—I meant *someday.* Someday a long time from now. But I shouldn't have—" She peered at him. "Are you okay?"

"Oh, sure. Just that it hasn't been that long since—well, did you hear I lost my wife?"

"Of course. Oh, Ed. You didn't get my card?"

He thought of the pile mounding on his dining room table, Robin trying to get him to deal with it. "I guess not."

"And I'm so sorry about your daughter, too."

Now this *really* startled him. "You heard about all that?"

She nodded. "You might think it sounds strange, but I've always kept up my subscription to the Gazette-Times. Like I said, this never stopped being my hometown and I followed people's stories. As much as you can reading the obituaries and wedding announcements, anyway. And then, that was quite a spread when Spark died."

Boy, he'd had no idea. The Garland family had been relieved when Julie Pomeroy went off to college and her parents moved to Portland. When you had something horrible you were trying to forget, you were just as glad to not have reminders in the presence of a person who'd been involved. So no one ever said her name. No one talked about her at all. But she'd followed their story all along?

"I actually met your daughter, Ed."

"Robin?"

"No, Shelley."

"Shelley!"

"Yes, she was so lovely."

"But…how?"

"Oh, a few years back I came up to help out with the grandkids in Eugene and decided to take a day in Corvallis. I went by the old house. I wouldn't have had the nerve to knock on the door, but she was right out there, working in the garden. Seemed like it was meant to be."

Somehow he found this vaguely alarming. "Did she know who you were?"

"Well, no, and of course, I had no way of knowing she was a Garland. Not with a hat covering that gorgeous hair. I just said I was an old family friend and had a lot of good memories of the place. So she started explaining she was

Spark and Charlotte's granddaughter. Absolutely lit up when I said I remembered parties in the Owl's Nest. Took me on a little tour, and all around the garden too. I told her the sundial had always made an impression on me: *Grow old along with me, the best is yet to be.* She said I could thank her for the fact that it was still there, because her husband wanted to get rid of it."

"Yeah, well, you know, I think that was a little tough on his pride, Shelley wanting them to live in the grandparents' house."

"It was a beautiful house. Still is. She said she loved a chance to show the garden off, because she worked so hard on it, but her husband was such a private type, they could never be on any of the charity tours."

"Yep, that's my son-in-law. He's a good guy though. Alice thought the world of him."

"Oh, it's so sad. How's he doing, anyway?"

Ed shook his head. "Not that good." He stopped walking and looked at her. "But Julie, I'm just surprised. That you didn't mind going there. Didn't it kind of bring it all back?"

"Well, of course, and I got more than I bargained for, didn't I? Because… Shelley. She was John's niece. She would have been mine. So when I read about the accident, that she'd died…Well, it was hard. And I couldn't talk about it to my husband. He always seemed to find it a bit threatening that I'd had this first love."

"Yeah, helluva thing. How did you ever get over that?"

She hesitated, but only for an instant. "I didn't. You don't. At the time I thought my life was over. But I was so young, and it wasn't, of course."

They walked awhile in silence. Then Ed surprised himself by choking out in a husky voice something he'd never before said aloud.

"When Alice died, I felt like I died too."

He felt the soft touch of Julie's hand on his sleeve.

"I know." She ducked her head, forcing his eyes up with her own. He found on her face the most interesting little smile. "But you didn't. You're every bit as alive as the rest of us here." And then she added, "That's something *I'm* happy about."

Whoa.

"So," she said, "do you ever go out to eat?"

"No. Not lately."

"Well, would you like to? You know the new restaurant downtown? Aqua? They make a terrific Margarita!"

He laughed. He hadn't had a Margarita since sometime back at Kona Village. He remembered liking it. Maybe it was time to try one again.

"And guess who eats there—Michelle Obama's brother!"

"The basketball coach?"

"Yes, I've seen him there twice already. Isn't that fun?"

Ed was just staring at her, mesmerized by the possibilities on offer here. Going down to that restaurant did sound good. People could do that, after all. Go out. Better than one more thawed casserole.

Just as they were almost back to the farmyard, a black cloud stalled straight overhead and let loose. But rather than fret over the threat to her hair and clothes, Julie Pomeroy simply laughed, as if this were the most perfect punctuation to the gloriousness of their hour's walk. Ed shrugged his right arm out of his yellow slicker, threw it over that pretty but impractical suede jacket of hers and the two of them picked up their pace as best they could.

"I'd offer you a ride," Ed said a little breathlessly when they'd made it back to the shelter of the barn's overhang, "but all I've got's my old truck here."

"But I think riding in your big old truck would be fun."

"Oh, I don't know. Your nice coat'll get filthy. I've had my daughter's dog in here."

She smiled. "I don't care."

"Well, okay then." They hustled through the pelting rain and he yanked open the passenger side door with an embarrassingly loud creak. "Let's get you home."

And that's the way they would tell the story ever after.

Ed, however, would always insist that the fact he went right down to Jack Scoville's the very next week and bought a Caspian blue 2010 Volvo S80 with heated leather seats and a genuine wood dashboard insert had nothing at all to do with any of it.

CHAPTER 15

Every family has a secret, one event or painful truth, the knowledge of which some family members possess and others do not.

Bridget had long known what the Garland family had worked so hard to keep from the world.

It came to her in the first year of her practice by way of a hunting buddy of Will's, a roofer, lying on her exam table, wondering aloud what was up with Will Trask's crazy wife. 'Cause Bridget was related, right? He'd just seen this Shelley girl do the scariest, most over-the-top meltdown in that shed thing of theirs. Wow. Maybe Will ought to dump her. No amount of money worth that shit!

At Bridget's first tentative, carefully worded inquiry to Shelley, it had all come pouring out. Had Bridget heard they'd had an uncle named John who died in a hunting accident? Well, listen up, it was worse than people knew. Not just a stray bullet out in the woods like the family wanted everyone to think. It was actually Uncle Pete who shot him. Shelley's mother told her. It was a secret, though. Even Grammie didn't know. Especially Grammie needed to be protected. Could Bridget believe it? Good, safety conscious hunters, supposedly, and yet he'd accidentally shot his own brother. And then she's not allowed to tell Will. Has to just sit there when he pooh-poohs her anxieties about hunting.

"So you can see why I freak out every time he puts on his camo and loads up his guns, right? And then to walk in on that big bloody thing hanging in the Owl's Nest. Yes, I admit it, I lost my temper. But I am *not* apologizing."

"Well, does John know about this?"

"No, and you can't tell him."

"What about Cindy and Robin?"

"No, and not even Ardis. That's what I'm saying. It's a secret and we have to keep it."

Bridget would hear a lot of confidences over the years from her patients, but never anything that hit so close to home. Jesus. Her own father-in-law.

Bridget and Shelley had done a lot of bonding that winter they were pregnant with Charlotte and Gar. Bridget loved having a friend with whom she could discuss nursery furniture without having to pretend to wring her hands over crib prices.

Also, they could analyze family personalities. A favorite topic became this question: What on earth had Pete ever seen in Ardis? They'd met at OSU. Looked like Pete just went over and scoped out who was getting a degree in Business and chose the most likely candidate for a sober, solid, executive assistant as his wife. Shelley's mom, in contrast, was so warm and gracious, so creative and full of life, it was just baffling why Pete hadn't hooked up with somebody more like her. Had he actually fallen in love with Ardis? Had this humorless woman—young—been completely different?

Bridget never would figure out Ardis, but after years of being on the receiving end of confidences divulged in her office, she thought maybe she understood about Pete. Sure, a person abused as a kid would be messed up six ways from Sunday; everybody knew that. But also, she'd seen people abuse themselves, accept punishment for mistakes they felt they'd made in the past. If the guilt didn't sicken them or send them spiraling downward with chronic pain, they might quietly declare themselves unworthy of happiness, and embark on a series of choices guaranteed to keep their lives appropriately sober and dutiful forever after.

Maybe Pete married Ardis as a penance.

But then, that was just Bridget's idea. Who was she to say?

Now she missed being able to confide in Shelley more than ever. Driving the outskirts of Corvallis in the bitterly cold rain, a mug of stomach-calming peppermint tea in the holder, it occurred to her if Shelley were still around, she might be sitting beside her right now, flipping through the real estate listing maps, instructing her where to turn. She'd have been on Bridget's side, right? Cheering on the divorce? That was the hope. But women could be disappointing when it came to sticking up for each other, Bridget had learned. When the reputations of the men and the family itself were at stake, sisterhood wasn't always so powerful. Sometimes it totally flaked out. Well, whatever. Shelley was gone. Off the hook. Never to be put to this test.

Bridget had the newly-released Susan Boyle CD in the player and joined the British star in belting out each song of hopeful defiance. How many times had she watched that YouTube clip of *Britain's Got Talent*? And when Susan said she was forty-seven and that idiot Simon rolled his eyes…What? Like it was a crime to be forty-seven? We should all politely drop dead at forty or something? And then the way Susan had shocked their socks off the very instant she opened her mouth with that thrilling rendition of *"I Dreamed a Dream."* Bridget teared up every time.

Simon What's-His-Face reminded her so much of John, always sneering, rolling his eyes at her. Which was actually just about the only expression beyond a blank stare she ever received from either her husband or her daughter anymore.

Well, she had news for them. She still had a dream or two herself. She stopped the car at a For Sale sign, squinted at the house, moved on.

She had a dream; she just wasn't sure what it was.

At first, in the glorious days of Fall, the newly single woman thing had been fun, sashaying around town so damned thrilled with her own bravado she half wondered why the paparazzi hadn't shown up, wanting her take on everything. *Oregon Girl Kicks Butt; Shows Wives of Cheating Politicians and Golf Stars How it's Done!* There should be a word for the way she felt, defined as a surprising burst of thrilled relief at finally making a long postponed but inevitable decision and then being pleasantly surprised to realize the emotional consequences were not going to be nearly so dire as feared. Caught up in the furnishing of her new little nest, she'd had many lovely days where it seemed just possibly she'd already done all the grieving required for her marriage while it was still technically intact, and now she had arrived at a state of much-deserved bliss.

Well, maybe not.

For one thing, when the dreariness of falling rain and leaves began, she could not help but notice she now lived alone. She'd lost her daughter, and not just to college. Charlotte had been holding herself coldly out of reach. Also, Bridget was sadly short on close friends. With Shelley gone, she had an email pal from PT school and her mother on the phone and that was about it.

Her mother had to be pretty sick of her break-up story, and Bridget knew her general responses by heart: She should stop beating herself up over where she'd gone wrong with Charlotte in the early years because clearly she'd done her best. She should give herself credit for finally figuring out John was never going to change.

"You're such a special person, honey. You deserve better. You've got so much to give. And you're still so young."

"Come on, you call forty-one young?"

"Yes, I do, and I suggest you remember this rule—a daughter should never complain about being old to her mother."

"Sorry. I just meant old for starting over."

"Oh, phooey. People start over at every age."

But how did she arrive at this point in her life so totally alone? She'd stood on the soccer fields all those Saturdays with the other moms, went to group coffees. Charlotte had been a competent goalie and a star student, so as long as the chat stuck to the kids, Bridget was fine. No need for the sort of spinning some poor moms had to do. But the husband hashover was a different game. People talked about husbands who refused to clean the garage or go to the gym. Nobody confided about affairs. Not to Bridget anyway.

Also, simply being a Garland had cut her off from people. At the baby group she'd joined early on, the women were sitting around nursing one time, discussing the mortgage rates they'd had to accept—shockingly high back then—and Karen Fraley had turned to her. "So, what's yours?"

Bridget had no skill in lying, and the notion that a person did not necessarily owe information to anyone who requested it had not yet occurred to her.

"Actually, we don't have one," she admitted. "A mortgage."

Every head in the room swiveled suspiciously toward her.

"What am I supposed to be saying," she'd come home asking John. "If I act like grocery prices are really busting my budget, that's just...disingenuous."

"Well, don't go to these henfests, then. What do you need those people for, anyway?"

Now, seventeen years later, she knew the answer: People needed friends.

Thanksgiving this year had completely blindsided her. Morosely eating her turkey drumstick in front of *House Hunters,* it hit her: When she'd married John, she'd married the whole Garland family. Okay, so she'd never got on with Ardis and Pete; being an only child, she *had* sort of fallen in love with the idea of a big family gathering around that Thanksgiving turkey. John's cousins had become her cousins, and now she'd lost them. No fair. And for today's holiday feast, they had Charlotte. Tempting as it was to imagine her daughter as their hostage, though, Bridget had to admit: nothing coercive about it. What girl wouldn't rather be at a big party with *her* cool cousins, Gar, Cody, and Kit, instead of sitting around with her moody old mother?

Honestly, bad call, turning down her mother's invite to Santa Rosa. If she'd known she was going to feel *this* lonely, she'd have braved the possibility of snow in the Siskiyou Pass and beat it down there to sleep in her old room a night or two, share a meal with somebody who truly loved her.

This past week had brought a cold snap, but about two minutes after she'd touched a match to the carefully laid fire, her landlady was at the front door, having spotted from the chimney that first tentative puff. Hadn't she told Bridget? The fireplace was not to be used. No such thing as a chimney this old being usable, not without being completely tuckpointed, and she certainly wasn't going to put that kind of money into a rental, as she was sure Bridget could understand.

So Bridget took the poker to the fire, separating the logs. Why were there fireplace tools anyway if you weren't supposed to use them? She cranked up the electric heat, but no matter how much the temperature rose, any semblance of coziness eluded her.

The workweek was more tolerable. She could lose herself in trying to figure out what was at the root of Mrs. Dodson's hip pain or Charlie Oldfield's elbow. Was it classic tennis elbow or did he have something more serious going on with his vertebrae? Or, as seemed true in so many cases, did he just hurt because he was sad? The hours passed as she put her hands on grateful patients, finding the tenderpoints, pressing, releasing the pain. Nobody at her office ever rolled their eyes at Bridget Garland, The Good Witch. And this was therapeutic for *her*.

Weekends seemed interminable, though, and she'd taken to escaping the gray light of Sunday afternoons for these little real estate hunting excursions. Not that she had a clue what she'd be entitled to look at, pricewise, although it did seem she would at last be learning about mortgages. Dividing their assets might leave her with plenty. Or maybe not. It was John's parents who'd given them the house, yes, but the lawyer still thought she'd be entitled to half its value. (And I should hope so, Bridget thought, after twenty years of cleaning the big ugly thing.) Her in-laws had contributed to her "advanced earning capacity" by paying her PT school tuition, and it wouldn't matter how grudgingly they'd done so, they could still make a claim of sorts. It was all just so horribly tedious and complicated.

Well, if today wasn't the most depressing house hunt ever. Not that much on the market. Why bother, sellers were probably thinking. Everybody's decorating and snuggling in for the holidays in the homes they already own. Who'd be idiot enough to be thinking of buying a house now?

Just a weary, not that wealthy, soon-to-be divorcee.

The dank dreariness of winter didn't help either. Definitely *not* real estate weather, as she'd heard Will Trask call the kind of sunny day when a skimpy row of daffodils might make the most neglected little shack look like a place with cheerful possibilities. But she'd also heard him say that this was the best time to look. Better to go in with eyes wide open, aware of every flaw. Things could only get better as spring bulbs popped up and clematis vines twined with softening effect over the lattice fences hiding the garbage cans.

Her print-outs—sadly, just three—represented the likeliest properties for a single woman who wanted some yard to grow things. However none of these, driving by, were doing anything for her.

She glanced at her watch. Twelve-thirty. She was out earlier than usual because the open house she had steeled herself to attend would start at one. She headed out to Brooklane Drive. She'd already done all her homework on this place online, even drove by once and hadn't been completely turned off. Rather than a discouragement, the half dozen handsome old Doug firs thickly snarled with ivy had actually spoken to her. *Come free us, Bridget! We need you!* The listing promised an acre and a half. You could do quite a garden and chicken set-up with a lot that size.

She stopped the car out on the road and reassessed the house, a 1920s bungalow. Kind of cute. She'd been reluctant to hook up with a real estate agent, fearing somebody'd give her the hard sell. But an open house with other people looking around? Maybe not so scary. So far there was just one car parked in the drive, a Lexus.

She glanced at her watch. She was early. It hadn't taken as long as she'd thought to drive across Corvallis on a rainy Sunday with little traffic. So, time to kill. She disliked that expression, time being precious, but there didn't seem to be a more benign equivalent. She flipped open her phone and called Charlotte, knowing her daughter wouldn't answer and that one more rebuff by phone wouldn't improve her own mood, but executing this practiced maneuver just the same. Charlotte was the teenager with the unfinished brain. Bridget had to be the grown-up. She wanted it on record she was not giving up. When her daughter's voice came on, she left her usual just-thinking-of-you message and pocketed the phone.

Now the front door of the little house opened and a petite woman in black slacks and a red turtleneck hustled out to hastily hang a Christmas wreath on the front door. Clicking down the porch steps, she retrieved from the trunk of the Lexus an armload of greens which turned out to be an artificial, pre-lighted garland. Deftly she twined it over the porch entrance, a plug was engaged and—voila!—lights twinkled with instant Christmas cheer.

So that's how they did it. Impressed, Bridget turned her Subaru into the circular driveway. The real estate agent/hostess picked her way past her through the gravel in her spike- heeled boots, carrying an Open House sign to add to the For Sale sign, along with a bouquet of red balloons.

She waved at Bridget. *Go on in* she seemed to be saying with a red lip-sticked smile.

Bridget got out of her car, looked at the house, and had a silly thought: a picture book she used to read to Charlotte. *Home for a Bunny.*

Feeling a lot like that bewildered little creature, she stood there and wondered: *Can this be my home?*

CHAPTER 16

Liza Madison checked her phone. Three o'clock. Okay, let's call it quits here. Hadn't she told the owners it was pure folly to have an open house this time of year? Especially out here in this mud hole. Never calling it that to their faces, of course, just trying to tactfully point out how much better their lovely home would show in the Spring. But they'd insisted. Even offered to host the thing themselves, which of course she'd never in a million years allow. She could just see them following people around, earnestly explaining the house's less than appealing quirks. *Right here behind the fireplace in this little cupboard is where we always keep a mouse trap. It works great! They never get inside the actual house.*

People rarely appreciated the role of a real estate agent in selling their homes, Liza found. So why, she often wondered, did they even engage one if they were going to be so stubbornly against taking advice?

And now, the production of an open house, the advertising, the staging, wrangling a playdate for Andrea—all to draw just one snooty young couple who obviously felt their first home should be their dream home and clearly this wasn't it.

Them and that Bridget Garland.

Liza punched off the CD she'd brought—a compilation of Christmas tunes rendered in tinkling music box tones. She unplugged her handy air-scenting device which made the place smell like these bakery cookies had come right out of this very oven. She slid the beautifully frosted Christmas treats back into the pink box. It would be hard enough to spin this meager attendance into something vaguely optimistic for the owners without leaving cruel evidence to the contrary. Of course she'd expense the cookies, but she'd leave them with the Petersons as a thank you for keeping Andrea.

In spite of the turnout, Liza felt cheerful. You never knew what might come of a single connection. Maybe she was actually one of the first people to hear this surprising news: a divorce in the Garland family!

Soon to be ex-Mrs. John Garland had hardly been out the door before Liza whipped out her BlackBerry and located their Witham Hill house on Zillow. Promising. A Zestimate of $537,000 = a sizeable commission. And almost six thousand square feet. Really, how likely was it that *the* John Garland would want to hang onto that big old thing in a neighborhood that—sought after as it was—would certainly be a bit on the stodgy side for a suddenly single guy like him. She had several listings in the Country Club golf course frontage development that could provide just the fresh take on a new lifestyle John Garland would find appealing.

And then his ex, this Bridget, already looking for a place. Frankly, pursuing the possibilities with the husband would undoubtedly be more lucrative. Bridget Garland hardly seemed like a person ready to cough up for anything yielding a decent commission. Not if she'd come out to see *this* place.

And hadn't she been a surprise? Liza had heard about her, of course, but only in passing, and always the intel had been limited to her physical therapy thing, how helpful she was. The house painter Liza used swore by her. Of course John Garland's handsome face was easily recognizable—wasn't he on the board of the local bank and other institutions where his photo showed up in the newspaper? But she couldn't say that she'd ever seen his wife. Not knowing that's who she was, anyway. She would have expected somebody more polished. Someone more appreciative of having the money to dress with some panache. Bridget Garland was, frankly, scruffy-looking. Her hair wild and all over the place. And when she'd had to kick off her clogs to come into the house, there'd been holes in the toes of her socks.

How had these two ever hooked up in the first place? A person could make the case that John Garland was, quite simply, married to the wrong woman.

Well, well. There's a thought. Could be that right now, the position of Mrs. Right was entirely up for grabs.

The idea of becoming a Garland certainly had its appeal, and while Liza Madison prided herself in never—well, never knowingly—dating married men, she wasn't in any position to turn her nose up at divorcees, being one herself. It was certainly preferable to a widower. Honestly, she was still smarting from that whole awful episode with that shirt-tail relative of the Garlands, Will Trask. Him and those bratty boys of his. Especially the older one. *Garland William Trask.* Please. Rich little snot. And being broken up with by email? Good riddance to all of them.

She would way rather compete with an ex-wife in the form of a pathetic person like this Bridget Garland than she would ever again even dream of dating somebody who was still married to a memory. Not that Will was fool enough to talk about his wife all the time or anything—she'd give him credit there—but people were always saying what a beauty Shelley Garland Trask had been, and you could just see that this guy was a long, desperate way from getting over her. Liza had persuaded him to stop wearing his wedding band—that's as far as she got. Any future women in his life could thank her for that. End of Story.

Okay, she was out of here. She slipped on her red leather jacket. She wanted to be gone before the owners reappeared, necessitating an annoying discussion, plus she wanted to stop by the office on her way home and look up a few more bits of info about the Garlands. She needed a strategic game plan here.

On the way out, she unplugged and pulled down the lighted garland, coiling it into the trunk of her Lexus.

Life was interesting, she thought, turning out onto Brooklane Drive. You just never knew what might come up. Wasn't it great she'd been blessed with such an optimistic, go-for-it attitude? She might just make lemonade here, turn a lousy open house into the opportunity of a lifetime.

ED GARLAND

CHAPTER 17

My God, it was beautiful morning. Sky pure blue. Sparkling frost on all the firs. Ed felt like he was in a glittered Christmas card as he drove Walnut Boulevard.

Everybody at the Timberhill Athletic Club wore orange and black OSU T-shirts and seemed extra pumped. Tomorrow was a Civil War for the Ages, the newscasters were calling it with unabashed bombast, the 113th football game between the Beavers and the University of Oregon Ducks, and never before had the outcome been so crucial, for the winner of the Autzen Stadium showdown in Eugene would go to the Rose Bowl. Nobody wanted to talk about anything else. Even the women. Amazing. These two gals on the treadmills beside Ed were going on and on, discussing past games, comparing players.

Ed was jazzed too, but for secret reasons of his own. He and Julie had booked a private game-watching party, just the two of them, at her place.

Julie enjoyed recounting how the odious real estate agent tried to steer her straight to a house at Stoneybrook, pointing out the advantages of being able to move right down the block to assisted living when she needed it. ("And she couldn't even hear the condescension in her own voice, implying it wouldn't be long!") Instead, Julie had insisted on seeing whatever was available in the College Hill district, then made a prompt offer on an adorable jewel-box of a cottage just a few doors down from the house in which she'd grown up.

What nicer place, Ed thought, to watch The War for the Roses than Julie's little love nest? So what if she didn't have a big screen TV? The game was just

— 141 —

an excuse anyway. Beavers? Ducks? Who cared? As Julie put it so promisingly, she was rooting for *them*.

Ed Garland was in love. And shocked at himself to realize it. How could life take such an outrageously wonderful turn? How did he ever get so lucky to wind up with this beautiful woman they'd all sighed over way back when? And oh, boy, wouldn't this have tickled his mom? Charlotte always thought the world of Julie.

Lost in all this, he probably had a sappy look on his face when he slowed and stopped the treadmill. He stepped off and turned right into Vic Colton from church.

"Well, hey, Ed." Slightly hushed voice. Pity and Concern. "Good to see you back here."

"Yeah, yeah." Ed swiped his face with his towel, hoping to swipe as well his smug little smile.

"You can't underestimate the benefit of exercise for giving you a lift, can you?"

"True," Ed agreed.

Sex is even better.

Criminy! He hadn't said that out loud, had he? Good thing he was already red-faced with exertion.

"Got a Civil War party lined up?" Vic asked.

"Oh, no. No."

"You're not watching the game? Come on, why don't you come over to our place?"

Damn. Fighting off all this Pity and Concern could be exhausting. Strange how it had seemed like forever he'd been alone, but now that Julie Pomeroy had lured him back to the land of the living, he realized it hadn't been that long since Alice's huge church memorial service. Was there some rule about being in mourning for a year? Sure, people wanted to see him stop moping, but he sincerely doubted they would approve of outright euphoria quite so early on the conventionally accepted timeline of grief. After only one restaurant rendezvous, he and Julie had been feeling like they had to sneak around.

Jane had scored prized Autzen Stadium tickets for the game, and poor Robin obviously wasn't going to be able to enjoy herself if he let her go off thinking she'd abandoned him, so he'd had to admit to his watch date with Julie, admit to Julie Pomeroy period. With Robin, though, he knew it was okay. She would always cover for him, keep a secret if that's how he needed it to be.

"We're having a few people over," Vic pressed. "Come on, Ed. We'd love to have you."

"No, no. Thanks, Vic. Sure, I'm watching the game. With a friend. *Friends.*" That sounded better, right? "I just meant, I'm not *partying*, you know."

"Oh, sure," Vic said gravely. "I understand. That'll come. In time. You hang in there."

Ed frowned, nodded. The men slapped each other's shoulders in parting.

Then Ed went back to thinking about Julie.

You, he warned himself happily as he tossed his towel in the hamper on the way out, you, Ed Garland, are a bad, bad boy.

CHAPTER 18

C limbers missing on Mount Hood again. Newspapers full of it. TV, radio. Internet too. All eyes on the mountain. Every year at this time, people did battle with the elements in Oregon and some lost. A few were deliberate adventurers like these climbers, taking on the mountain's most challenging face in the risky month of December, but more often it'd just be a guy hauling his kids out to find a Christmas tree and then getting stuck in the snow. Or like that poor family from San Francisco who couldn't believe there wasn't a better route to the coast through the rugged Siskiyous. GPS units. Don't get Will Trask started. People breaking down in the wilderness by following these error-riddled computerized systems instead of relying on maps, some pre-trip research, and their own God-given brains.

In the valley, the weather couldn't be more desolate. Not frigid enough to snow, just wet and cold enough to make the elderly ache and entertain thoughts of moving to Arizona before the next winter rolled around. People who'd moved from places technically colder back East would swear they'd never been so miserable in Michigan's lake-effect snow storms as they were now in Oregon's oppressive, bone-chilling dampness.

Things looked ugly, too. With Summer's screening greenery long dead, every scrap of litter in the ditches was revealed. Yards displayed rusted oil drums and trashed cars. Vegetable gardens featured white plastic buckets and pipes, tattered tarps disintegrating into non-biodegradable bits in the mud. Even the nicely-kept spreads along the way looked bleak. Bottom line—no place needed the cover of darkness relieved by Christmas lights more than the rural Willamette Valley.

Will was driving out to cut Ed a Christmas tree, get it set up at his house. He and Shelley and the kids had done this for years; recently he'd kept up the tradition alone. This was the first time, though, that Cody hadn't even wanted to come. Something going on with his friends—that movie just out: *Avatar*. Will drove up Woods Creek Road and pulled in at the gated Garland Forests property where they'd all been cutting Christmas trees these past years. But when he picked up the rock by the gate post—no key. Shit. And it was starting to rain again. Well, he had keys for some of the other properties. Bound to be some decent eight-footers somewhere. He got back in the truck, started the engine.

And then—wait a minute. Wasn't Benton County the goddamned Christmas tree capital of the whole world, cut trees on every corner? Not like they were going back to the forest to grow another year if they didn't get taken home and tricked out with ornaments now. Besides, who gave a rat's ass anyway where he got Ed's tree?

He backed the truck around and headed down into town. Just past the Welcome to Eden Mills sign—a thick round disk of tree trunk, carved and painted—he spotted the first Christmas tree lot and pulled in. A couple of guys in pitch-smeared jackets held their hands over an oil can fire. They looked up, nodded, in no rush to leave the warmth.

Will passed leaning piles of Doug firs, the ones that looked like they'd been put through giant pencil sharpeners, and headed for the Grand firs. People got all excited about the Noble firs, and now, word was, they had some exotic new variety growing in hopes of being the next big fad—Nordman firs. But give Will a good old Grand fir any day. They had a natural look, not so densely pruned. And you couldn't beat their smell—almost citrusy.

Tilting one tree forward, then another, he flashed back on a year when he and Shelley had been dealing with frozen, broken pipes and hadn't felt up to the cut-your-own outing. The shame of it, a tree-growing family hauling the kids to a commercial lot. But it had reminded them all of the Christmas-tree-buying scene in their favorite movie, *A Christmas Story*. Will, much to Shelley's chagrin, had started imitating the film's salesman: "This ain't no tree!" He pushed one aside and marched to the next, Gar and Cody gleefully taking up the chorus, "This ain't no tree! This ain't no tree!" Shelley'd been left to roll her eyes at the salesman, shaking her head in apology. Of course his trees were perfectly fine.

They'd started out cranky, Will recalled, thanks to their long running impasse over the pipes, Shelley lobbying to just pay a pro to get in there and insulate them properly once and for all, Will insisting, as he did every time they froze and broke, that he could handle it and he would.

"It's too bad your dad's gone," she'd said that day. "I bet if I'd asked nicely he'd have come over and fixed these pipes for me years ago."

Damn. Talk about a low blow. First, it was annoyingly true. His father, although rarely motivated, was perfectly competent in undertaking home repairs, and had always found Shelley cute enough that he was glad to show up with his tool box and play hero. Did this make Will grateful? No way. If his dad has been as quick to help out his mother, maybe there wouldn't have been so much bickering around that house growing up.

And now Shelley was Will's wife to do chores for. Or *not* do chores for, damn it.

And she knew perfectly well bringing it up even after his father was gone—*especially* after—counted as fighting words.

So Will already felt defeated setting out that day, knowing she was right, that if he'd followed through as he'd promised the last time, water wouldn't be flooding all over the basement bathroom today. It further dampened his spirits that they were wimping out on cutting their own. Now, these years later, he regretted having to remember and acknowledge how he'd approached that shopping expedition like it was just one more tedious chore on his to-do list. It had actually ended up pretty good, after they'd got to goofing around. Sad, what a short time in your whole life it amounted to where you got to be the fun dad with kids at Christmas. That he'd wasted any of it being a grouch seemed criminal.

Now he pulled out the biggest Grand fir he thought his truck could manage, paid, and got one of the guys to help him load it.

Well, what the...? Will could see it in Ed's front window as he pulled into the driveway up on Country Club Hill. A prissy little Noble fir—flocked with fake snow, even. How'd that happen? Ed and Alice hadn't managed a tree on their own without his help in quite awhile. That Ed on his own would suddenly get ambitious seemed highly suspicious.

Will went up and knocked on the door. No answer. Tree's lights'd probably be on if anybody was home. He stepped back and looked at the fussy thing again. That, he thought, is a tree decorated by a woman, plain as day. Could Robin have done it? Well, sure, she could have cut the tree, delivered it in her truck, maneuvered it in and all. But this just did not look like any kind of Robin-ish decorating job. Robin Garland was a woman who took great pride in the design and construction of forest road culverts; she was not the type to delight in the artistic distribution of colored globes on a Christmas tree. Jane, either.

Well, now what? Bridget's? This sucker was pretty big, but she did have a high ceiling in her living room, and she was usually a good sport about stuff like this. Also, to be honest, he never minded an excuse to go by and check on her.

When she opened her front door, though, he saw that once again he'd been aced out. To her right was a three-foot tree, already decorated.

"Well, I can see you don't need me either," he said.

"What."

"You already have a Christmas tree, so you don't need the one I'm hauling around." He glanced back at the tree his truck bed, then hung his head.

"Will, are you *trying* to sound like Eeyore?"

"Who? I'm not trying to sound like anything. It's just that I'm driving around with this big-ass Christmas tree in my truck and now nobody needs it. Just makes me feel kind of...pathetic."

"And you've already got a tree up at *your* house?"

"Uh, no."

Bridget sighed. "Well, then, see, Will…you *are* pathetic." She pulled him inside. "I'm just having lunch. Then we'll go put the tree up at your house, okay? If it's that big you can't do it by yourself, right?"

"Guess not." Wow. Kind of embarrassing, being caught without a Christmas tree of his own. He still had a kid at home. What kind of a father was he?

"I hate my lawyer," Bridget confided as they sat there in the breakfast booth eating chicken soup. "One more man, telling me how I messed up. Says I should have got my financial ducks in a row before I walked out."

"He can't help you?"

"No, it's not that. He loves my case. Rich family? Son clearly in the wrong? Honest to God, Will, when he heard there was no pre-nup, I thought he was gonna jump up on his desk and do the happy dance. But the thing is, he's making me dig up all this financial stuff for him, plow through all these bankers boxes."

Will looked around. He didn't see any boxes.

"No, they're not here," Bridget said. "They're at the Witham Hill house. You know, the place I swore I'd never set foot again? I did give it one Saturday but I think I'm done. I mean, Charlotte's completely covered so, just for myself? I don't care. It's not worth it. What if the world ended tomorrow—is that how I'd want to spend my last day?"

Huh. This gave Will pause. He never wondered if he was happy doing something anymore, like if it would be a worthwhile way to spend his last day. He just put his head down and moved forward, avoiding the stuff he didn't want to do, doing what he thought he was *supposed* to do. Like get Christmas trees for people.

"And Charlotte won't return my calls. That's fun. Course, she's been blaming everything on me since she turned thirteen anyway. Last time we really talked she goes, 'You never even tried, Mom. You always wear those Earth Mother sandals when you know how Dad likes women in spiky heels.'"

Will leaned to the side and looked under the table. "I'd call those boots."

"Will! Don't you get it? The point is, what's this guy saying in front of his daughter that she even knows this? That is just wrong on so many levels."

Will grabbed his mail from the box and let Bridget into his house through the side kitchen door, feeling apologetic for the chill, the stink of dirty dishes in the sink. Sad contrast to her place, always warm and smelling good, with hot food cooking or those spicy candles she lit. He started tossing the mail on the kitchen desk piece by piece. Bills. College flyers for Cody. (Nice, a reminder his younger son wouldn't be around much longer either.) A Christmas card from Northstar Surveying. One from the bank. And one from Pete and Ardis. This would be their annual letter. He opened it.

"Uh, Bridget? Looks like you're still officially part of the family." The letter featured a formal portrait, taken last spring in celebration of Pete and Ardis's fiftieth wedding anniversary. It included all three generations, Bridget smiling beside John. "Wow. *You* in a black dress."

"Ardis made me wear it."

"They're just sending this out like everything's hunky dory?"

"Looks like it, doesn't it? Well, John hasn't stopped trying to talk me out of it, you know. Maybe they're still hoping I'll cave and they won't have to think of some graceful way to mention a divorce in their Christmas letter next year. But that portrait sitting cost a ton, which of course Ardis made sure everybody knew. So I guess I can't expect them to not use it, just because of me."

"They could have Xed out your face."

Her eyes flashed. "Gimme that." She grabbed a Sharpie from the kitchen desk and scribbled a thought bubble above her own head in the portrait.

Help! Bridget in the picture thought. *I want out!* John now sported horns.

Will laughed. "Sweet. So, are you doing Christmas cards?"

"Like, just from me? Not this year, that's for sure."

She was looking at the messy pictures on his fridge, most of them curling up or hanging by one ineffectual magnet. A far cry from the collection Shelley used to take pride in carefully curating. Bridget detached one, held it for closer examination.

"I took that," Will said. Alice walking a forest road with Ed and Robin, Mattie the Mutt a yellow blur. "Ed told me it ended up being the last picture of her. That's how she wanted it."

Bridget winced, shook her head, pinned the picture to the fridge again with a Kona Village magnet. "So, yeah, it was always John making me do the cards and our list was people we were *supposed* to pay attention to, you know? How about you? You kind of gave that up, didn't you?"

"Shelley used to do 'em. She'd do one for us with a family picture."

Bridget laughed.

"What."

"Well, you say that like I wouldn't know. Don't you s'pose we were on Shelley's list? You guys were on my fridge for years."

"Really?"

"Yeah. Actually, I took them when I left."

"Oh," he said. "Well, and then she'd do a business one for me, these cards with forest pictures on them. You know, a guy planting a baby tree in a clear-cut."

"But you're not doing that now?"

"Nah. Honestly? The people I work for do not give a rip."

Bridget drifted off into the living room. "Will!" she called back. "These paintings!"

He followed to find her slowly turning herself to take in every wall.

"When did your house turn into an art gallery?"

He shrugged. "Couple years ago. I thought you'd seen 'em."

"When would I have?"

"At a family thing?"

"Oh, Will." Bridget looked at him with great tenderness. As if this house had been the setting for any family gatherings at all since Shelley died. "Well, I *like* them."

"You do?"

"Yes!" She laughed. "It's just so…I don't know. I never would have thought you'd be the guy to get into art."

He watched her examine each painting up close, check out the artist's signature, then stand back for a more all-encompassing view.

"Gar says they'd look better if I got rid of the wallpaper."

"Yeah?"

"What do you think?"

She cocked her head, carefully hesitating. "I think he's probably right." She ended this on an up tone, though, like yeah, that made sense not *Oh, my God, how could you be so dumb?*

"He says you're the one who knows how to get the old stuff off."

"Yeah, I stripped layers of wallpaper out of pretty much every room in the Witham Hill house."

"Is it hard?"

She made a face. "It's messy, is what it is. You get that steamer going, everything's wet. You'd have to haul all these paintings upstairs so they wouldn't get wrecked."

"But it's not an impossible job?"

"No, you just have to get in and do it. It's like anything else, the hardest part's just getting started. Well, and it's definitely a two-person job. Although actually the reason I know that is from doing it by myself all those times and thinking how much easier it would be with another set of hands. If you decide you want to do it, I'd be glad to help. We could rent a steamer." She stood back and scanned the room. "Then you could go with this great color called 'straw.' A soft gold. You see it all the time in the craftsman-style restorations. Great backdrop for your paintings."

Whew. She had so much energy.

"That sounds…" That sounded *exhausting*.

"Well, whatever. You don't have to listen to me. Let's get this tree up, shall we?"

"Right. Let me get the stand from the basement."

But when he came back up a few minutes later, she wasn't in the living room.

"Bridge?"

She came walking out of the bedroom. "Will. Will, Will, Will."

"What?"

"Tell me those aren't Shelley's clothes still in your closet."

"O…kay." His entire body flushed. "How about those are my new girl-friend's clothes?"

Bridget gave him a look: Mournful Accusation.

Hey, so what if he was still grieving, damn it. What business was it of hers?

"Who said you could snoop, anyway?"

"I wasn't. I didn't mean to be. I had to use the bathroom. Your closet door was open and…I couldn't help it. I saw…pink stuff."

"Okay. So?"

"Will, you haven't sorted her things yet?"

"That's right, Bridge. This was a death, not a divorce. So, no, I didn't just open the windows and throw all her stuff in the yard, okay?"

She waited a moment, took a breath. "I know it's different."

"Okay, then."

"But it's been—what?—four years?"

"I can count."

"So, do you need help with it?"

"No!"

He knew four years was a long time. But this was his wife. His life. His pathetic *no* life. He felt awful enough without having somebody point out just how badly grief had paralyzed him.

"You know what, Bridget? It's nice of you to offer to help, but suddenly I just don't feel like putting up a Christmas tree. It's wet anyway. I ought to let it dry out a little on the back porch."

"Oh, okay. Well." She shrugged. "Wanna get me out of here, huh?"

"Bridge."

"'S'okay. I don't blame you."

She picked up her jacket and headed out the back door toward the truck. "But you'll still have to drive me home."

"Yeah, I get that."

"And I just want to say one more thing."

"Okay." He made a point of not looking at her. "Spit it out."

"I miss her too, you know."

CHAPTER 19

helley's clothes there—what a shock. Bridget hadn't realized how bad Will was still hurting. Thought maybe he'd even been dating. Seemed like a couple years back Charlotte said Gar told her about Will hooking up with some real estate agent he and Cody couldn't stand. By the time Bridget heard it the woman was history, but she'd assumed it meant Will was out in circulation again.

Obviously not. A closet of your dead wife's clothes didn't look like getting on with it. And, weirdly, here's where Bridget found herself missing Shelley herself. *Honey, we've gotta talk. You would not believe how stuck this guy is on you.*

She felt so bad for him. He deserved to be happy. Yes, agreed: Shelley had been a sweet, beautiful person, Will's devotion entirely justified. But Bridget had always wondered if it worked both ways. Had Shelley appreciated Will?

In every way?

Bridget had never forgotten that time at Kona Village when the guys had the kids out snorkeling. Temporarily freed from child-care, she and Shelley had stretched out on beach chaises by the Talk Story Bar and explored a bit too thoroughly the menu of fruity, decorated cocktails available just a staggering step or two away. Hey, it was vacation. Mellow and boozy, they had relaxed especially deeply into the sort of intimate confidences probably best exchanged only before drinking even more, the better to sufficiently eradicate any specific recollections upon sobering up.

"Will's after me for sex all the time," Shelley had complained. "I mean, I love him, and I want to be a good wife, but honestly. When people use the word desire? I've got no idea what that even means. He never gives me long enough to see when *I* might be interested. It's like, how can you ever get thirsty if somebody's always rushing to fill up your drink way too fast?"

Ten years had passed since Shelley'd tossed this off, and although Bridget might have wished she'd forgotten it, she hadn't. Thought of it every damned time her iPod playlist came around to Bonnie Raitt singing about the hazards of advertising your man. *Women be wise…keep yo mouth shut….*And now, seeing Will tending this everlasting love shrine to Shelley, as if dying had elevated her to sainthood…Well, no use speaking ill of the dead, as people said, but on the other hand, what's the point in painting the past as more perfect than it ever was?

"Will," she said now, as he pulled up in front of her house. "I'm so sorry. I really…I know it's completely different with you and Shelley and I shouldn't have said that."

He just sat there. Looked straight ahead through the rain-streaked windshield.

She waited.

Nothing.

"Okay, then." She got out of the truck and made her way up the paved walk. On the porch, as she stuck her key in the lock, she realized Will hadn't pulled away. What, was he having second thoughts? Wanting to talk after all? She gave him a moment, but the instant she pushed her door open, he pulled away from the curb. Okay. Just doing the gentlemanly thing, making sure she got in okay.

Inside, she closed the door, leaned back against it.

So, she knew the secret about Pete Garland and the hunting accident and she'd always had this secret too—Shelley's revealing remark. What was the good of knowing it though? It wouldn't help anything to tell him. And as for his closets, she herself had taken twenty years to pull the plug on her own ridiculous marriage, so really, she had no business thinking he just needed a kick in the butt from somebody like her to get his life back on track.

Okay, so what the hell had she been trying to get done here when Will showed up with a tree tall enough for the White House and a crippling psychological hang-up big and obvious enough for a Psych 101 textbook? Ah. On the dining room table—the cute Asian-style padded jacket she was sending her mother for Christmas. Top to-do list item: Wrap and ship.

She'd phoned down to Santa Rosa a few days ago with a suggestion: How about she flies down for Christmas and they put in some serious mother/daughter time? Bridget was surprised when her mother hesitated. Turned out she was seeing some guy. Insisted it wasn't a big secret, but admitted that Bridget phoning with stories of lonely weekends had made her less than comfortable bringing it up. But now of course if Bridget wanted to come for Christmas, she definitely should. Well, Bridget knew the pause that meant mixed feelings, and she sure didn't want to get in the way of a good thing her mother might have going. She'd have to pivot, generationally, turn in the daughterly direction and insist on Charlotte signing up for a couple of hours of quality holiday time.

Yeah, and good luck with that.

Bridget had already made an effort at decorating, deliberately situating the tree against the side window where she'd see it when she pulled into the driveway, and then, the Martha Stewarty candle stand she'd placed in the empty fireplace. Nowhere close to the cheer of a good wood fire, but it helped.

She had psychological protection plans in place, too. She would avoid being alone on Christmas Eve by walking the two blocks over to the Presbyterian church. She would book PT appointments every day but Christmas itself. That'd make people happy. They'd half expect her to be taking more time off for her family and be pleasantly surprised to get in at the last minute. And there *would* be calls. People always got stressed around the holidays, making whatever was hurting hurt worse.

Now she went over and hit PLAY on her Bose. Alison Krause: *"Get Me Through December."*

Yeah. That.

The doorbell rang.

A flutter of hope. Will wanted to talk after all? She trotted back and opened the door expectantly.

Nope. Instead, John. She sagged.

"That was Will Trask just left," he said, "right?"

"Yeah, so?"

"Oh, come on, Bridget. Don't be that way."

"What way?"

"Cold. Look, can I at least come in?"

She glanced at the window of the house across the street for the lift of her landlady's lace curtain. Bridget wanted to provide an entertaining scene for this nosy woman even less than she wanted John in the house. With a sigh of annoyance she pulled the door open and stepped aside. She wasn't actually afraid of him like some women had to be of their stalking exes. She just did not want to go over all this again.

"So exactly why is that guy hanging around?"

"He's not hanging around. We—" Wait a minute. Since when did she owe John any good-little-wifey explanations? She cocked her head and squinted. "You just can't stand him, can you."

"Oh, I have no problem with Mr. Trask."

"Right."

"Other than the fact that from the word go he's been one colossal pain in the ass. Just so desperate to prove he didn't need his pretty little wife's family behind him. Commercial fishing. Why didn't he just stand on the dock, beating his chest, hollering, 'Macho macho me?'"

"John!" She laughed helplessly. "Why do you even care? That was so long ago. He only did it for six months but you still can't get it out of your head."

"Maybe it's about family pride, okay? That s.o.b. turned us down when Dad and Ed offered him a position. Not to mention my cousin Shelley was a lady in every sense of the word. You expect me to be happy to see her marry this backwoods hick?"

"Oh, brother," Bridget said. "That's really how you see him, isn't it?"

"Damned straight. You think that's so far off? You ever see the hovel in Eden Mills where he grew up?"

"Hey, did you have a reason for barging in here? Something beyond lecturing me about Will Trask? Because I'm trying to get some things done." She turned her back and started unrolling wrapping paper on the table.

"I really just wanted to talk."

"About what? The depositions?" They were slated to spend what might amount to a full day each being queried by their opposing lawyers. "You know, I really cannot can't stand my lawyer." He'd asked if she had anything to wear to this meeting other than a flannel shirt and jeans. A dress? A little suit? "I have a set of scrubs," she'd told him. Not amused.

"Bridget. Is he hitting on you? Because if he is—"

"Oh, for God's sake," she said over her shoulder. "You would think that, wouldn't you?"

"I still care about you, Bridget. If I thought somebody was giving you a hard time—"

"What." She turned to face him. "If you thought that, what? I guess you've always figured giving me a hard time was *your* job, huh?"

"Oh, come on, Bridget."

"No, he's not hitting on me. He's *mad* at me because I don't want to cooperate with his plan to get every last nickel of Garland money I'm entitled to no matter how long it takes."

"Oh. Well, Mom wouldn't like me saying this, but that's just being a good lawyer."

"But I just want out. As fast as possible. I can't stand wasting the precious time of my life going through tax records."

"Oh, honey, me neither. Why don't we just bag this? You don't really want to go through with it, do you?"

She turned back to her wrapping.

"We're talking twenty years, here."

He put his hand on her arm; she shrugged it off.

"Yeah, I can count." And years weren't the only thing.

That first time he'd cheated, she'd been outraged. Because—wait a minute—initially he was the one who'd chased *her* all over campus. Wore her down with the persistence of his pursuit. His was a love for the ages blah blah blah. And the harder she was to get, the more she had unwittingly turned herself into the very prize he most wanted to prove he could win.

After his first "indiscretion," she had fallen into an agony of painstakingly comparing herself to this other woman—a hot-looking aerobics instructor, the one with the ridiculous implant job. Hey, this was Corvallis, Oregon, for God's sake, not Hollywood. Still, Bridget tortured herself. What did this other woman have that she didn't? Come on, she was a C cup. And hers were real. That wasn't good enough for him?

It engulfed her completely, the quest to save her marriage, a giant project complete with counseling—out of town, of course. The counselor and John together entreated her so earnestly. It would be hard, these two men pointed out, but if the marriage were to be saved, she would have to give it time, work at learning to trust again. She and John would never make it if she couldn't acknowledge his appeals for forgiveness, his sincere efforts at reconciliation. How could a man possibly stay married to a woman intent on being suspicious the rest of their lives?

And so she had tried. And she hadn't left. But she had never truly trusted him again. And this happening at the very time they'd have been thinking about a second child meant that somehow, Bridget just couldn't seem to get pregnant again.

Funniest darned thing.

Then, years into the marriage, when he started slipping again and again, she began to see how it was. This was *so* not about bra sizes. It was about a guy like John never being able to stop setting his sights on fresh new prizes. And every time she caught him it was the same—the confrontation, his attack-as-defense strategy, the lying, the insistence she was mistaken, more proof she wasn't, followed by a certain contrition and promises it would never happen again blah blah blah but of course it did. She found out about that woman who ran the U-cut Christmas tree farm right before they all went to Hawaii for the double fortieth anniversaries, and then it wasn't that long before the blonde running for state representative showed up in their lives. Far from being overly suspicious, Bridget had actually tried hard *not* to find out. After all, how many times could she look the other way without exhibiting some shred of self-preservation and taking action? This wasn't even about her, she saw now. Or sex. It was simply that John Garland would never be able to resist a woman who would stoke his ego the way he seemed to so desperately need.

"I warned you," she said, taping the wrapping paper seam. "I told you I wasn't going to be one of those women who leaves and comes back and leaves and comes back. If I finally couldn't take it anymore and moved out, that was going to be it. I've done the Big Beg scene way too many times already. You beg for another chance, I beg you to be a better boy."

"But I never thought…"

"Never thought I'd do what I said? Because you don't do what you say you'll do?"

"Bridget." He put his hands on her shoulders. "Honey, I really miss you."

She pulled away, flushed and dismayed by her own body's inner betrayal. She missed him too, in some ways. That's why she hadn't wanted him in the house, she remembered now. She couldn't be letting him touch her.

"I think you should go," she said. "Wait, let me rephrase that: Go!"

"Okay, okay." He held up surrender hands. "But can I first take a peek at the room you've fixed up for Charlotte?"

Like he cared.

She was probably a fool to waste time setting up a room for Charlotte, anyway; she had no interest in coming over here. But one of Bridget's patients had quoted advice from a book about getting along with your kids as they became adults, something about keeping your mouth shut and your door open. Thus, a designated room, left deliberately plain, for a daughter who seemed unlikely ever to visit it, much less do any decorating.

Bridget waved toward the short hall. "It's the one in front, to the left."

"You're not giving me a tour?"

"You can hardly get lost." She cut a length of ribbon.

John's voice came from the hall. "Ho! What have we here? A big brass bed."

"That's not her room! You can just stay out of there."

"You always did like that song," he said, reappearing. "*Lay, Lady, Lay.*"

"Shut up."

"Come on," he sang, "let me help you break it in."

She made a face. "What makes you so sure it hasn't been already?"

"Whoa." A flicker of interest passed over his face. "Well babe, I guess because I know you."

"Don't call me babe. I never liked it before and I like it even less now."

"Sorry," he sang, not sorry.

"And you *don't* know me."

Except in this way, damn it, he did. If after all the times he'd been unfaithful to her, she'd never yet run out and hopped in the sack with somebody else for a round of revenge sex, how likely was it she'd start now?

"Bridget, Bridget…Can't we just talk?"

"No! There's nothing to say. Nothing I haven't heard from you a million times."

"I know," he said with perfectly calibrated chagrin. "And you're right. I've been a total jerk and I don't deserve your forgiveness. But is it so wrong of me that I want it? Doesn't that say something good about me that I at least know whose approval is worth having? That woman was *nothing*, but you won't even let me explain. Believe me, she is not worth breaking up over. And I don't want to. I mean it—if you give me just one more chance, things'll be different from now on."

She dropped the ribbon. He was making it hard to concentrate. Not that she hadn't heard all this before, of course. And every single time she'd wanted to believe him. She wanted to believe him now. Was it possible? Could a guy screw up regularly for twenty years and then somehow stop? Was there a place on the internet where you could type in all the cheating data and come up with the odds of things going better the next time around? Because, admittedly, all things being equal, she'd still rather check off *married twenty years* instead of *divorced and alone.*

"Come home, Bridget. It's awful there without you."

"Yeah?" Her voice came out low and uncertain. "Cry me a river."

"Come on, honey."

He reached and turned her around. He did look stricken. He looked like he meant it.

"I hate that house," she said.

"We'll get a new one. Anything you want. I know you've never liked that place and you're right, it's been unfair of me that you never had more say in it. This time you could design a house and we'll have it built. You could even do a log house. Isn't that what you always wanted?"

"You mean it?" He'd actually been paying enough attention to register that yes, a log house was, in fact, her dream? Never before had he tempted her with a peace offering like this. Maybe actually moving out had knocked some sense into him.

"Yes, I really mean it. And Bridget, look around. Divorce wrecks people's lives. I'm talking about family. When there *isn't* divorce. Everybody sticking together. Having people who are there for you. Going through all the ups and downs together, whatever happens and, you know, at the end of the story, still being there with the one you started out with. You don't really want this to be the story of a marriage that fell apart after all this time, do you? You don't want to be people who just...lost heart? Gave up? Especially when it could still be about a marriage that hit rocky spots but the two of us held it together?"

Dammit. He knew so well how to do this. He knew the very words to use and the hypnotic way to say them. He made it all sound so good and sensible that you had to keep reminding yourself why it was such BS, coming from him. If you let him keep it up, before long you'd forget, as she'd done so many times before.

"I love you, Bridget. You know that, don't you? I'm not saying I haven't been a jerk."

"You've been an asshole."

"Okay."

"You've been a total prick."

"That too. There, now. Feel better, saying it?"

"No. Not really." But she found herself acquiescing, letting him put his arms around her.

"Bridget, you've got to believe me. I'm just saying that nobody else has ever for one minute meant to me what you do. You know that, don't you?"

Actually, she did believe that. She just wasn't sure how much good it did her on a day-to-day, go-out-and-screw-up-again basis.

"You're such a politician," she murmured. "You could be up there giving those speeches like they do."

"Oh, Bridget." He laughed a little and held her, completely missing the hint of insult she'd intended. But be fair. Can you honestly expect a guy to notice any negativity if you're letting him get his hands down your pants? This is what she missed. This is what turned her back into a fool every damn time. Why couldn't she just—

"Actually," he mumbled, "on the subject of politics…"

"Mmmmm?"

"Since you bring it up, people have been telling me I ought to run for state representative."

She froze.

"They think I'd be good. They think I could win."

Damn. She yanked his hands out of her jeans.

"Right." She shoved him back. "You could win with a nice little wife by your side—"

"No, Bridget—"

"But not with some bitch suing for divorce." She started pushing him through the living room to the front door.

"Bridget, no. This is just what's happening in my life right now. Everything I said about wanting you to come home is the truth and has nothing to do with the other. I swear to God."

"Right! News for you—your swears to God mean nothing. I'll bet you've already been thinking about making me wear high heels. And one of those dumb Sarah Palin suits."

"No! I never said that."

"Oh, look John. Give it up. It's too late. And too bad for you, because now that I'm out of the house, I found out I'm happier." She grabbed his arm and started dragging him to the door. "You may miss me or you may be lying, but I'm done trying to sort you out and the truth is, I have not been missing you."

"Okay, so this *is* about Will Trask, then, isn't it?"

"No!" But suddenly it hit her. "Well, yeah, actually in a way, maybe it is. 'Cause tough shit for you, John—here's a guy who never cheated on his wife. Never would no matter what. And after everything you've put me through, a guy like that looks pretty damned good to me. Just the *idea* of a guy like that. Just the living, breathing, walking around proof of the possibility of male decency." She opened the front door.

"Bridget, that's not fair—"

"Fair! Gimme a break. What does that word even mean to you?"

"You really don't think I've ever tried to be fair?"

"Oh, for God's sake. You know what? You're only right about one thing. I do want a log house." She pushed him out onto the porch. "But I don't want live in it with you. And that brass bed? Forget it! You're *never* sleeping in that with me. You're never doing *anything* in that bed with me."

And with that she slammed the door.

And bolted it.

CHAPTER 20

The marked-up fiftieth anniversary family portrait from Ardis and Pete lay accusingly on Will's kitchen desk. The whole deal was so sad, he thought, the way things had gone down for all of them. The amazing fortieth anniversary gathering at Kona Village had hardly concluded before everyone—in the grip of some kind of instant nostalgia—had begun looking forward to staging a repeat for the two couples' fiftieths. Will and Shelley had even talked about it on the flight home, discussing what they thought Gar and Cody might be like at sixteen and eighteen.

But what a wallop a decade can pack.

First, Cindy having a miscarriage just two weeks after they got home. Shelley was close enough with Cindy to hear and pass on to Will the details of the swift aftermath, Phil's hastily tossed up roadblocks to parenthood. That clod. No more hope of babies for Cindy. Even adopted ones. Cindy was pretty broken up about it.

Next, Will's dad dying.

Then losing Shelley and Alice.

Some of this seemed random, and Will couldn't call his dad dying a tragedy. Between smoking and drinking, Dan Trask probably lived longer than he had a right to expect. But for Will, losing his wife and mother-in-law in succession did not seem unconnected. Was there some kind of domino effect in force? Who was next, Ed?

When their lives had all seemed golden and charmed, Will now realized he'd been stupidly assuming this was a credit to his family as smart, hardworking people who made good decisions. They weren't folks letting drugs and alcohol drag them down. They didn't drive recklessly. They got their flu shots.

But then a car crossed the center line with the slamming news that—guess what, dummy—shit still happens.

Pete and Ardis, too, would have voted for everybody having their babies, staying alive and married and going back to Kona Village. Instead, with Alice in hospice last spring and a lavish double fiftieth trip or even a modest party out of the question, they'd done what they'd thought appropriate, gathered everyone for a sober-looking fiftieth anniversary portrait.

And now that picture was already out of date; Ardis was losing her treasured bragging rights to status as a family completely unmarred by divorce.

Will admired Bridget in the picture, glad she'd kept the Sharpie markings off her own face. She may have resented wearing that dress, but she looked good in it. The black set off her rosy cheeks. Even in a posed studio portrait she looked healthier and more alive than the rest of them. Will took scissors from the drawer and with three or four deft snips freed her, tucking the tiny picture in his wallet.

She'd only been trying to help today. And she was right: he was way over-due on dealing with Shelley's clothes. People died and whoever was left had to take care of their stuff. That's just the way it went. What made him think he was somehow entitled to a pass?

He went down to the basement and scrounged for clean boxes. In the bedroom, he started pulling out Shelley's dresses, still on their hangers, and laid them across the unmade bed. What was he supposed to do with these? No daughters, her mother gone, a gay sister who wore her one navy blue dress rarely and with reluctance. Shelley and Bridget had been close enough, but he couldn't see Bridget in any of these. Probably never wore pink in her life. And anyway, weren't people creeped out at the idea of a dead person's clothes? Or was that just if the people were old and the clothes were out of style anyway? Was it not the same if you died young and had beautiful things like Shelley's?

He phoned Robin, pacing the house. He explained what he was up to, then listened to what was probably a pause of surprise.

"I guess I assumed Mom helped you with that," Robin finally said.

"She probably would have. I never asked." Alice hadn't brought it up either. Face it, neither of them ever wanted to do anything that actually acknowledged Shelley was gone.

"I took Mom's things down to the OSU Thriftshop," Robin said.

Will let out his breath. Relief. She wasn't going to lecture him.

"It's like a consignment thing, but if you don't care about the money, they put it toward a charity."

That sounded about right. You couldn't go throwing nice stuff like this in the garbage.

"We put the Art Center's number on Mom's things."

"I'll do that too, then," he said. "You know Shelley always went along with whatever your mom said."

Another pause.

"Will? You want me to come over and help? I wouldn't mind."

"That's good of you, Robin, but I guess I ought to do this myself."

His sister-in-law was quiet, maybe giving him time to reconsider. He could hear Mattie whimpering in the background.

"Don't feel bad," she said after a moment. "I don't know how long it would have taken Dad to deal with Mom's stuff on his own. I pretty much just went over there and started doing it."

"Well, thanks. I appreciate that."

Signing off, he picked up the first lavender dress, held it at arm's length on its hanger and waited for it to hit, the onslaught of some tidal wave of sorrow he feared as he remembered her wearing it. He gave it a moment. Funny. Couldn't picture her in this one. He looked at the others, sheer ruffly things in pastel shades. He felt a little guilty; he didn't remember these. Was that because she had so many clothes a lot of them hardly ever got worn?

Maybe, he thought, carefully folding the silky gowns into the boxes, it was just because these dresses weren't her real, everyday life. Like most women around here who weren't clocking in at an office or a classroom every day, she had lived her life in jeans. Even when she did put in a little office time, helping process permits for people who wanted access to various Garland Forests tracts, she'd worn jeans and a green logoed hoodie like the other girls Ed and Pete hired.

But then he found that long peachy-colored thing. The Hawaiian dress. As far as he remembered, she had only worn it that one time at Kona Village. But...he thought of the painted coconut. Yeah, he remembered exactly how the fabric had felt against her thigh as he pushed it up...Now he smothered his face in it, breathing deep, hoping...

Nope. No trace of the tropics.

No scent of coconut.

It had been too long.

No Shelley.

And another thing, now that he thought about it. He couldn't so easily hear that lilting voice of hers. Used to be he could imagine whatever she'd say about anything, like she was watching over his shoulder, sweetly determined to register her opinion about whatever was going on. But not so much anymore. Everyone around him was moving on. The boys were growing up. It was getting harder all the time to figure out what she'd have had to say about their various issues.

Still, he couldn't ditch this particular dress. He rolled it up and stuffed it into one of his own drawers. Saving just this one didn't brand him as too sick of a puppy, did it?

He hurried to finish up. Like Bridget said about stripping wallpaper or really, any project—starting was the hardest part. He'd dreaded this task for so long, he'd refused to even think about it. If he'd known he'd could get through it without completely falling apart, he'd have done it sooner.

"Whatcha doin', Dad?" Cody was standing in the bedroom doorway.

"Just taking care of a few of your mom's things."

"Oh."

That was it. Just "oh." Kids always seem to think whatever their parents do is normal, and don't sort out the weirdnesses until they leave home and compare notes with the rest of the world. Will wondered if maybe someday Cody'd be telling this story to his college roommate: *Well, I didn't think much of it at the time, but here's my dad, finally clearing out my mom's clothes and dude, she'd been dead, like, almost five years.*

"So," Will said, "how was the movie?"

"Awesome! You better go. I'm serious. *Avatar's* like nothing you've ever seen before."

"Okay." *Okay,* as in, *I register that,* not *Okay, I'll be sure to go.* Will hadn't been to a movie theater in years.

"Hey, Dad? Is that tree in the truck for us? It's huge!"

"Yeah. Wanna help me put it up?"

"Sure. Hey, can I order a pizza?"

"You bet."

Will folded in the tops of the two cardboard boxes and stacked them by the back door. The hard part was over. These would go to town first thing Monday.

Right now, he had a Christmas tree to put up.

CHAPTER 21

H is office phone rang too fast and furiously to check caller ID. The instant he put it back on the hook it rang again. Or his cell went off. "Will Trask," he'd answer. "Will Trask." Chasing this recent spikey timber market was nuts. His clients were looking for a boost in cash flow by setting up logging shows, but only if Will, as their agent, could nail down a less than abysmal price per board foot. Since the price spikes into decent territory seemed to last a day or two at best, trying to get the contracts all signed at the most advantageous moment did a job on his nerves. His transactions kept the FAX machine downstairs humming non-stop.

Now his cell nagged again, that dumb little jingle.

"Will Trask."

"Well of course I know it's you!" He held the phone away from the assault of his mother's voice. She sounded hysterical, already in the middle of a frantic story about something happening at Stoneybrook, and *now* what did he have to say about this being the absolute nicest, best place for her?

"Mom! Mom, stop! Back up." She was always launching in like this, as if caller ID not only identified her, but also delivered ahead the back story on whatever she was ready to rant about. "Now try to calm down and tell me slowly. What happened?"

"Well, don't you know? You always know everything that's going on."

"I didn't see anything in the newspaper."

"Well, it only happened last night! And I just have to wonder how you're feeling about moving me here now."

"Mom—"

"A couple of thugs threw a rock right through the big front window in the middle of the night and broke in!"

"Oh, gee…"

"They went in the office and stole some purses."

"Well, Mom, are you okay? Nobody got hurt, did they?"

"No, I'm all right. We all slept through the whole thing. And they already caught them, too. But it's scary, Will." He heard her sniffling.

"Okay Mom, I'm going to come over, okay?"

"Well, I think you should." She hung up.

Damn. He stuck his head in Kim's door. "I gotta go calm my mom down. They had some kind of a break-in over at Stoneybrook."

Will got in his truck and headed out. Wasn't this supposed to be the new year? A year better than everybody agreed 2009 had been? Nothing good happening so far. This break-in business. Some idiot taking a high-powered rifle and shooting out the light at the historic Cape Meares Lighthouse the other day, damaging the irreplaceable antique lenses. And of course the earthquake in Haiti, just so horrendous, dwarfing every local problem. People talked like this ought to put things in perspective, and maybe it did to the extent that everybody felt guilty for whatever they'd been bummed about, but it certainly wasn't a thing to cheer anybody up.

He drove along the highway from to Eden Mills to Corvallis. This grim January weather didn't help. No, it wasn't the bitter cold they'd been enduring back East. But those Eastern snow storms, when they cleared, left a world of dazzling light on bright snow, right? The unrelenting oppressiveness of the gray Pacific Northwest this time of year was a grim challenge to anybody appreciating an occasional ray of light. Day after day, the sky one huge smudge of a worn-out pencil eraser.

Will turned off Country Club Drive and drove past the Stoneybrook entrance sign and fountains. Couldn't those low-lifers have picked someplace else to break into? His mom hardly needed additional ammunition in her arsenal of gripes. Will had done his research, felt sure Stoneybrook was the best nearby assisted living facility, but before ever poking her cane over the main door's threshold for a tour, Betty'd decided she didn't like it. Not that there was any other place she preferred.

"Do you want me to call Val," Will had asked her, "and see if she's got any ideas about places up in Spokane?"

"Will! I wouldn't dream of letting you do that! Don't you know how busy your sister is? They *both* have to work, you know."

Right.

"Well, we're agreed you're not doing that well on your own, right? So what's the matter with Stoneybrook?"

"Oh, honey. Stoneybrook's for rich people."

"Come on."

"I won't fit in."

"For Pete's sake, it's not like you'd be living there as some kind of charity case. I'd be paying."

"I know, and I don't want you to have to."

"Well, don't worry about it, Mom. I'm doing okay. Make you feel better to know it's almost like Garland money in the end? Ed's so generous with the kids' college funds. That means I can take care of you."

"Oh, but wouldn't your father just have a fit? Thinking the Garlands were supporting me?"

"Mom, Dad's gone."

"And what would Shelley have thought?"

"Shelley *wanted* me to take care of you." And had been a saint, as far as Will was concerned, patiently ignoring his mother's digs. Shelley couldn't buy a new piece of furniture without Betty reminding them how much better off the two of them were than she and Dan. "I had to save up three years for my new sofa. Oh, I know, it's different for you two, but I have to wonder—if you can have everything the minute you get married, what do you have to look forward to?"

As if the only things in life worth looking forward to were new sofas.

To be honest, of course, hadn't he felt the same when Ed and Pete flew everyone to Kona Village? Uneasy about being with people who seemed like they must be members of some other species? It had taken time to figure it out and get used to it, the idea that rich people—at least rich Oregon timber people—were not necessarily flashy types who flung money around buying stuff; they were also the plainest of the plain, people who could buy a new sofa any time they wanted, allowing them to quickly learn what a small part a sofa might actually play in the quality of a person's life. They could afford to pay for experiences, things that made life nicer and more comfortable, like first-class plane tickets or an apartment in the best assisted living facility in the area. And the real key: they could pay without worrying. Was that so horrible? Was that a crime?

So, finally, his mother had moved into Stoneybrook two years ago. About five minutes after the last lamp was set on the last end table, she started in with what would be the first of her incessant critiques. "You know Will," she'd say, "these people just don't dress up for dinner the way you'd think. I mean, if they're rich." She made a game out of reporting to him every person she met who was obviously above her in station. "I *told* you it would be like this," she took great delight in reminding him. "This new fellow was a CEO of some big company back East, come out here to retire near his daughter."

"Yeah? And, so?"

"Well, what am I supposed to say at dinner to somebody like that?"

"Oh, for Pete's sake. How about, 'Is the apple crisp any good today?' These people eat, don't they?"

"And it just disgusts me, Will, how these women flock around a new single man."

"Nobody says you have to get in on that."

"I know." She'd give him a look. "But you expect me to live here with people like that."

It was worse than arguing with a teenager. She was so confident Stoney-brook was where he wanted her, she could indulge in nitpicking to her heart's content. Ha! Wouldn't it be fun, he sometimes fantasized, to show up with a moving truck and call her bluff?

Today he found Betty in her neat little second floor apartment where she sat him down, fussed over a cup of instant coffee, and made him hear all the details about the break-in again. People were just so upset! And what a wonder nothing worse happened than a few purses getting stolen.

"There's people walking around these halls at night not quite all with it, if you know what I mean. If those crooks had run into somebody…" She trailed off, not about to put something so awful into words.

"Well, I see they've already got the glass guys down there repairing that window, so that's good."

"Oh, of course. Don't I tell you? These people used to be president of this and that. They're not going to put up with a broken window."

"But, Mom, that's good, isn't it? Would you be happier in a place where the management just says, 'Tough. We'll fix it when we feel like it?'"

His mother sat back and tsked, shaking her head. "I don't know why you always have to get so mad every time I say something about rich people. I'm just stating facts. Sometimes I think you're turning into one of them."

Will stood up. "Anything I can do around here for you before I go?"

"You're leaving already?"

"Well, I've got work to do, Mom. You don't want me turning into a rich guy who's got time to sit around with his mother all day, do you?"

A wounded sniff. "I'm an old woman, Will. And I'm your mother. I wish you wouldn't take that snippy tone with me."

Will sighed. "Sorry, Mom."

"And I think you forgot something. This month's spending money?"

"I gave you that, Mom."

"Are you sure?"

"Yep."

"Well, I could use a little more. There's a bus going over to the casino tomorrow and I signed up."

"All right." He sighed. "Whatever." He pulled out his worn wallet and tugged off the dirty rubber band.

CHAPTER 22

Kit Garland had to go up to Corvallis, and she was mightily peeved about it. She never felt comfortable there. Okay, it wasn't like she had to walk around wearing a big name tag reading GARLAND, but whatever she did in life, whatever path she took, she knew she could never live in that town. Even if she changed her name, people would figure it out.

Thank God the name wasn't the same big deal in Ashland. When you're sitting up in a tree, chained to a platform so the Neanderthal loggers don't dare cut it down, you really hate to be letting on to the other protesters that you're from a family who's made a fortune by doing that very thing…cutting down trees.

It was creepy enough, now that her roommates had caught on that her parents actually owned the Ashland house they were all living in, had bought it specifically for that use while Kit was in college, that the rent checks she was collecting were being sent to her mother up in Seattle. After the initial surprise they were mostly chill about it, but once in awhile, when the crap was piling up deep all over the place, dirty dishes overflowing the sink onto the counter, recycling burying the official bins on the back porch, and obviously somebody should do something about it, they'd start sniping at each other and invariably the dirty words would be lobbed her way. *Our little junior landlord.* She suspected they talked about this to each other behind her back.

"We're not the only parents doing this," Greg and Susan kept assuring her, sounding apologetic.

Plenty of people had figured out that buying houses in college towns wasn't the worst investment. But they didn't seem to grasp the uncomfortable position it put her in. In an added weird twist lately, she'd noticed herself somehow wanting to defend them. Okay, so they were sort of rich. They weren't bad people. Sometimes she felt like telling Jake and Roseanna they could just take their minimal rent money and see how far it would go at one of the slumlord places other students were packed into, old houses where windowless basement closets were rented out as "rooms." Kit knew plenty of people who were paying twice what her roomies were for half as much space. Couldn't they show at least a smidge of appreciation instead of resentment for the sweet deal they were getting?

The housing issue was nothing compared to the whole Garland Forests thing, though. She just couldn't imagine what she'd do if her compadres in Earth Alliance ever put it all together, that she was a goddamned Garland, a family who'd been raping the land for generations now.

Well, that's how *they'd* put it, anyway. Everything with them was always so black and white. You either loved and protected trees or you cut them down. She doubted they'd be willing to consider the possibility of people standing on some kind of middle ground, people who planted and nurtured trees that— yes—would in all likelihood be harvested at some point in the future, but in the meantime cut trees that first sprouted from the earth before they were born.

And the individual members of her family, most of them, weren't bad people. For awhile, when she realized that actually, her tuition money could probably be traced right back to a loaded log truck (well, say a dozen), she had been pretty down on everybody, but by now, having conversed with more of them as individuals at various family gatherings, she'd noticed herself softening up a bit.

She'd adored her grandmother, Alice, who'd once even said she thought it was just fine what Kit was doing, that somebody ought to speak up for the old-growth trees. And last time Kit had gone out fishing with her grandfather, Ed told her all about some secret, beautiful falls on the Yaquina River they owned, how hardly anybody even knew about it, but they were planning to do some kind of a swap with the state of Oregon so maybe someday it could be a park. The Garlands didn't want to cut down the trees and ruin that place. They were not, in spite of what her Ashland friends might have guessed, in the business of simply setting out to destroy the earth. And Aunt Robin was cool as hell.

Even her Uncle Will, who for awhile she'd been thinking of as a bloodthirsty hunter and despoiler of the wilderness, turned out to be a bit of a softie. After Grandma Alice's funeral in June they'd all gone back to Uncle Pete's. Nobody thought Grampa should be expected to handle it at his house, apparently. It was just family, and nobody paid any attention to who was drinking what. She'd been completely freaked with grief and desperate to be alone, but when she took her wine down to the basement where they used to play with the miniature log trucks during the family foundation meetings, Uncle Will was down there by himself too. She was so mad about everything, she sat down, let him re-fill her glass (he'd swiped a whole bottle from the buffet apparently) and promptly picked a fight. Yeah, she sat in trees, she told him. Somebody had to protect the earth from people like him who'd like to cut down every last tree and poison everything with those horrible herbicides

"Hey, I hate that stuff myself," he said. "Knock my lights out trying to get my clients not to use it. I mean, two hundred yards away I was standing one time when they were loading it onto the helicopter. Jeez, the stench. And you know it kills baby animals."

"Well, duh. Why do you think I'm so against it?"

He wasn't listening. He was off on his own memory track. "Found a blinded fawn once. Jesus. Made me sick."

His eyes were red and welling with tears, but she was a little drunk and upset herself, not ready to let him off the hook.

"What's the point of worrying about baby animals dying if you're just going to go out and shoot them in the end anyway?"

He looked at her askance. "Well, Kit, my idea's to let 'em grow up, run around in the woods and have babies of their own. Then someday if I go out there and chase one down for my freezer, well, at least that critter got his shot at being part of it all for a little while, just like the rest of us, right? If you don't see the difference between that and saying 'Oh, hell, nuke all the newborns,' well then you're not as smart as I always thought."

Surprised her uncle had ever thought about her at all, Kit felt her throat close. "Okay, okay." She threw back her remaining wine in one shot. "Uncle Will?" she said after a moment. "I can't stand it about Grandma."

"Yeah, me neither." He looked as miserable as she felt. "I can't stand it about anything."

Aunt Bridget came down the stairs then and caught them both falling apart.

"You guys," she said, all concerned, sinking down by Will and putting her arm around him. "Are you okay?"

Will waved at her. "We're just crying about animals."

Bridget looked to Kit for confirmation on this and Kit said, "Well, it's about Grandma, too."

Bridget nodded, a hand on Will's back.

"It's my fault," Will said, and Kit noticed he was even drunker than she'd realized. He was almost sobbing now.

"What are you talking about?" Bridget said.

"Alice."

"Sweetie, cancer's nobody's fault."

This was heavy. Kit felt like she was witnessing something she shouldn't. Like this was rated for Adults and she wasn't old enough. And it struck her: Aunt Bridget called Uncle Will sweetie.

"I would lay good money," Will said, sniffing and having to choke it out, "that if Shelley and I hadn't had that car wreck, we wouldn't be having a funeral for Alice today."

After that, Kit would never feel the same about Will Trask. She certainly couldn't see him as the villain her Earth Alliance group would make him out to be.

Now she sighed as she stuffed a few tattered clothes into a backpack. Too bad it was winter and no sane person would be going around sleeveless—she was itchy to get a reaction to her first tattoo. Ha! How could the family object? A nice fir tree on her biceps. But then, a tat was probably nothing compared to what she'd stirred up with that picture in the paper last Fall. Uncle Pete made a snide remark at Thanksgiving, and when she complained to her mom, Susan said he'd already phoned and tried to lecture them on their many mistakes in raising her.

It was such a drag, Kit thought now, having to lie to people about where she'd be spending this upcoming Martin Luther King weekend. Like anybody would even know what a family foundation meeting was in the first place. Just the most boring thing ever. Hey, maybe this year she ought to really perk things up. Maybe climb onto that big old polished wood conference table and demand a grant for Earth Alliance.

Well. She yanked the zipper closed. Maybe someday.

God. What a weird life.

CHAPTER 23

Being forced to put the annual Garland Family Foundation meeting on his calendar was not a gripe Will had ever been able to lay on Doug at Taco Time. He couldn't complain to his mother. He really couldn't talk about it to anybody. Rich People Problems! Who'd believe him anyway, what tedious, contentious work it could be to give away money? Even when professionals in Portland were being hired to pre-sort the grant requests.

In earlier years, before the building of the new headquarters, the meetings had convened at Pete Garland's huge house, with Ardis fretting over the selection of a babysitter to ride herd on the youngest generation in the basement rec room. Should they try for someone mature but perfectly discreet, or just settle for good-hearted, young and so naïve as to be clueless as to the nature of the meetings going on upstairs? No secret the Garlands gave out grants; plenty of local non-profits hoped every year to be on the receiving end of one. But the Garlands wouldn't want to hear their debates quoted around town, nor did grant recipients need the details of how it all went down.

No need for babysitters anymore. Since members of the younger generation were expected to grow into their roles as stewards of the philanthropic trust Spark Garland had set up, they were now encouraged to sit in on as much of the annual meeting as they could stomach. Will had especially appreciated his sons joining him at the headquarters meetings the past few years, because although he himself was, according to the bi-laws, still a voting member even without Shelley, his connection to the foundation itself now felt more tenuous, and his sons' involvement made his presence seem slightly less awkward.

So, yeah, he always wished he were anywhere else on the Winter day of the annual meeting, and now this added bummer: No more Bridget. No co-conspirator with her flashingly-fast crossed eyes at him whenever her husband or in-laws said something she simply could not let pass. Yep, he was on his own now. Nobody could replace her. Even Robin, who agreed with him on most matters, usually seemed busy trying to keep Mattie quiet under the table. And no tempting his sons in even the most subtle mockery. Will had to be a good role model, and the Garland Family Foundation annual meeting was not the place to goof off.

Ordinarily Will tried to steer clear of the new headquarters building, this being the location of John Garland's office, so each time he *was* required to show up, he always got a fresh take on the set-up. *The Forests of the Future Start Here* was the motto, with wood, obviously, the dominant architectural theme. The walls were paneled in an attractive pattern of the various species grown in Western Oregon and today, as Will led Gar and Cody to the formal conference room, he pointed out to them how much of this being pretty was thanks to their grandmother, Alice.

"It's nice she got some fun out of them building this," he whispered, "finding this art stuff." Not only did Alice manage to score an original Ken Brauner (many of the other timber offices around the state had to be satisfied with his giclee prints, she'd explained to Will later), she'd also tracked down a Montana wood artist by the name of Ron Kelly and commissioned a gorgeous panorama of wildlife at a forested stream, all done in various shades of inlaid wood.

As soon as the family had taken their places around the huge Doug fir conference table and Uncle Pete opened the meeting, Cody stuck up his hand.

"I think this year we should just give all the money to Haiti for the earthquake orphans."

John Garland looked to the ceiling. "Moving right along…"

Will tensed. *How many votes for me just climbing over the table and choking the s.o.b.?* At sixteen, Cody was proving to be a sensitive soul, and the Haiti earthquake coverage had hit him hard. Did John think his own daughter Charlotte so superior, sitting there next to her Aunt Cindy, already texting under the table?

Kit Garland, slouching sullenly in her chair, eyed Cody from under her black bangs and swiveled her wrist in a languid thumbs-up.

Robin gave Will a look: *good kid you've got there.*

Ed Garland cleared his throat. Cody was his grandson, after all; it was his place, not his brother's, to explain to a new young member the complications of philanthropy.

"That's a fine idea, Cody. And I'm sure we'd all like to do that. But Spark arranged things with rules about who we can give the money to. If we sent it all to Haiti right now, the other people counting on using it for college tuition and such would be in trouble."

Cody's black brows went together. "But couldn't we send a little?"

"Well I'm sure everybody here will be chipping in personally for the various aid efforts, right?" Ed looked around the table and Cody's aunts and uncles gave the boy quick, earnest, oh-my-goodness-of-course nods. "And there's a part of the trust set up to go to a couple of the relief charities in Portland on an annual basis, isn't that right? Mercy Corps and Medical Teams International?" He looked to his brother Pete, who confirmed this with a nod. "So you see, Cody, our family's chosen to handle it so that the doctors who can really help down there will be able to jump on a plane and go without having a bunch of fund-raisers first."

Will studied his son's face. Was he comforted at all? He and Shelley had never agreed on what to tell the kids about the family money. Cody once asked if they were rich. Some kid at Tree Planting Day said if he was the great-grandson of Spark Garland, then he was. His mother told him so. Shelley'd been livid. It wasn't nice for people to talk about other people's money. And of course they weren't rich, she'd insisted, invoking what Will had come to think of as The Doctrine of the Denial of Wealth.

Sure, their personal bank account wasn't that impressive, but didn't she get it? They had security. They had a roof, and food, and they didn't have to worry about getting sick and being unable to pay the doctor's bills. To Will, after growing up in Eden Mills, that was rich. No matter how bad he and Shelley blew whatever they tried, they would not wind up under a bridge, dumpster diving for dinner. Will thought his kids should understand they were lucky and be grateful. He finally decided that what Shelley really meant when she said they weren't rich, though, was that they weren't evil. That just because the family owned thousands of acres of land, it didn't mean they lived in a way that would thrill and horrify people, and put the Garlands in a trashy magazine or voyeuristic TV show. She wanted the kids to feel that it somehow didn't count as rich if you were decent and boring and guilty rich. If you were Northwest timber rich and drove a dirty truck.

Will couldn't even begin to imagine what she'd be saying to the boys now that they were getting older and couldn't be put off with the simple explanations they'd used when they were little.

Now Greg Garland opened the notebook in front of him on the table.

"Dad and I have been discussing a suitable memorial gift for Mom. We thought something in the fight against cancer would be good, in light of..." He cleared his throat. "Robin and I have made several trips to various research hospitals here in Oregon and also Washington and California. We're finding it's easy enough to endow a department chair, but we were really hoping to place the money somewhere where it could do the most good."

While Robin patted Mattie under the table, he went on to explain about a project in what they called epigenetics, a new field where they were hoping to figure out what switched certain genes on and off. The University of Southern California Norris Comprehensive Cancer Center had a program that sounded very promising.

"Epigenetics." Gar said. "Wow."

Heads turned.

Will smiled. "You know what he's talking about?"

"Yeah, we did a whole unit on that last year in AP Science. It's the coolest thing."

Everyone looked to Will, as if he should somehow explain this son of his.

Proud as hell, he regarded Gar with baffled amusement. "I don't remember you ever talking about this."

Gar shrugged. "I didn't think you were interested and also—" He ducked his head apologetically—"I didn't know if you'd understand it."

Will laughed. He was perfectly happy to be Dumb Old Dad if it gave him the privilege of claiming this brilliant boy as his own. He narrowed his eyes at John Garland. *In your face.*

Greg went on with his report. He'd obviously knocked his lights out trying to distill the science of this proposition into language the Garlands could all understand.

Now there was a mystery of genetics for you. How could Greg be such a good guy and have a first cousin like Bonnie Prince Johnnie? Was it Alice's genes vs. Ardis's? Greg had obviously put so much into this research. And it wasn't like he didn't have anything else to do—he was a tenured professor up at UW and currently writing a biography of 19th Century Scottish botanist David Douglas, whose story, he kept insisting, didn't get near the attention in the wider world it deserved.

Will watched Ed, head down, eyes fixed on his tablet of yellow legal sheets, still blank. Must be hard, Will thought, to have Alice brought up.

"Of course we wanted to do something more personal and closer to home for Mom, too," Greg said. "She always admired the garden they put in over at the hospital in Lebanon. She talked about studies showing that looking at nature helps people recover faster."

"And keeps them from going crazy," Robin put in.

"Right," Greg said. "Mom actually started doing some of the planning for this in the weeks before…" He had to stop and take a big breath. "So we're proposing a start-up fund of a half-million to get this project going up at Good Samaritan. It would be a room that opened into an outdoor space. We've had meetings with the administrators and we feel this would be enough to launch the thing, and then we'd be hoping for others in the community to step up and supplement this."

"Not because we don't want to bankroll the whole project," Robin said, "but because we wanted to let the community in on it. Mom had so many friends. I'm thinking people would welcome a chance to be part of something like this. Do it in her honor."

Solemn nods all around.

"And although we've always generally agreed we don't need to be slapping the Garland name on everything we fund, this case seems a little different, and we thought of calling it the Alice Garland Garden of Healing."

Ed's voice was hoarse. "She'd have liked that."

Will was watching Robin. Funny. He'd have expected more sympathy from her directed to her father; instead, she seemed to be making a point of not looking at him at all. She just kept glancing at Jane.

"And by the way, Will," Greg said, "in Mom's papers on this we found some notes. She had it down there she specifically wanted you to help pick out the artwork."

"Oh." Everyone looked at him. He swallowed hard. "Yeah. Okay."

Kit started to cry, startling everyone but Will, who flashed her a sad wink. Alice's death had turned out to be an unexpectedly keen loss for so many of them, with people a little surprised to learn they weren't her absolute favorite. That's how effectively, how privately she had rooted for each in turn. Marrying into a family where some, like Pete and Ardis, insisted on life roles being lived out as prescribed, nobody had been better at encouraging each person to feel free to be themselves than Alice Garland, and for a few moments, everyone gathered around the table seemed to be pausing for thoughts of her.

"Okay, then," John said abruptly. "Are we finished with this? We need to move on."

Will clutched his pencil. Wasn't that pretty damned rude? He glanced around. Yeah. Not his imagination. Greg and Robin both looked appalled. This wasn't just some random piece of business. This was their mother.

"Now, I think most of you," John said, "are probably aware that I've been encouraged to run for state representative in the primaries this May."

Yeah, yeah, everyone knew. Maybe this is just what John Garland *should* do, Will thought, be a lousy politician, because all he had going was his publicly affable nature and the ability to scoop up the check for the rounds of drinks and golf, fine traits for a politician, useless for a husband and father.

"Because of this," John said, "I've been doing my homework, taking the pulse of the community. I've had a lot of prominent people approaching me with their concerns. One of the issues is the Garland Grants for the graduates of Eden Mills High."

Will frowned. What could anyone be concerned about? Seemed like the entire community had always been grateful for the support this gave the kids of Eden Mills. Not to mention all the real estate agents' enthusiasm for pointing out this amenity attached to every property in the Eden Mills School District. Great PR for Garland Forests. So Ed looked puzzled too, like he couldn't quite think where John was heading with this.

"Here's my concern," John said. "The student body of Eden Mills High— well, I'm going to say it—it's *degenerated* from what it was when Spark first set up these grants. He wanted to help the children of the timber industry, sons of loggers." Patronizingly, he gestured toward Will. "Like our own Will Trask here."

Will flushed. He wasn't ashamed of having worked the woods himself, but he certainly never felt like bragging on the fact that his whole college education had been at the expense of the Garland family. And here were Gar and

Cody, looking at him questioningly, making Will twist uncomfortably in his seat, wishing he hadn't stalled on spelling out this bit of family history to them.

"But now," John said, "we've got kids taking advantage of these grants who have nothing to do with the timber industry. Their parents can be with Hewlett-Packard or one of the other high tech firms that coat-tailed it into the Willamette Valley. They're buying into the Eden Mills district specifically to take advantage of these grants."

"I'm not sure why that's a problem," Ed said. "Are we supposed to penalize them for knowing a good deal when they see it? Their property taxes support the school system, don't they?"

"But Ed, these are just not the kids Spark wanted to help. They have pierced noses, for God's sake. They have blue hair. They are forming gay support groups."

Robin's winced, turning to Ed. "Dad?"

"Jeez, Uncle John," Kit said. "You think just because Garland Forests pays people's college tuition we should be dictating how they do their hair? Maybe you think we oughtta say how everybody votes. Or who they can marry."

"Now don't *you* get going," John said to Kit. "I wasn't going to bring it up, but you're a perfect example of what I'm talking about...biting the hand that feeds you."

"John!" Greg said. "That's not—"

"Just whose hands do you think are feeding her," Susan cut in. "She's *our* daughter." She gave Pete a pointed look. "And we're proud of her."

"Okay, sorry sorry," John said dismissively while Kit went red as if she weren't sure whether she wanted her mother's pride or not. "So let's try to stay on track here," John continued. "As I was saying, it's the whole culture of the school over there that's concerning. They've got science teachers actually demonizing the timber industry at the same time their hands are stuck out for Garland money. They wanted a pool? We gave 'em a pool. They needed new grandstands? We wrote the check. When Spark set up the tuition grants in the late sixties, most of the kids taking advantage of it *were* the children of people in the forest products industries. But that is just not the case anymore, and this whole thing has developed into a culture of entitlement. Now you've got people in the Eden Mills School District sending their kids to college on Spark's nickel so they can learn to how to stop the timber industry in its tracks. You've got kids with parents who're members of the Greenbelt Land Trust!"

Ed's palms braced on the table. "And what is your big problem with the Greenbelt, if I might ask?"

Pete lifted his head and stared at Ed. "Since when do you *not* have a problem with the Greenbelt?"

"The point is," John said, bypassing his elders, "it's our money."

"It's *not* our money," Will interjected.

John rolled his eyes. "Well, it's not *your* money, logger boy, that's for sure."

"John!" Ardis said.

"You listen here," Ed said, "the one thing Spark always talked about was knowing exactly where that money came from. Not just the timber, but the labor of the men who logged those trees and worked that mill. He heard you using the word logger like a dirty word and I'm betting you'd be the first he'd want to kick off his foundation board."

Everyone froze, pale statues around the table. Charlotte had actually stopped texting.

"And believe it or not," Will said, "I can read just fine and I've looked at those by-laws myself. It was Spark's money. Money he wanted given away. That's all we're here to do."

"Right," John said. "And it's up to us to say who ought to have it. Otherwise, he could've just let it all be distributed when he died, right?" He turned to Pete. "Isn't that always what you've said, Dad?"

"Well, yes, he did entrust this responsibility to us." But Pete was not looking happy at the way this was going.

John jerked his chin. "I'm just saying Spark'd be turning over in his grave if he saw some of those kids applying for his grants."

"I'd say he's turning over in his grave listening to *you*," Will said. "Spark didn't know what the future'd look like. No more than the guys writing the Constitution did. That's why you got us living guys trying to sort this stuff out, not the dead ones."

"You should read some of their application essays, *Mr.* Trask. They're an insult to Spark's generosity."

The kids were all staring. Grownups weren't supposed to argue. Not like this. Loud. Vein-throbbing, hands-shaking mad. Weren't some kind of lines being crossed here? Even Mattie the Mutt was picking up on it, wimpering at Jane's feet.

Will snorted. "I'm not so sure Spark woulda worried that much about a clueless sixteen-year-old kid dyeing his hair. And the school's not that bad. Don't they still have that Forestry program going over there?"

"Yeah. Talk to the kids in it and you'll find out the teachers are giving them a hard time about it. These teachers are favoring the kids with the nose rings. They're all busy signing on as advisors to the gay support group."

"John!" Will stood up. "For God's sake, you do know your cousin here is gay, right?" Because for the second time John's intonation on *gay support group* had been laden with the sort of loathing you'd reserve for people suspected of taking delight in the torturing of small animals.

"None of my business," John snapped. "Not anything I'm supposed to be talking about." He gave Robin a pointed look. "Right?"

Will saw Phil gulp. Nice. Ten years since he got clued in about Robin and it still freaked him out.

Robin sat still, her voice quavering. "I am so sick of this shit."

"Robin!" Ardis said. "The young people!"

"The young people know that word, Ardis."

Kit spoke up. "Know bullshit when we hear it too."

"I've put up with this for years," Robin said to John without actually being able to look at him, "but I don't see why Jane has to sit here and listen to it now."

"Well, you're right about *that*." John's temple pulsed. "Jane *doesn't* have to sit here. That was *your* idea, not ours. Dad and I have been discussing this. The bi-laws state that voting members are family and legal spouses, not partners or significant others or whatever you're calling her."

"Goddammit," Will said, "They're as married as the State of Oregon allows, and just as soon as people like you stop voting down gay marriage, I bet they'll be the first ones down at the courthouse."

"Oh, please, do not get going on—"

"And furthermore, Spark was huge fan of Robin's. Huge! We don't know what he would have thought about blue hair, but we know for a fact he thought Robin was great. Didn't you ever notice that? So if she wanted Jane here, I think Spark would have approved."

Robin registered stunned gratitude at him before turning to Jane, sitting there suffering a brave new level of married-into-the-Garlands misery.

"Excuse me," Jane whispered, standing. "Mattie needs to be out of here."

Oh, God, so do I, Will thought. Couldn't somebody take *him* for a walk? He'd gladly submit to a collar and leash if it meant escape.

Mattie's nails clicked on the wood floors.

"If it makes any difference," Cody said, finally breaking the stark silence, "we have a gay support group at Corvallis High too. I'm in it."

John smirked at Will. Like *yeah, your kid would be.*

Jesus, Will thought. And all this before they'd even busted open the stacked up bankers boxes full of grants to argue over.

It was going to be a long day.

Maybe a long year.

A long, nasty life.

CHAPTER 24

Will never minded putting on the Day-Glo vest marking him as a team leader for the kids on Tree Planting Day, but now, out here on one more cold, rainy day, he had the same notion that had taken him by surprise at the foundation meeting: Nothing was the same without Bridget. Damn. He hadn't even realized how big a part she'd been playing for him in these family-related events until she was gone.

"And to think I never have to go again!" she'd crowed when Will told her about people practically coming to blows at the recent meeting. Divorcing a Garland was apparently not going to be the same thing as being widowed by one of them. "I *will* miss Tree Planting Day, though."

He thought of her out here just last year, cheeks flushed, misted hair escaping her bandanna. Shelley had begged off participating early on, only half joking she was still suffering from the trauma of all those childhood Tree Planting Days in the rain. But Bridget had loved it. She always said that actually getting in there and planting the trees was the purest, best part of Garland Forests.

Will braced on the steep slope and looked across the draw to an adjacent section where an adult crew in yellow slickers was actually seeing to the proper establishment of the so-called Forests of the Future. Yep, Mexicans doggedly doing the back-breaking work while this gang of white ten-year-olds enjoyed the privilege of pretending.

"It's starting to rain," one whined.

"That's what we want." Will swung his hoe-dad. "The trees love the rain."

The kids didn't, though, and the unrelenting downpour eventually cut this year's planting day a bit short. Working in the rain was one thing; listening to kids gripe about it was another. Will got home earlier than usual.

Gar's Honda was in the driveway. Hey, great. Maybe they could get some kind of take-out. Dinner alone was getting old. Mostly, when Cody had soccer or something, Will just nuked whatever was in the freezer.

Gar wasn't in the living room. And funny, the washer and dryer weren't running either.

Will went over to the stairs and called up. "Gar?"

He heard some banging around and took the steps to the landing. Then came what sounded like muffled swearing, followed by Gar's voice, tense and insistent.

"Just a minute, Dad. We'll...I'll be right there."

We? What the—? Will stumped back down, knocking mud clods off his boots all the way. Then he just stood there in the living room, waiting the longest time for his son to appear.

"Uh, hi Dad," Gar finally said over the banister. He was wearing his old *No Fear* T-shirt, black with a white skull and crossbones, an interesting contrast to what was apparently the most angelic expression he thought he might get away with. From above him on the stairs he pulled down an embarrassed girl. "This is Hannah."

Will may have managed a nod; he'd never be sure, trying to remember later. But as for some pithy parental directive? Forget it. Struck dumb with astonishment, he was pretty sure he never said a word. Not about the situation anyway, which was perfectly clear. Even if their clothes hadn't been hastily pulled on and done up, their flushed faces and messy hair said it all.

"Uh..." Will's eyes darted around, as if avoiding the brazen evidence might somehow help. "I just...I just had to drop by and pick up the...the..."

Gar waited. "But you're done planting?" he prompted.

Helpful little twerp.

"Yeah. No. No, that's right, we're not done. So, uh...nice meeting you, Hannah."

Will jumped in his truck and backed out faster than he should have. But he had to get away. Then, out on the road it hit him: What a wuss, running away again. Chased out of his own house. Should have stood his ground, kicked the kid's butt, pulling a stunt like that. *No Fear.* No shit. And shouldn't he? Have some? Be a little more worried what his dad would do if he caught him like that? Will knew *he* would have at that age, having a girl in his own bedroom. Christ. But then, wait a minute, at Gar's age, he was out of that cramped little house on Applegate Street for good. He'd thought of himself as a man. He wasn't afraid of his father. If his dad had taken a swing at him, he'd have swung back.

Oh, hell, he really didn't know what he was supposed to do about something like this.

And now, here he was, out of his house with his clothes all caked in mud. Aimlesssly driving toward downtown Corvallis. Hungry. He ordered coffee shop meals in less than pristine work clothes all the time, but showing up anywhere this bad would be over the line, even for him.

Bridget's. He'd go over there. She wouldn't mind. Even if she wasn't around, he could park on her back porch for a few minutes until the coast was clear at home. But he hoped she *would* be there. Somehow he just wanted to talk to her about this. Get some advice. She had an eighteen-year-old kid. Maybe she knew what you were supposed to do when they threw something like this at you.

When Bridget appeared at her door he said, "Don't laugh, I'm a walking dirtball."

"Wow, you are."

"And I'm kind of freaking out because...Hey, look, why don't I come around back and at least not trash your carpets?"

On the back porch he sat on one of the Adirondack chairs she had recently acquired and pulled off his muddy boots.

Bridget leaned against the door jamb. "So how'd you get like this?"

"Tree Planting Day. Rain."

"Well, come on in the kitchen."

"Are you sure? I'm dropping dirt clods all over."

"I don't care." She steered him into the breakfast booth. "Sit. Now what is it you're freaking out about?"

"Oh, nothing," he said sarcastically, signaling with big eyes the outrageous drama he was about to reveal. "Just that I came home and caught Gar in bed with a girl!"

"Oh." She turned to the fridge to hide her smile.

"What. It's not funny!"

"It's not?"

"Huh. You're a big help."

She cocked her head. "You want a glass of wine?"

"Why not?" he said, annoyed but wanting the drink.

"Sorry, no choices." She poured him a glass of her Elk Cove pinot gris. "I always drink this same stuff."

"S'okay."

"So will you let me feed you? I was just going to fix a steak."

"You don't have to do that."

"I know, but if you don't stick around and eat this second one, I'll just have to throw it in the freezer. You might have noticed it's hard to buy groceries for one."

"Well, in theory I'm still cooking for Cody, but the kid's hardly ever home." He took a taste of the wine, checked out the label. "Nice elk." He smirked. "Looks like one I remember shooting."

"Oh, shut up."

He tried the pinot gris. "Good. Good enough for a muddy guy like me, anyway."

She smiled, took a sip herself, then went back to the fridge for vegetables and started putting together a salad.

"I don't know why I'm so upset about Gar," he said. "Maybe it's because I keep thinking I should have the Big Talk with the boys, but I never get around to it."

"Looks like the cat's out of the bag now."

"Jesus, I don't want him to go getting some poor girl pregnant!"

"Well, if it's any consolation, I think the kids these days have all heard the drill about condoms. Charlotte certainly has. I've made sure of that."

"Yeah, well, good for you."

"Come on, I didn't mean it like that. I just meant you're not his only source of information."

"Huh. Let's hope. I just feel like such an idiot, running out of my own house. Like I was scared! What am I scared of?"

She turned to look at him. "I don't know, Will. What *are* you scared of?"

He winced. "Don't do that. Don't talk like that."

"Like what?"

"The way women do. Where you say things but you mean other things or you mean more than just those words and we're supposed to figure it out. And we can't."

"Okay, okay."

"At least *I* can't."

She sat down opposite him, put her hand on his. "Take it easy, Will. I won't talk about it." She aimed at him that direct, steady look of hers, then gave his hand a conclusive pat and went back to fixing the meal.

He sighed, starting to relax a little. Took a sip of wine. He didn't know why it should panic him, the idea of his son pairing up with somebody. That's the way it was supposed to go, wasn't it? The boys should grow up?

"I have to admit I miss the Jenn-aire," Bridget said. "I have to use the broiler for these."

He watched as she bent over the open oven and slid the pan in. He couldn't help appreciating the way her rear looked in jeans. And with nobody else to catch him, he could get away with staring. Like you never could with women's breasts. Stare and they'd be annoyed as hell. Although if they were going to wear those bras that propped them up like that, it seemed like that's what they wanted. Who could figure?

She shut the oven and turned around.

Damn. Bridget was one pretty woman. How come he'd never thought much about that before? Well, except that Hawaii thing. Mostly he'd always just enjoyed how funny she was, but even that part he'd never really put into words, even just to think. Maybe it was because Shelley was his wife, the most beautiful, and he'd always judged other women by how far they diverged from her—the creamy skin, the reddish-gold hair, so rare.

But now he thought it was nice Bridget's hair was plain brown. And the fact that she didn't see fit to mess with it color-wise just made her seem confident in a way you didn't see so often in women. And her eyes were gray, nothing exceptional. Her cheeks were pink like she was always busy taking deep breaths and being really alive. He smiled at her, getting a bit of a buzz.

"What," she said, smiling back.

He grinned a little goofily.

"You okay?"

"Oh, yeah."

She made a face like maybe she wasn't so sure about that and then turned away. "I'm thinking about getting a grill for the back porch if I'm still here by summer."

"I thought you guys had one of those great big fancy propane suckers."

"You can't really think I'd want to go to the mat with John on that. The cheap ones are good enough, anyway."

"For sure." He looked around. "Have you done something in here? Changed stuff?"

"I painted. This is that color I was telling you about—straw."

"It's nice."

"And I made the curtains." They were done in an old-fashioned print of red and yellow fruit on a blue background.

"I like it," he said, not really understanding how a person chose these different colors and patterns but admiring the way it all combined to make it feel good to be sitting here.

She wrapped a crusty loaf of bread in foil and popped it into the lower part of the oven.

"Amazing," Will said.

"What."

"Apparently not a single part of this meal is being prepared in a microwave."

"It's pretty basic, really."

"I guess. I've just gotten so microwave dependent."

"Well, you should come over for dinner more often. It's no trouble to fix a little more, and I'm trying really hard to keep eating healthy. I don't want to get going on all that frozen stuff just because I'm on my own."

See? She was doing it again. Saying things. And what did it mean? Was "Come over more often" supposed to be flirty? Like a real invitation? Or did she just feel sorry for him, pointing out how deplorable it was for a single person to never eat anything but frozen entrees? Better change the subject.

"We missed you at tree planting today."

"We?"

"Me and Ed. Well, Robin probably missed you too." He shrugged. "But it was Ed who brought it up."

"He did?"

"Why'sat surprise you? You know he's always liked you."

"I guess. I did always think it was too bad *he* wasn't my father-in-law. You definitely married into the better side of the family."

"Won't argue with that. Today he said Spark would hate knowing they were letting you get away."

"Aww, really? Now Spark I feel bad about. Kinda glad he's not around to see what's happened. Remember what he said at that anniversary dinner? 'Don't get divorced!'"

Will scoffed. "He'd have been rooting for you all the way, Bridge."

"You think so?"

"Sure. Ed says he's probably turning over in his grave that his own grandson, his namesake, for cryin' out loud, went and treated you so bad."

"Oh. Well, that's sweet."

"Not to mention Spark was very big on the idea of a guy cutting his losses. If a patch of trees wouldn't grow, he just figured it was bad ground or a crappy seed source. Whatever—it wasn't working. He believed in moving on, get something going that would thrive. You know, don't look back. He liked that Chinese thing—the best time to plant a tree was twenty years ago. The second best time is today."

"And that's what it says, specifically—twenty years?"

"Yep."

"Wow." She sighed. "Twenty years. So was John the wrong tree or the wrong ground?"

After they ate she persuaded him, dirty as he was, to come out and sit with her on the sofa. She had these little candles set in the fireplace. When had she managed to light those? They smelled good. Made it nice. To think he had a perfectly good fireplace at home and never even lit a fire. He sank into the sofa cushions. He'd probably already had more wine than he should have to make this safe, but he couldn't go home yet, and he liked talking to Bridget. Just don't look in her eyes, he reminded himself. If everything stayed light and he didn't give her a chance to really get to him, he'd be okay.

"So how's your house hunt going?" he said as she refilled his glass.

"It's not. I went to an open house back in December that kind of put me off the whole thing. The agent put me off, that is, not the house."

"Who was it?"

"Liza somebody? With Town & Country?"

"Aw, jeez. Liza Madison, right?"

"Yeah. You know her? She was so pushy. And just all over me about why I was looking, my life circumstances and stuff. When I mentioned getting divorced, she kind of…deflated, like, oh, okay, this woman's not going to have any money. But when she caught that my last name was Garland, I swear her eyes bugged out in dollar signs like some old-timey cartoon. It was scary!"

Will laughed. "That's Liza all right."

"And what is it with women getting haircuts like that? Where it's all razored off short in these precise angles? Seems like you've have to go sit in the salon about every other day."

"Not to mention it looks like crap. Compared to long hair like yours, I mean."

Wait. Was he not supposed to talk like that? Somebody complained on TV that women were supposed to cut their hair however they damned well pleased and shouldn't be thinking about if men would like it. But, he wondered: Was it okay to like it if they were already doing what they wanted?

He felt relieved when Bridget went on, not looking annoyed.

"That house could've worked out for me," she said. "It was actually a lot like this place. But I kept stalling on following up with her and the next time I looked, it said 'under contract.'"

"There'll be another one, but yeah, you wanna steer clear of her."

"She has me steering clear of real estate agents completely. I don't seem to be getting very far on my own, though."

"Well Bridget, I can take you to see houses if you want."

"Really? I thought you hated showing houses."

"This'd be different. This would just be you and me." And then she was just looking at him, that way she did, so he hurried to add, "I found Robin and Jane's house, you know."

"Yeah?"

"Course, that was the easiest deal in the history of real estate. They took one look at that big flat fenced yard and said, 'Sold!' I practically had to force them to check out the inside. I think they've been really happy with it, though."

"But I don't want to look at any subdivisions of ranch houses like that, okay?"

"Absolutely not. Not for you. So tell me what you *do* want."

She perked up. "Shall I get something for you to take notes?"

He laughed. Like he'd have to write down anything that had to do with Bridget and what she said about real estate. "Spit it out," he said. "I'll remember."

So she took another sip of wine and began laying out her little back-to-the-land fantasy.

When she listed *log house* as one of her so-called boxes to tick, he said, "Are you sure? I don't want to sound like John, stomping on your dreams, but log houses do have some issues. If you're somebody who worries about how many trees you're cutting down, there's a hell of a lot more wood in one of those than in a regular house. And the maintenance is a pain. They don't just sit there looking like a big old Lincoln Log set forever. Unless you keep slapping stain on them, they weather unevenly. Kim had one listed that was just full of bugs. Little holes all over it."

"Hm. Well, maybe it wouldn't have to be all logs. Just so it was the rustic look. Like a lodge. Guess I just never got over wanting to play pioneers, you know?"

He smiled. Playing pioneers with Bridget might be fun.

"I've been watching the ads," she said. "I'm learning to decode the language of real estate."

"Oh, like *Bring your tools* means *It's a dump?*"

"Yeah. Also the names of things. So, here's one I've been wondering about: Why are trailer parks always *Such and Such Estates?*"

"Uh, wishful thinking? Aspirational, if you like bigger words?"

"And you guys: Heritage Realty. Ever thought about that?"

"You mean like how it's supposed to make you think you could buy a great old house and expect to get the heritage along with it?"

"Yeah, exactly."

"Well, I've seen that with people. But you can't buy somebody else's history. You have to put in the years there yourself."

"I guess you could look at it another way, that people might like the idea of buying a property they hope their kids would think was worth inheriting."

"Yeah, okay. Like, traditions have to start somewhere."

She grinned. "Haven't I seen that in some ad? *Traditions start here…at Muskrat Ranch.*"

"Not bad! You want a job writing ad copy?"

"Well, I wouldn't come cheap, you know. And anyway, maybe I should get my own real estate license. I'd call my office…" She looked over at the flickering candles…"*Home for a Bunny Realty.*"

"Oh, shut up!" he said, laughing. "I don't think you show the proper respect for my profession."

"Yeah? Well, you don't either!"

"Okay, okay."

"Oh, one other thing about my dream place. I need some apple trees."

She then confessed she had a $1200 cider press on order from some amazing craftsman down in Veneta.

"You've ordered an apple press and you don't even have any apple trees?"

"Well I did when I ordered it! Remember that big one in our back yard? This guy's presses are in such demand, you have to get on his list a year ahead. And it was one of those things John didn't want me to do. He was always telling me why all these ideas of mine made no economic sense. He'd just stopped me from ordering a cute wooden rain barrel. So when I saw this story online about Cider Bob, I went ahead and ordered one of his presses. I had this lovely vision of standing under the apple tree on a mellow September afternoon, making this...this elixir of the gods."

He smiled, eyeing her sideways. "I think a cider press is a great idea."

"Yeah?"

"Hell, yes. There's tons of apples around here go to waste every year." He was thinking about the Gravensteins that must fall into the meadow grass at Hopestill Creek. "And don't forget, I've got a tree in my backyard."

She was smiling at him. That's when he made the mistake of looking into her eyes as he clapped his hand on her thigh.

"You know you can have my apples."

CHAPTER 25

You can have my apples.

     After Will left, Bridget threw herself backwards over the sofa and just laughed out loud. He actually said that! You can have my apples! Said it in total innocence, his freakin' hand parked firmly on her thigh. Too bad she was sure that poor, sweet, forthright Will Trask never uttered a double entendre in his life. Not knowingly anyway. And didn't seem to recognize the suggestion of one when it came up and bit him on the butt, either.

If only Gar hadn't called right then, prompting Will to jump up for a fast exit. She'd have enjoyed explaining that a man can't go saying things like that without giving a woman ideas.

Because—oh, my God—yes! She'd love to take on his apples.

Meanwhile her ex, whose phone calls she tried not to take, had developed a habit of emailing her on the slightest excuse. Did she really not want any more of the furniture? Could she please be in touch with his parents? They were having a hard time believing she didn't care to mount the fiercest court case possible and he was tired of trying to convince them.

Now John wanted to be in touch. Now more than when he actually lived with her. He seemed disappointed she'd decided not to fight him for every nickel, almost crestfallen when she blew him off with the news that life was too short to sit there diddling with his stupid bankers boxes, looking for proof of all her financial contributions. Time was more valuable than money, and he'd already gotten too much of hers; she wasn't about to give him any more of it.

As his campaign for re-engagement ramped up, she backed away—didn't always respond to his emails. And if she didn't "forget," she'd delay. If she saw his name on her phone, she rarely answered.

But one day she came home from work and found a message on her computer about a house he was thinking of buying: *What do you think?* with an attached link.

Her brain said *don't,* but she couldn't resist. She hit the blue underlined words. An impressive-looking house popped up. Honestly. He was contemplating a million-dollar mansion for his own empty nest? She clicked and enlarged the pictures on the screen. Damn. Obviously she'd never want to live on a golf course, and Country Club neighbors weren't likely to appreciate her potential chickens and flapping laundry in any case, but this house…Well, it *was* kind of a lodge-style thing, at least the interior. Lots of wood beams and paneling, an incredible soaking tub with a stained-glass window behind it. Hey, she could have warmed up to a house like this.

Wait a minute. Was he baiting her? He understood, didn't he, that she was one hundred per cent gone? So was this a last ditch effort to tempt her back or just *Nyeah nyeah, look what I'm gonna do.*

She phoned Will. "Can I take you up on your offer to go house hunting?" If John was moving forward, why couldn't she? Was she going to waste away in a rental with no garden space while her ex sat in his soaking tub looking out over the 15th fairway?

"Sure," Will said, sounding like she'd reached him somewhere outside. "Lemme guess. You want to check out the 1918 fixer on Spring Lane."

"Will! How did you know?" She was actually holding in her hand the newspaper ad for that very property.

"Well, it's what you've been saying you want, right?"

But what Bridget really wanted, she realized now, was Will. Pacing the house, waiting for his truck to pull up, she was obviously way more excited just to see him than she was in checking out this property.

Ever since that *You can have my apples* bit, she'd been a mess. And now she'd figured it out. If you wanted to see Will Trask, you had to ask a favor. He couldn't accept them, like when she tried to offer dinner as repayment for all the truck errands he'd already done. But he could give. He'd always be right there on the spot if you said you needed him.

And oh, yes, she did need him.

Because face it. She'd always had a thing for Will. Well, as much of a thing as you allow yourself when you're a good girl, play by the rules, and a person is completely off-limits. Which is to say, you're afraid to even let yourself think about him.

But she had.

That time at Kona Village? After Shelley complained about Will's...appetite? Only a couple hours later Bridget had to sit there on the beach and watch Will out there in the surf with all the kids, tossing them around. Charlotte eating it up. Why couldn't her own father ever give her that kind of attention? And where *was* John, anyway? Oh, right, the can't-miss-this-opportunity round of golf over at the Four Seasons. With people he'd only met at the bar the night before. And here was Charlotte, shrieking with glee as her uncle, not her father, horsed around with her, bucking her off his broad back into the waves. When Will had come dragging up out of the surf, seawater sliding off the muscular planes of his chest and thighs, white teeth flashing from his bronzed face, Bridget clearly remembered having to roll over, claw the sand for her book, and make a serious point of minding her own business. She was thinking that apparently she had never seen that much of his naked body before. She would have remembered.

Well, Will still looked as good as ever, ten years later. Tramping the woods apparently did more for a guy's physique than riding in a golf cart. John was still handsome, true, but look at the huge contrast where it really counted: Two goodlooking men, one a lousy cheat, the other loyally sticking to a woman four years gone.

That's what I want, Bridget realized. A man who knows how to stick. Except get him sticking to me.

From the living room window she saw his truck pull up, watched him come around the tailgate. She loved how he looked in that vest of his, always so square-shouldered. Man, she'd go look at anything with this guy. If it meant jumping in the truck with Will Trask in charge, she'd sign on to check out a dilapidated trailer draped in crime-scene flagging.

She opened the front door and skipped down the stairs, smiling.

The Spring Lane house was vacant. When Will pushed open the front door, a wave of cold, musty air hit them. No artful staging here. What you see is what you'd get. As they started through, it became apparent that each room stood in a different state of completion, as if it were a museum exhibition of the stages of a remodeling project. The main room was sheetrocked, but not yet taped or mudded. The small but nicely redone kitchen was missing only a light fixture over the sink. The wires dangled overhead. If you ignored your peripheral vision, you could almost imagine behind you a tidy, finished home.

"Nice view," Will said, standing at the sink window.

"It is." Bridget came up beside him, close enough her shoulder grazed his. A better, more beautifully framed view of Mary's Peak hardly seemed possible. And on the nearest rise in the foreground, a new young patch of forest.

"You ever see the mountain on a morning when it's just snowed," Will said, "and the way the light hits it, you can see every individual tree?"

"Yeah." Bridget leaned toward him. "Lovely to have right out your kitchen window."

And then lightly, casually, it seemed, maybe even unconsciously, Will threw his arm over her shoulder.

She held her breath. God, she missed being touched. How long since anybody put his arm around her? All day at work she touched other people. She could see how much it meant to them, especially the old ones who were alone. Quite a few of them came to her just for that, she suspected. Just for the healing power of simple human touch.

But who was there now to touch her?

Just as she thought *Please don't take your arm away,* he did.

"They say a view like that around here's worth $25,000," he said over his shoulder as he moved away. "Or on up into blue sky."

Bereft, she hesitated, her follow-up question a faint echo. "Blue sky?"

"You know, like, price-wise, sky's the limit. Never know what something like that might be worth to the right person."

Bridget followed and watched as he easily took the stairs. Just for a moment, the two of them looking at Mary's Peak, it seemed he'd forgotten himself. Out of habit or muscle memory, his arm had wanted to be encircling someone.

Any good reason it shouldn't be her?

She climbed the stairs after him.

In the bedrooms upstairs, the foil-backing of the newly installed pink fiber-glass insulation remained exposed.

"Looks like they were doing a thorough job," Will said. "Taking it clear down to the studs."

Back downstairs, the bathroom revealed what the owners had started with. The vintage fixtures that might have provided some charm if restored had been removed years ago. Now going to mold and rust was a slapdash seventies-era renovation featuring a stapling of flooring vinyl as the tub surround.

Will flushed the toilet. "Works!" he announced cheerfully.

"Goody." She regarded the blackened squiggles of liberally applied caulking with dismay. "You should see the bathroom in the place John's getting ready to buy."

"What."

"Oh, stained glass. A huge soaking tub."

"Is that what you want?"

"I don't know."

"Because you could do that here. If you're gutting the whole thing, you can do whatever you want."

Bridget gave him a sad look.

"What's the matter?"

She hesitated. Shouldn't be anything the matter.

"It's just that—well, jeez, Will. All those years we had to live in that house I hated. Now, *without* me, he's suddenly going to be open to all these new possibilities? Suddenly he's got no problem telling his folks he wants to ditch the Witham Hill house?"

"So what do you care? He does what he wants and you do what you want, right? And you wanted a project." He waved at the bathroom. "Here it is in spades."

"I know, but being able to strip wallpaper and pick out paint colors is not quite the same as messing with plumbing."

"So get some pros in here. They'd be glad for the work right about now. The new wiring's all in, says here in the listing. And finishing up this sheetrock's no big deal. You could do it. Shelley and I did that."

"Yeah?" But that was two of them. Doing it together. She stood once more in the middle of the living room with her hands in her back pockets, arching to look at the ceiling. "This is just...house interrupted, isn't it? Why do you suppose they gave up on it? Whoever it was."

"Divorce," Will said.

"You know that? Or you're just saying?"

He shrugged. "Liza told me."

"Liza Madison?"

"Yeah, she's the listing agent."

"Great."

"Did you know she's gonna sell your old house?" Will asked.

"No!"

"Yep. John gave her the listing."

Bridget groaned, then caught herself. "Actually, I guess I should be glad to have a little shark like her on the case if half that's going to be mine."

"Good point."

"Boy, she just seems to have her finger in everything, doesn't she?"

"Oh, yeah. And I'll bet if you check, she's the agent on the house with the fancy bathroom you're talking about too."

Outside, Bridget followed Will along a path in the grass to the far corner of the overgrown, two–acre property. So overwhelming, trying to make judgments, be practical, confident, clear-headed.

All she could think of was Will in his Carhartts, striding ahead of her.

He pointed at a blackberry bramble overgrowing a pile of debris in the corner of the property. "You could put your chicken coop right out here."

"I guess."

He kicked a board stapled with rusty wire. "Looks like maybe they even had one at some point."

"Mmm." The place wasn't too bad, considering what else she'd driven by. Listings of properties with an acre or two tended to be either part of a new upscale subdivision or littered with rusted-out old trailer houses. *Liveable while you build your dream home!* many said. One touting a *Dream Home Staging Area!* turned out to be a non-permitted shack all but dissolving into a muddy hole in the middle of the lot.

Will was frowning at her. "Figured you'd get more excited."

She shrugged, giving him a wan smile. Could he please be a little less clue-less? Get the message she was trying to send with her hungry eyes? What if she came out and said what she was thinking: that when you hadn't been properly touched in such a long time and a guy like him put his arm around you, well, was it really going to be that easy to concentrate on the comparable dollar-per-square foot prices of recently sold properties? Her defiant little daydream of a cute chicken coop just wasn't cutting it at this point. In fact, nothing sounded that great if she had to picture doing it alone.

"So what about the house itself?" Will said as they started back. "Like it at all?"

"I guess. If we…if I threw a lot of money at that bathroom and all."

He sighed, suddenly sounding impatient. "Bridge, what's up? It's not like you to be so wishy-washy. I always figure you're the most decisive woman I know."

"Well, what do *you* think about it?"

"Oh, you know me. I warned you I don't care about houses. I only started watching these listings because you were talking about it." He glanced toward the house. "It's okay, I guess."

"So much work though."

"You're not scared of work." He stopped. "Maybe you just don't like the idea of jumping into the middle of somebody's else's plans. You wouldn't be weird, to feel that way."

"Could be part of it, I guess."

"Maybe you'd be happier finding a piece of land and starting from scratch. You ever look at the bare land listings?"

"No."

"Really? We've got a nice piece listed up on Hopestill Creek Road. I've had this hippie chick from California phoning me all winter. Just psychotic over the place, begging me to hold off showing it to anybody else. But I'd show it to you. Be a beautiful spot for your lodge thing."

"Oh, Will." Sometimes she got the feeling he saw her as braver and more independent than she really was. Hard to see herself masterminding the building of an entire house on her own. A house way out in the woods. She squinted toward the house at hand. "Think *you* could live here?"

He rolled his eyes, exasperated. "We're not talking about me."

Bridget turned away. Yeah, unfortunately, apparently they weren't. The big dummy. Maybe she was a fool for thinking he'd ever for one minute thought about her the way she thought about him. And now he just wasn't getting it. Nothing he suggested by way of plans was going to sound any good to her at all unless it had a "we" in it.

His cell went off and she glanced back irritably. "That is the most annoying ringtone I've ever heard."

"Yeah, well, I'm trying to make sure I hear it, not get all cute." He flipped it open, held it to his ear. "'Sat so?" He flashed wide eyes of significance at Bridget. "Okay, I'll tell her. Thanks." He snapped it closed. "Liza's got an offer on this."

"What! But it only showed up in the paper yesterday."

He shrugged. "Might have been on the website longer. And didn't you see those agents' cards on the kitchen counter? You've not the first one here. Maybe it's just what somebody's been waiting for. Can't dither around in real estate. If something's what you want, you've gotta jump on it."

"I thought I was, getting out here so fast."

"Well, you know, they've extended that first-time-buyer tax credit. Maybe that's what's going on. People are looking to get in under the wire. But this offer hasn't been accepted yet. And Liza says it's a bumpable buyer, anyway."

"A *what?*"

"Like they've got contingencies. This offer's only good if *their* house sells or something. So the owners of this place'd definitely be happy to look at an offer from you, too."

"Oh, right. No pressure."

"I could drive you over to Liza's office."

She glared at him.

"Sorry. It's just the way the game's played. You've still got time to top them."

"Will!"

"What?"

"I'm not making an offer on this place!"

"Okay. Fine. Nobody said you had to."

"But you're pressuring me."

"Bridget! I do not give a rat's ass if you buy this place or not."

"Oh, thanks."

He made a what-the-hell face, lifting his hands, looking to the sky for guidance.

She turned her back on him and found the path skirting the house. "I'll bet you're not mean like this to other people you show properties to."

"I'm not related to those other people."

"You're related to Robin."

"Well, *Robin.* Jesus, if you could be as easy to sell as she was…"

Huh. Good for Robin. *She* was finding a yard for her dog, not trying to figure out how to make Will Trask part of the sales package.

"Anyway," Bridget said. "You're not related to me. Not anymore."

"Don't act crazy, Bridget. You know very well I can't treat you like you're just anybody. And I don't think I'm being mean."

"Well, is it my fault I don't understand how all this stuff works?" Suddenly suspicious, she stopped. "Wait a minute." She turned around to face him. "How do I even know you're not just faking this other offer?"

"Bridget."

"Well—"

"That's low. I can't believe you'd say that. Even think that. I'm trying to help you. When you phoned I dropped everything to get down here. Now I'm in trouble for it?"

"You're right, I'm sorry. I know you could never be like that." She turned to walk again. "But I think you should just take me home now."

"Whatever," he said to her back, obviously fed up. "Just…anytime. Anytime you wanna look at someting. Any time you want to go out and mope around about a place—"

"I'm not moping."

"—and look at places you don't want until you think somebody else wants it—"

"Will!"

"And then that makes you want it—maybe—but you don't want to do anything to try to get it—"

"Shut up!"

"Any time then, I'm your boy."

CHAPTER 26

Sierra Sunderland had done her homework on the subject of winter in Oregon. For the sake of meeting up again with this long pined-over real estate agent, she'd sacrificed every iota of fashion sense to wear ugly rubber rain boots and the sort of Patagonia parka that seemed de rigueur around here. So everything being wet along the path into the Hopestill Creek property was no surprise. She hadn't quite anticipated, however, the way each blade of grass, each leaf on every bush, would hold a tiny cup of rainwater to be released when brushed against. Now the cashmere tights above her boots were soaked.

And then…Somehow the property just didn't look the same.

And neither did this guy, this Will Trask.

After he'd first brought her up here in September, she'd gone back to Marin enveloped in a dreamy glow, absolutely in love with this fabulous property, rhapsodizing to her friends over the secret meadow in Oregon that was clearly her destiny. She'd been seduced by the name itself: Hopestill Creek. Even the name of the agency, Heritage Realty, seemed like a good omen.

One friend's husband was impressed she was considering moving to Corvallis. Did she know this was the town where a group protesting the war in Afghanistan had set some kind of record by having at least one person with a peace placard out in front of the Benton County Courthouse every single day at five o'clock? And they'd kept this up for over eight years? A bit embarrassed she actually *hadn't* heard this, Sierra pretended she had, and quietly added the info to her lovely little Story of Oregon.

Now she tried to remember—had she told absolutely everybody about this guy, the agent? Oh, probably, and it was disconcerting to realize how much he'd somehow become such a huge part of the whole fantasy. When he came down the stairs from his office that first time, she'd been totally knocked out, he was so handsome. And leading her up into the woods he'd seemed so ruggedly healthy and vigorous, simple in some ways but smart about everything important, so wonderfully opposite of every guy she'd run into at Burning Man. Guardian of the Forest, she'd come to think of him. Keeper of Dreams. When she'd phoned him from back in California explaining about the probate hassle, he'd seemed so understanding, so willing to be part of her grand plan by agreeing to hold off on aggressively marketing the property, give her a chance to get back here, take a final, confirming look and make a formal offer. To be honest, a couple of her calls had probably been just for the pleasure of hearing his husky voice. Bit of a turn-on.

But now he wasn't saying a damned thing. Totally cold and broody. Walking behind him through the dripping woods, she felt like she was in an episode of *Lost*. Was she trying to get off the island or back *to* the island? Had she made a huge mistake, attempting to conduct Adventures in Real Estate while under the effects of that top grade weed she'd scored leaving the festival in Nevada?

The meadow, wisped with fog, did not lift her spirits.

"Not the best day to check the view again," Will Trask finally said.

Duh.

"It was beautiful yesterday."

So helpful to know. Seemed like people were forever saying that in Oregon. *You should have been here yesterday.*

"Do you want to go down by the creek?"

She didn't want to do anything.

"Well, I'm gonna take a quick look."

Left her there to slap her arms around herself in a vain effort to generate warmth. What kind of a salesman was he, anyway? Surely he'd noticed she was having qualms. Why was he going off to the creek instead of trying to talk her back into love? Reassure her about the rain letting up eventually, remind her what a great, guaranteed investment a twenty-acre buildable parcel would be? Watching him return across the meadow, she had to wonder: Did this guy ever sell anything at all?

She'd stood there long enough that when she glanced down at her boots, a slug had attached itself.

"Euew!" Balancing on one foot—no problem, thanks to yoga—she dislodged it with the toe of her other boot and scraped the ugly thing into the grass.

Will Trask watched. "Had one of those on my kitchen floor the other day."

Seriously? She shuddered. Maybe she wasn't cut out to live up here.

"So what do you think?" he said. "Still like it as much as you did?"

Was he for real? He couldn't tell?

She gazed across the open area of new green grass poking up through the dead brown blades of the previous year. Took in the menace of those thick, spiky blackberry canes arcing around the trees he'd claimed were a homestead orchard. How would you ever even begin to get rid of those?

She wasn't a total air-head, okay? She understood about seasons. Even native Californians realize it isn't sunny all year long in quite a few other places on this planet. Yes, she knew those trees would bloom. And yes, this *was* the field in the pictures, sure to be sprinkled with wildflowers come May. And, yes, when the fog lifted, that mountain out there in the Cascades would no doubt still be anchored firmly in place.

But what if she couldn't hack it, the long rainy season they had to endure here for the sake of a couple of months of sun shining on green forests and fields? She might get depressed. Because it wasn't just that this twenty acres looked different than she remembered. The first wave of gray dismay had actually hit the very minute the plane landed on Eugene's rain-slick airport runway. Oregon had been gorgeous in September; now it revealed itself as the land of people biking around swathed in plastic rain tents.

She sighed, resigned. "I guess I'm ready to go back."

Here she was, almost thirty-five, and what did she have going on? Nada. She didn't even feel fully grown up, and God knows her parents would be the first to agree on that assessment. She'd been so determined to show them she was capable of doing something solid and mature with her inheritance, that she wasn't going to be a spoiled little rich girl forever. Well, moving up here clearly wasn't going to be the thing to prove it. Too many bad omens. This just wasn't her destiny after all.

"Shit!" She pitched forward, ankle caught on a blackberry vine, that other variety lacing across the ground like a trap of tripwires. Pushing up on her bare, wet hands, she yelled *Hey!* at the back of Mr. Guardian of the Forest. He turned, registered she'd fallen, came back and reached down. But, honestly, that hesitation. The way he'd assessed her lying there an instant too long before reacting.

"You okay?" he said, pulling her up.

She didn't answer. He didn't seem to notice.

Bracing against him, she extricated her boot from the thorny snare, then let him lead the way out. She'd thought she was going to do something bold and decisive today. Now she felt so stupid, huffing along, struggling to keep up. Was there a face-saving way to tell him she'd changed her mind? He was going to be mad, losing his commission after he'd held off trying to sell this to anybody else.

No, wait. Come on. Like he'd care that much one way or the other. The well-worded excuse she needed was for herself. For her parents, when she got home. They were the ones forever pointing out how much trouble she had ever committing to anything.

Well, of course she did. Who with any brains didn't? Every single thing that came along in life needing a major commitment was always such a gamble. How were you supposed to make such momentous decisions when nobody could ever tell you how things would turn out? Maybe living up here would be fine or maybe she'd hate it. But she was the one who hadn't been able to commit to schools, jobs, men, or even—a growing regret—that one ill-timed pregnancy.

So how could anyone who knew her be surprised she couldn't commit to a patch of hillside dirt and a handful of trees?

Even if it did have a goddamned river running through it.

CHAPTER 27

Donna Hudson spotted Will Trask's white Ford pickup in the parking lot of Heritage Realty. *Finally.* For Pete's sake, she'd been trying to track him down for weeks, checking the lot every time she drove into Eden Mills on errands. And now, darn him, just as she signaled and pulled in, he came out and headed for the Ford, keys dangling at the ready.

She scrambled out of her car and hustled after him. "Will!"

He turned. "Donna. Hey, howya doin?"

"Doug wasn't kidding about you." She was panting a little. "Starting to think you don't spend any time in this office at all."

"No more'n I have to!"

She held up a paper grocery sack of stuff she'd been leaving in her car. "Did some cleaning out. Had a couple of things for you." No way was she prepared to just throw the sack in his office, not when she had these things that needed saying.

"Oh, okay." Will looked up and squinted as raindrops started pinging them. "Better come on back inside."

"You looked like you were heading to an appointment."

"Did I?" He grinned. "Good. I work hard giving that impression." With a light touch to the small of her back he steered her toward the entrance.

"Will, really? No appointment at all?"

"Only with a place up on Hopestill Creek to check for fish!"

She shook her head. "You and Doug are so much alike." She caught herself. "Were." She sniffed. "You know what I mean."

"Yeah." He held open the glass door for her. "Well, our coffee's not *too* bad this time of day. I'll grab us some. Go on up." He nodded toward the stairs. "You remember which one's mine, right?"

The reception room part was pretty fancy, Donna thought, but Will's office seemed to her just what an office of Doug's might have looked like, if Doug'd been a guy who needed one. The usual desk and file cabinet. Hunting and fishing pictures. A map of Oregon. An arrowhead collection in a box frame. On his desk, a soft-focus picture of his wife, looking like an angel. Donna wasn't sure how those high-priced Corvallis portrait studios did that, but it sure was effective. Will's wife had been pretty, sure, but maybe not quite as perfect as this picture had her. And of course now, frozen in time, unlike the rest of them, she was forever young.

On a shelf Donna spotted a framed five-by-seven that made her heart thump, a shot of herself and Doug in front of their new house, the day Will handed them the keys. She edged around the desk to pick it up for a closer look just as Will came in with the coffee.

"I didn't know you had this," she said, turning around to him.

"Didn't I give you guys a print? This one's been sitting here since right after I took it. Shelley framed it for me." He set the steaming mugs on his desk, dragged a chair up for her and switched places with her to take his own chair. He nodded at the picture. "You remember what Doug said that day?"

"No, what?" She loved hearing Will say Doug's name. So many people made the mistake of figuring she'd feel better if they didn't talk about him at all. What, like it'd be a painful reminder of something she'd managed to forget? So wrong. If any of Doug's friends had one more memory to share, one more word to quote, she was all ears.

"Doug said, 'I just bet you never thought a dumb old logger like me would wind up with a house like this!'" They both laughed, and then Will said, "You know, don't you, that I never thought of him as a dumb old logger?"

"Yeah, but that's how he thought of himself. And he was happy about it."

"Nobody could lay out a set of logging corridors like him," Will said. "Got engineers over at the college have to learn that stuff out of books. How to get the angles right and all. He just had a knack for it. And getting a crew working together like he did?" Will shook his head. "Wade's got big boots to fill. But he's doing okay with that, isn't he?"

She smiled. "Oh yeah. Got a lot of Doug in him. Well, anyway, I'm sorry it's taken me so long to go through his things, but you know how that is."

"Sure," Will said, looking down, his voice low.

"Okay, first this." She pulled out a tan twill shirt. "This was practically brand new and too big for those skinny boys of mine. Figured we could help keep you out of pink."

"Donna." He raised his hand as if taking an oath. "I never wore that shirt again after you schooled me on it."

"Really?" She was touched.

Next she pulled out some little square snapshots. Doug and Will, ten-year-old boys, grinning faces poked out the peeky holes of a ramshackle fort Will's mom had let them throw together.

"Wow," Will said. "Look how we trashed the backyard. My mom musta thought it was cute, though, if she took the picture. I'll have to show her this."

"I guess you took the other one here, since it was in the same envelope and Doug didn't have a camera when he was little." Donna handed him a faded Kodachrome print, two rainbow trout, laid on a stump.

She looked at Will. They both laughed.

"Not even a hand," she said. "I mean, where was this? Who caught them?"

"Who cared?" Will said. "It was always all about the fish. Least that's what we thought then."

They were silent a moment.

"And then there was this." Donna pulled out a little scout knife. "You gave it to him."

"I did?"

"You don't remember?" A little disappointing.

"Donna, you gotta gimme a break. I'm getting old."

"Hey, watch your mouth. We're the exact same age."

"Only by the numbers. Hey, you're the best looking grandma I know."

She felt herself blushing. People had been saying her hair looked good, the way she'd finally cut off her long braid and let Dixie down at the salon fluff the rest around her face. Doug always liked her hair long, so chopping it off while he was still around wouldn't have been very nice. She couldn't tell if Will had actually noticed the change, or if he was just dishing it out like he always did, being kind, making people feel good.

"Here." Will opened his top desk drawer, dug around and pulled out a chunk of lead. "My lucky fishing sinker, because Doug gave it to me. I've had it thirty years."

Okay, she got it. Gifts received and cherished remembered better than gifts given and forgotten.

She held out the knife. "I tried to give this to the boys, but they insisted you should have it. They're the ones told me Doug was always saying it was from you."

Will took it, closed his hand around it and lifted his eyes to hers. "Thanks, Donna."

"Maybe your little guy Cody would like it. He's old enough now, right? Seven or eight?"

Will smiled, but sadly. "Try sixteen."

"Oh, for Pete's sake."

He shook his head. "Goes by so fast, kinda takes the wind right outtaya, doesn't it?"

"Yeah." She took a sip of coffee. "Will? You know Doug cared about you a lot."

"Well, yeah. And I cared about him. Best fishing bud ever."

"Ever since Shelley died, he's been so worried about you. Well, I have too."

Will cleared his throat. "I don't want you worrying about me."

She hesitated. "You feel like you're doing okay, then?"

"Sure! Sure."

"And you been on your own—what?—three years?"

"Actually, almost five." He coughed, tried to turn it into a laugh. "But who's counting?"

She leaned forward. "Sweetie, what are we gonna do with you? Doug used to talk about it all the time, how you just looked like you were going for some kinda lifetime prize of loneliest old coot ever."

Will looked surprised. And pained.

"And the thing is, Will, I feel like maybe I can say this to you when nobody else can. 'Cause I know how it is when you've lost somebody. Everybody tiptoes around you 'cause they've heard that stuff about you can't go telling people how long they get to grieve and when they ought to stop. But after a point, Will, you do have to start living again, don't you?"

"I'm living."

She pressed her lips together. "You seeing anybody?"

"Are you?" he shot back.

She was making him nervous, she could tell. He was wishing she'd leave. But she just had the feeling Doug would want her to come down here and say it to him straight.

"It's only been six months for me, Will. You can't really compare."

"Yeah. S'pose not."

"Doug used to talk about it all the time," she said. "The way you were acting."

"Never said anything to me."

"Well, he wouldn't, would he? Men don't. But now I kinda feel like all the stuff he was saying, how he wished you'd find somebody new, and what a waste it was to go on being lonely and unhappy when the world was full of other people who needed to find new people too…Well, it's like he was saying that to me. About us. Like leaving a message if anything ever happened."

"That's real nice for you, Donna." Will couldn't seem to look her in the eye. "But Doug was my friend, not my spouse. He's not really the one I'm… You know."

"You don't think Shelley would have wanted you to go ahead and be happy?"

Now he did lift his face. But he still didn't seem to have an answer. He just looked miserable.

Poor guy. He was such a sweetheart. Her sister-in-law always talked about how goodlooking he was and warned Donna she ought to grab him before he went online and every single woman around started swiping right on him. Or maybe it was left. Donna didn't know about all that. Anyway, here Donna and Marcie had lost their husbands on that same day, in the same accident, and Marcie already had some guy. Yeah, Marcie felt a little guilty, she said, but wasn't it an Oregon tradition? Like when the pioneers who'd buried their husbands and wives along the Trail married up with each other when they got out here? Only now they could meet-up online.

But Donna couldn't think past Doug yet. When she got to that point, Will would probably be the first guy she'd consider.

Maybe in a year or two.

The way he was acting, she had plenty of time.

CHAPTER 28

"**D**onna Hudson showed up and chewed me out today," Will told Bridget over a plate of lasagna, once more having found his way to her cozy kitchen booth.

"Donna? Who's that?"

"My friend Doug's wife. Widow. Remember that fishing accident on the coast last summer? She thinks I ought to get out there and join the old dating game again."

Bridget widened her eyes, pressed her lips together.

"Bridge!"

"Well, maybe you should."

"Thinks she's entitled to give me a hard time 'cause the three of us all knew each other since kindergarten."

"Hm." Bridget regarded him with half closed eyes. "I'll bet she likes you herself."

"Are you crazy? No way! Now you really don't know what you're talking about."

"I'm just saying." She forked up some lasagna.

"Saying what?" *Damn, she sure knew how to push his buttons.*

"That women *like* you, Will. Or hadn't you noticed?"

"Women like to yell at me. I'll agree to that."

"Oh, come on."

"No, I mean it. You would not believe some of the speeches women have delivered to me."

Liza Madison's final blazing tirade had permanently burned his brain. Such memorable staging, the way she'd hunted him down at Cody's soccer game and dragged him off along the sidelines for an ear-blistering. Nobody broke up with *her* by email, he remembered her hollering. And he needed a shrink in the worst way. So did his kids. They were the most deplorable sort of dysfunctional family unit. Those boys had suffered the tragedy of losing their mother and now he seemed determined to just keep making the whole situation worse. Obviously none of them would be mentally healthy or one bit happy ever again.

What was he supposed to say to a curse like that? He'd spent a long time writing that break-up email. It was hard. So tricky, dancing around the truth. Is that what she wanted? *Dear Liza, my kids clued me in you're a bitch.* He'd honestly thought it'd be easier on both of them by email, imagined she'd be as grateful as him to skip a scene like this. Breep! Wrong! That woman wasn't signing off until she'd given him the tongue-lashing he deserved. Even practiced it, he bet. She was like a skinny little bomb in high heels and a blazer, exploding by the soccer field where the parents of Cody's friends must have wondered what the hell was going on. Will was left with a memory of her contorted mouth, glazed for battle in red lipstick, spewing a lot of ugly words.

"You poor thing," Bridget said now. "Somehow I'm having trouble picturing this Donna really hauling off and letting you have it on the subject of widowers jumping back into the dating pool."

"Well, I didn't mean her. Donna's nice."

"She's probably just concerned about you, like everybody is."

"Yeah, well I wish everybody would just *quit* being concerned about me." He put his hand over his wine glass as Bridget reached to refill it. He'd stick with one. Past that and it would just be that much harder to keep his wits about him, the way she sashayed around.

"So, is she pretty?"

"Who?"

Bridget cut her eyes to the window and back. "Donna?"

"Well, yeah, she is." *Pretty enough for your slimy ex to hit on,* he thought, but why go there? "Honestly, Bridget, it's not like that. She's like a sister to me. We're pals. She'd probably be insulted to have people hinting she might feel that way about *anybody* at this point. Doug only died last September."

"Okay, okay. Take it easy."

Will twisted his neck to the side, wincing as he massaged his right shoulder with his left hand.

"Something pinched there?"

"No. No, I'm fine."

"You don't look fine," she informed him. "Looks like you're hurting."

"Just a little uptight, is all."

"About anything in particular?"

"Ha! You want my list? The economy? The fact my son's got a girlfriend I worry's gonna make me a grampa before my time? My mom on my case? A depressed father-in-law?" Of course he wasn't going to list the major stressor of this very moment—sitting in Bridget's kitchen, getting off on being around her, confused as hell over just what he thought he was doing showing up all the time if he wasn't going to act like a man and make a play. He'd have to stick to safer claims for being uptight. "I got a call from some joker at the newspaper, wanted to interview me about the Garland Foundation."

"Hey, me too. He asked if it was true all the tuition grants were going to be pulled. So, is it?"

"Well, not if most of us have anything to say about it, but John's shooting his mouth off around town, saying that. Like he's floating trial balloons, trying to see if it'd work for him politically to take that line."

Bridget shook her head, poured herself more wine even if Will wasn't having any.

"I have the feeling they're writing up some big story," Will said. "But I mean, I'm with you, I'm not talking. They're probably bugging Ed, too."

He circled his shoulder again.

Bridget stood up and wiped her hands on her napkin.

"Come'ere," she said.

"What." A little alarm buzzed through him.

"Let me see what's going on with your neck."

"Naw, I'm all right."

"Will, don't be silly. You know all the construction guys say I'm the very best in town at this."

As if letting her get her hands on him in her own private kitchen was the same as it'd be in her office, all medical and businesslike, everything draped in starchy sheets.

He stalled. "I'll bet you wear a white coat at your office."

"Nope."

"You don't?"

"Nope. I wear this." She opened her arms. She had a plaid flannel shirt over a lacey, low cut tank top that Will was afraid to look at. Also a handful of painted beads on a leather choker around her neck.

"Seriously?" Will said. "With your shirt…open like that?" Because it just made him want to slide his hands right in there under the flannel, all the way around her.

She laughed. "Well, okay, Mr. Propriety Police. Yeah, actually I do button it up."

He stuck his tongue in his cheek. "Seems like a good idea."

"But basically, it's my practice, I can wear whatever I want. Nobody's ever complained. Come on, stand up. Let me check this out." She took his arm and tried to pull him up.

"Bridget! No."

"You're that scared of letting me touch you? It's not like I'm trying to make you lie on the bed or anything. I can check it out right here. This is what I *do*, Will. I want to find your tenderpoints. That's what we call them. I've seen you doing that with your shoulder before. You probably had some minor incident where you jerked it. It's like your nervous system gets caught off guard."

Ha! *She's* what had his nervous system off guard, talking about his tenderpoints, for cryin' out loud.

"Come on, don't be so stubborn. Maybe I can help you feel better."

He flushed red hot to the roots of his hair. Yeah, she probably could.

He stood up slowly, carefully. "Bridget, don't do this."

"What?"

"What. You know exactly what you're up to."

"Do I?"

"Uh huh." And what the hell was *he* up to? Why did he torture himself like this, coming over here when he knew very well she'd just make him horny as hell and he'd have a whole lot of trouble trying to keep himself in line.

"What then," she said, easing closer. "What am I up to?"

He sidestepped her, but even as he did so he was wondering if he was totally nuts. What kind of a way was this for a guy to act? He should get it wherever he could, right? And to hell with the consequences. Well, call him a mental case, he *did* debate the consequences. Look what an ugly mess that had turned into with Liza. And Bridget was in such a weird, vulnerable spot herself, muddling through this divorce. Sure, he wanted to get laid, but it seemed like sex could be just the bomb to explode the comfortable little…friendship or whatever it was they had going, this thing where he actually had somebody to talk to again. He couldn't stand to give that up.

"So, uh, what'd you do with my jacket?"

She nodded at the peg rack by the back door.

He grabbed it. "Great dinner," he said, "but I promised Cody I'd...I'd play Settlers of Catan." He was backing through the dining room toward the front door, thinking it was lucky he'd stopped her with the wine or he'd never be able to take his own advice and get himself out of here.

She leaned in the kitchen arch, regarding him with a look he interpreted as not that far from disgust. "Settlers of Catan."

"Yeah. Great new game the kids found. You should come over some time and play with us. Okay. Gotta run. Take care."

"Oh, Will." She shook her head, clearly, thoroughly exasperated.

He really had a talent for that, he thought, almost jogging out onto the porch: exasperating women.

CHAPTER 29

Bridget stood dreaming at the display of gardening implements on the wall in Robnett's Hardware. New, shiny tools always spoke to her of projects—flagstone paths leading out to charmingly fenced vegetable gardens entered through arbor gates crowned with roses.

The chat overheard from the little store's three aisles was all so upbeat, everybody in a can-do mood. How else could people feel on a gorgeous Saturday in March when it had finally stopped raining?

She wanted to feel can-do, too. But do what? She shifted on the creaky wood floor. She was a renter. She wasn't allowed to tackle her own idea of "improvements."

Ellen Sterling, one of her patients, came down the aisle and stopped to visit.

"How's your son doing?" Bridget asked. The poor woman's body had been knotted with stress over this troubled kid, addicted to opioids ever since being prescribed Percocet after a wisdom tooth extraction.

"Well, you know," Ellen said. "One day at a time. But thanks for asking."

Bridget nodded. She was The Good Witch, a keeper of secrets. She had to be; people told her things. They never intended to; she wasn't a shrink, after all. But once they were in her examination room, lying on the sheet-draped table being asked in her gentle, concerned way whether they'd been under any particular stress recently, they'd find themselves pouring out their heartbreak, all the dreams they'd had that somehow didn't seem to be coming true. So many had difficult, elderly parents who never appreciated what they were trying to do for them. Or adult children who were painfully distant and resistant to hearing their hard-won wisdom. Everybody had a story, and she listened sympathetically to all: The grief of losing a spouse. The bewildering inability to get pregnant. The bitterness of divorce.

Hey, I got a raw deal too, she wanted to chime in.

Nope. Not professional.

Now, next to her, a guy with elaborate braids was checking out a power drill. When he turned, she realized she knew him. Len Something. A nurse up at Good Samaritan who used to be a logger but ditched woods work after famously riding a Komatsu shovel loader down a steep side, later sheepish at having miscalculated the grade, but stubbornly proud he'd only rolled the machine once, at the bottom. Once was enough to bang him up pretty good though. She actually knew two or three guys like that, loggers who had taken a hard look around and seen more job security in patching people up than in trying to keep busy logging trees in a waning timber economy. Healthier, too, not being the guy with all the broken bones.

"Hey, Bridget, I been thinking about you. What's all this about the Garland Grants getting yanked?"

She couldn't remember his last name, but obviously he remembered hers. That's how it was if you were a Garland.

"Hey, Len."

"If I hadn't got one of those grants, you know, I'd still be logging." He grinned. "Or dead."

"Yeah, well, I hear it's not all decided or anything. I'd sure vote to keep 'em going, but I've got nothing to say on it. Pretty soon I won't be a Garland at all anymore except for the name."

"Yeah?" He squinted at her, a quick, futile attempt at faking surprise before admitting he actually had heard something about the divorce.

So, people knew. Somehow, word of the split was getting around. Other women from the soccer sidelines approached her hesitantly at the grocery store, their freighted *How are you?* revealing they'd already heard there was cause for concern.

Bridget turned back to the tools. Hey. An electric hedge clipper. Just like Will used to have. Didn't *that* bring back memories. She'd hated the ivy hedge at the Witham Hill house from the first, and felt proud of her gut instinct when a later OPB program explained that English Ivy is ruthlessly invasive and everyone ought to wage war on it by all means possible. Will had loaned her his power tool and John came home to find her doing battle with the hedge, the driveway already piled with clippings. "What the hell you think you're doing?" he tried to shout past her earplugs. When she pulled them out, he read her the riot act for being out there dressed in work clothes and goggles like somebody they'd hired. Pointed out that the ivy was actually covering a cement wall, and it was just lucky he got home before she hit it with the blade. And shouldn't she have at least discussed this with Ardis first? When she started defending herself, he called her a banshee and stalked inside, said he wasn't about to stand out there arguing like a couple of low-class trash types.

Now Bridget stared at the electric pruner—same brand, even—remembering how she'd jumped in the car and driven it back to Will's, made a point of hanging at their house long enough to make sure her bully of a husband knew she wasn't coming home to cook his dinner.

"Hey Bridget!"

She turned. Ron Ruggerio, one of her patients. He stood there bouncing slightly on the balls of his feet, happy to see her.

"Hey, Ron. You haven't called for an appointment in ages." Not a bad-looking guy. Divorced, if she remembered right.

"Shows you how shot the economy really is." He grinned. "Not enough work to even wreck up my shoulder like usual!" He was a sheetrock finisher who typically showed up once a year for a few sessions of her magic fingers and to get scolded about keeping up with the exercises she'd given him. "Nobody's building anything."

Nice smile. And definite charm, this light-hearted spin on the positives of unemployment.

Hm. Maybe she should think about dating her patients. Was that unethical? She hadn't given it one thought as long as she'd been officially if miserably married. Married women didn't date anybody. But now she wondered. She knew a ton of guys in construction. Sometimes felt she was single-handedly keeping the entire county's construction crews firing their nail guns. These were good guys. Most of them fit. And not a one of them was a slimy lawyer on the side. But, of course, very few were single, and never for long if they did temporarily find themselves claiming this status.

Flirting had never been her strong suit, nor would twenty years out of practice likely have improved this particular skill set. Which was so unfair. While she in her faithfulness had let all her social skills with the opposite sex go completely to rust, John had been keeping his polished to perfection.

"So what are you up to today?" she tried.

"We're building a deck," Ron said.

We.

She hated that. "We" without explaining, like you were supposed to know. He and his buddy? His kid? Hey, maybe he meant that dog tied up out front. Some guys talked that way.

No luck. A human female in jeans now approached.

"I found the wheelbarrow I want, honey." She looked vaguely familiar to Bridget, as most people around here did by now. "They've got them chained up around the side."

Maybe Bridget should get a dog. At least then she could say "we." But she didn't want a dog. She wanted a man.

Forcing a smile, she got introduced. Honest to God, she actually saw the woman—Janine?—check out Bridget's bare ring finger and slip her hand possessively around Ron's arm, an arm which Bridget happened to know from personal experience was very nicely muscled. And, if she remembered right, sported a charming blue swallow tattoo.

Okay, I get it, he's yours.

He couldn't put a patch on Will Trask anyway.

Ha! Like Will was one of her choices, if only she decided he was best.

"We got married last summer," Ron offered.

"Congratulations."

"So what are *you* up to today?" he said.

"Oh, just the usual," she said lightly, turning back to the tools.

Just hanging around the hardware store, trying to figure out what the heck to do with my life, all by myself. Only that morning she'd sat there and filled out her sad and minimal 2010 Census form. One white woman in this place of residence. She had to wonder—would her 2020 census form say exactly the same thing?

"Take care of this guy," she said back over her shoulder to Janine. "Remind him to do his exercises."

Face it, Corvallis was not a good place to be single. Great for families, sure, and Robin once confided the town had a reputation for being lesbian friendly. Lot of good that did Bridget.

She stared at the tools again, spacing out. Ridiculous, that she should feel so achinglyly alone in this store today. It's not as if she'd ever come here anything *but* alone. John believed in hiring others to do your house and yard projects. They had never once been the couple earnestly debating the baffling varieties of hose nozzles. She couldn't even form that picture in her mind.

She could see Will here though. She'd taken to fantasizing about doing projects with him. At night she'd watch those HGTV shows where they were mucking around in people's yards. *Will could do that,* she'd be thinking, watching a guy put up a gazebo. She'd always loved watching Will out there at the crack of dawn on Tree Planting Day, lashing the shelter frame together out of fir poles, throwing that thing up like he was some kind of latter day Daniel

Boone. And then the Lowe's ad would come on: *Let's build something together.* "Yeah, come on, Will," she'd mutter at the TV. "Let's build something together."

Once, she'd reminded him of her offer to help him get rid of his rose-patterned wallpaper, but he put her off, gave her a load of bull about wanting to do it for sure someday, just not now.

What have you got against *now*, she always wanted to say. Darn him, he was making her crazy. Always coming over, wanting to hang around. Was it so weird of her to start thinking they could be a couple? That maybe in some deep, underlying, been-there-forever way they already were?

Finally she reached up and took down a little hand hoe. It had a sharp point on the front, perfect for pulling up ivy. Maybe if her landlady wasn't laboring under the misconception that the jungle of the horrible stuff she had going in the backyard was somehow a good thing, she'd be willing to let Bridget hack away at it.

God, she had to do something.

She took the hoe and a pair of leather gloves up to the old-fashioned cash register.

"Looks like you're ready to rip into something," the clerk said affably.

If only he knew. While he swiped her card, she glanced up at a sign on the wall: *One Hundred Years of Hardware: Serving the needs of our changing community.*

Dammit anyway, she thought, *I would so like to have my needs served.*

With so few things in life being either purely good or purely bad, Bridget appreciated knowing English ivy was bad, period. In eradicating it, she felt confident that at least for that moment, she was doing the right thing. She was going to save these trees.

Late in the afternoon, sweaty, breathing hard, she lifted the pointed hoe and—mid-swing—jumped at the sight of a man's boot.

"Damn!" She yanked out her earbuds. "Will! You scared me to death."

"Sorry," he said, laughing, not sorry at all. "Hey, I hope you don't wear those things walking around town. Being able to hear is an important survival skill, you know. There's a reason animals don't wear headphones when hunters are stalking them."

"Very funny."

"Seriously. You could get hit by a car. Or what if some guy comes up from behind and grabs you?"

She eyed him, sincerely hoping there was a reason that image popped into his head. She pulled off her baseball hat, wiped her face, tried to catch her breath.

"So what are you listening to?" he said.

"You don't want to know."

"Come on, I do too."

"Okay." She gave him a frank look. "Bonnie Raitt. '*I Need Someone to Love Me.*'"

"Oh." He recoiled like she'd punched him.

"No, wait." She pulled the iPod from her Carhartts pocket, checked the screen. "Sorry. It's actually"—she looked back up at him—"'*Love Me Like a Man.*'"

"Oh. Oh, okay."

"Want me to sing it for you?"

"No!"

So cute, blushing like that, completely unnerved. Well, he asked for it.

Oh, Jesus. Will Trask.

Every time she hadn't seen him for awhile she'd starting thinking maybe she'd been exaggerating this whole crazy thing, remembering him as better than he was. She kept expecting him to show up and disappoint her, but then, no, standing right in front of her, big as life, he'd have that same damned effect on her as always. He was the real thing. She had it bad. He didn't even have to touch her and she still hadn't felt so under a man's power to instantly fire her up since she was fifteen and Steve Baker had shown her just enough of what was what at his basement moving-away-to-Washington party to leave her hot and swooning all the rest of the summer.

She just had to switch gears here. Turning away from Will, she bent and swung her pick to catch a thick rope of ivy, yanking it up.

"I love this thing." She regarded the tool admiringly. "Just bought it today. It's Japanese."

Will nodded, surveying the yard, the huge piles of the vines she had heaped up all over the grass.

"Woman, you are a Force of Nature."

"Yeah? I like the sound of that." She wound the rope of ivy into a coil and frisbeed it onto one of the piles. "Better'n what I got called by the last guy who caught me hacking ivy."

"I remember that."

"You do?"

"Bridget. You—mad—is pretty memorable."

"When I brought your electric pruner back?"

He laughed. "You threw yourself around our kitchen for a solid hour, hollering about him."

"Yeah, well, you know, I don't think that was totally about the ivy. I think it hadn't been that long since I found out about that Jennifer person. No, wait. It must have been that other one, because I'm pretty sure Jennifer's when I got that guy with a tractor in to plow up the backyard."

"What!"

"Well, I wanted a garden."

He shook his head, smiling. "We've got to get you your *own* garden, Bridge."

She regarded him bleakly. We? The two of them? Or was that just real estate sales talk? He wasn't saying get *ourselves* a garden.

"And didn't anybody ever tell you tenants aren't supposed to have to work this hard on the yard? If they do any work at all?"

"Yeah, my landlady thinks I'm crazy." She looked up at the last tree still bearing a bushy green coat up its trunk. "But these trees don't care if I'm a renter or an owner, right? They just want the life-sucking stuff out of here." Then she swooped the pick again. "So what are you up to?"

"Uh, actually, Cody's been telling me this new movie *Avatar* is some kind of cultural touchstone or something, and I had to see it if I didn't want to become a complete fossil."

"Oh, nice. Sounds like the way Charlotte talks to me. Well, when she used to talk to me, anyway."

"And Gar was there and said I should see if you wanted to go. Like tonight."

"Oh." She straightened up. Smiled. "So would this be like a date?"

"No! No, no. Jeez." He laughed awkwardly. "Don't go worrying about that. No, this'd just be like, hey wanna help save me from fossilization?"

"Right. Well, I just thought maybe you were gonna try keeping that Donna happy, tell her you went out."

"No, Bridget," he said, "that was not my thinking. More like it's been so long since I've been to a movie, I don't even know for sure where that new theater is."

She peeled back her glove to check her watch. "And I'll bet you're looking for dinner, right?"

"No!" Insulted she'd even think it. Except, "Well, I guess it *is* getting to be time, isn't it?"

"Uh huh." Good grief. This guy was in denial on everything from his deepest existential dilemmas to whether he was hungry or not. Did he even know the word *yes*? "Tell you what—can you go pick up a couple of steaks?" That would be fast, and his favorite. "I just bought a grill the other day. I'll fire it up. By the time you get back I'll be cleaned up and ready to throw 'em on there."

He was hesitating. "Is that okay, Bridge? You did say one time you didn't mind me coming over. And you said weekends for you were…you know."

"Of course it's okay. I didn't mean to sound like it wasn't. And you're right—I get lonely. So I'm glad you came by."

It's okay, *honey,* is what she wanted to say, sidling up and winding her arms around him. But she always had to hold back. Everything seemed to scare Will Trask. The only way he'd keep coming around is if somehow he could keep from *noticing* he was coming around.

Why clue him in and break the spell?

CHAPTER 30

"Oh my God, you guys. Oh my God!"

"What, Char? What's the matter?"

Panicked, Charlotte Garland tried to sink in the last row of the movie theater, but no way. You couldn't hide in a place like this. Not with this stacked up stadium seating.

Lifting her Coke from the drink holder, she shoved it at her roommate. "Take this," she instructed. "And move!" She flipped up the armrest and threw herself across the adjacent seat, face down.

"Char! For God's sake."

"Don't look! It's my mother."

"Where?" Brit said.

Charlotte peeked up and winced. "In the denim jacket. With the bandanna?"

"Oh yeah," Brit said. "I remember her from the day we moved in."

The theater was not that big. Only a half dozen rows down to where her mother and Uncle Will, Charlotte saw, were parking themselves.

"And that's your dad, right?"

"Brit!" Charlotte pushed up just long enough to give her roommate dagger eyes. "What. Have you not heard a single thing I've said since Fall term? My parents are getting a divorce, remember? So no, of course that's not my dad."

Brit looked puzzled. "But isn't that the guy who was at the dorm helping you guys on move-in day?"

"Shh!"

"They're not even looking up here, Char. But I'm sure that's the guy who was hauling your boxes."

"That doesn't make him my father."

"Euuw." Erin wrinkled her nose. "So your mom, like, brought a date to help you move in?"

"No!"

"Ohmygod, I would so freak."

"No, no, they weren't dating then. They're probably not even dating now. Not really."

"So, when do I get my seat back?" Brit said.

"Hey, do you even know the meaning of being supportive? What, you want me to get down on the cement floor?"

"Oh, come on, Char."

Her mom with Will Trask. Suddenly, right there as she stared at the seat-back six inches from her face, Charlotte knew. This *was* a date.

"I have to go," she said. "Soon as the lights dim, I'm outta here."

"No, you're not," Erin said wearily. "You've already paid. And extra for the 3-D. They're not giving you your money back."

"I don't care."

"You gonna walk?" Brit asked. "'Cause there's no way I'm giving you my car keys."

"Thanks a lot," Charlotte said, consoling herself with picturing some future scenario where Brit was the one desperate for a getaway, begging for the keys to Charlotte's car—the new Beemer her dad had promised her if she lost twenty pounds.

"Dude's not that bad," Brit said. "I mean, for an old guy. If he's like, my father's age."

"Oh, please shut up," Charlotte pleaded.

"What," Brit said. "What'd I say?"

"Well, the creepy part is, he's my uncle."

"Oh," Brit and Erin said simultaneously, heavily made-up eyes big and ominous at each other.

"And they're like...*related?*" Erin said tentatively, as if preparing to be properly horrified if that were the case.

"Well, not really," Charlotte admitted. "I mean, I call him my uncle but he's...well, he's like an in-law. My dad is...was...cousins with this guy's wife. But she's dead. That wife."

"Oh." Erin sat back, utterly confused. Charlotte caught her giving Brit a look. *So, do you get why she's flipping out?*

"Okay forget it," Charlotte said. "You guys can't possibly understand. I'm sorry I said anything." As if there were any way she could have stayed calm and kept her mouth shut.

"Come on, don't be that way," Brit said. "Really, Char. We're here for you. You know we are."

But Charlotte Garland would not be mollified. What did they know? They were lucky. Erin's parents were still together and Brit's divorced so long ago she was completely used to it by now. Now, when it mattered. No, *she* was the one with the lousy luck to have a mother who'd decided that a perfect time to call it quits on a twenty-year marriage would be right when her only child started college. How selfish was that? Here was Charlotte, launching into one of the most stressful periods of her whole life and suddenly her mother just decides that no, this is really *her* time, and she's going off to lead the life *she* wants. God! Shouldn't people her age *act* their age? Understand that, hello? Sorry, but they just aren't the star of the show anymore? And it wasn't like Charlotte was the only one who thought this way. She could tell her Grandma Ardis was completely on her side and totally thought Bridget had blown it big time. Aunt Cindy, too.

When the lights went down, Charlotte pushed back up, allowing the other two girls to shift next to her again.

"He's got his arm around her," Brit reported.

Charlotte clamped her hands over her ears, squeezed her eyes shut. "TMI."

The trailers seemed to go on forever, but finally, the screen directed the donning of the 3D glasses and the movie started. Charlotte glanced longingly one last time at the lit-up exit sign and, resigned, tore open the plastic packaging containing the glasses.

This was her third time to see *Avatar*, so most of it went right past her. As the blue-skinned Na'vi fought to save their world, she scarfed popcorn, brooding about her crappy life and the mess her mother had made of everything. Bridget probably didn't even remember how hard freshman year was. Well, it wouldn't have been the same for her, would it? Bridget, in college, wasn't yet lugging around the Garland name. Not like Charlotte. Man, that one old prof with all this hair sprouting out his ears, right away picking up on her name and asking if she was related to *the* Spark Garland, who'd been *his* professor. When he said this, she'd been so confused, so startled at being asked to picture this old guy as somebody ever young enough to have needed a professor of his own, the real horror of the whole thing hadn't settled in until later. The appalling truth: She could never just be herself around here. She was always going to be the great-granddaughter, granddaughter and daughter of three generations of well-known Garland men.

Not that she hadn't seen this bullet coming and tried to dodge it. Hadn't she knocked her lights out fighting to get into Yale, the only other college in the country with a School of Forestry the Garlands had to admit was probably as good as OSU's? The deal was, her dad and grampa wanted her to give Forestry a shot. At least as long as she didn't have some other all-consuming passion of her own she just had to pursue. Which she, like most people she knew, didn't. Now she wished she'd faked something, just to get herself out of this town. Why couldn't she be like her cousin Kit, just sign off on the family crap? Nobody was making *her* join Garland Forests in lock step with everyone else. Just too bad for Charlotte she had to be the only child of the guy in line to head the whole thing. Her father would want her to step right into a management position. And oh, by the way, please remember to be terribly grateful that he, John Garland, was proud to say he was not sexist in the least and, as he had pointed out so many times, planned to confer upon her this responsibility even though she *was* a girl.

Ever since April when she found out she had not been accepted to Yale but would be strung along on their waitlist all summer, she'd been a hot mess. Was she moving back East or not? When it finally became clear Yale was not in the cards, going to Oregon State could only be regarded as settling. She had no sense of exuberance at starting college. She felt defeated before she'd begun.

Then, thanks, Mom. What a nice touch. She's barely settled in the dorm and she gets the news she's about to be the child of a broken family.

And now look: she's already packed on the dreaded freshman fifteen pounds and it isn't even the end of the year. Her father commented on it, said it looked like she was taking after Aunt Cindy. Ouch. Not a happy thought. (And by the way, why was he always so mean about his sister? Cindy had given Charlotte far more attention and support than he ever had.) Right after that her face had erupted in the most disgusting crop of zits—industrial strength acne like she'd never had in her life. Thanks, Dad.

Every once in awhile during the movie, when she'd think of some other friend who might be more satisfyingly sympathetic than Brit or Erin, or at least would for sure want to hear about the unbelievably awful situation she was in, she'd pull off the 3-D glasses, hold her phone down next to her seat and text them. Only made the whole thing worse, though, when not a one of them texted back. They were probably out partying with guys. She hated it when people turned their phones off. *Hey, loser! While you're trying to reach me with your lame little update, I'm actually doing something fun! In real life!*

Her only response came from her cousin Gar, to whom she'd texted:

AAAHHHHH!!!!YOUR DAD AT AVATAR WITH MY MOM!!!!!!

Big comfort *he* was, texting back: EXCELLENT!! MY IDEA!!

Oh, God. So weird to realize: If her mother weren't the whole problem here, she'd want to run right down and hug her. She hadn't seen her in months, this mother of hers who—admit it—she loved a lot. Her throat got tight, thinking how Bridget was always such a good listener, and Charlotte could remember a time when she'd have been welcome to wail out her troubles, enjoy a big fat dose of motherly, I'm-always-on-your-side sympathy. But over the winter, Charlotte had worked so hard at the mother/daughter separation thing, she had clearly given up rights to claiming this person as her champion. At least for now. Good job, the way she'd done this to herself.

When the movie's hero opened his eyes—AVATAR!—and the lights came up, Charlotte slid down out of sight onto the cement floor. Standing, Brit and Erin regarded her with a certain disdain. Which was so incredibly annoying. Like they never had things that upset them and she had to hear every detail over and over. Plus, every time Brit had some drama going, she'd show up at the dorm with a carton of Haagen-Daz and make Charlotte eat it with her. No stretch at all, Charlotte felt, to blame at least ten of the pounds each of them had gained on this one nasty little habit of Brit's.

"Do you know this person down on the filthy theater floor?" Brit asked Erin. "The one going all emo?"

"It's not that dirty," Charlotte lied, as if that were the point. She had every right to go emo. "And I am absolutely not moving until the whole theater's empty. You watch and tell me." She lay there inhaling the smell of Coke and crushed chips, conscious of her friends' feet shifting back and forth as they acted as sentinels. God. She would never forgive her mother for putting her through this. If only she'd gotten into Yale. If only she weren't stuck here in Corvallis where it looked like she might be set up for a front row seat on her mother's new love life.

"Okay, they're getting up. Check it out—he's still got his arm around her. Hey I'm sorry, Char, but I have to say it. Your uncle's kind of hot."

"Will you *shut up!*" Charlotte stared at the back of the next row of seats, purely appalled. Suddenly she had the most random and disturbing thought. Would this whole incident have bothered her quite so much if she'd been here with a hot date of her own?

CHAPTER 31

His mom and dad looked so worried when they sat him and Gar down and told them Grampa Dan Trask had died. Like they were afraid he was going start crying or something. Was he supposed to? Cody didn't know what to think. He and Gar didn't see Grampa Dan that much anyway and when they did—was it okay to say this about a dead person?—he wasn't always that nice. Or he'd be *really* nice, and start talking about fun places he promised to take them, like a pool in a secret creek he knew about that had a rope swing over it. Gar had caught on, though. "He says those things when he's drunk, Cody. Don't start believing him or you'll just be disappointed." Turned out Gar was right—they never did swing out over that super cool swimming hole they'd so many times been encouraged to imagine.

So, when Dad explained how Grampa'd had a heart attack, but he was old and that's how it went and everything, Cody's mind was already jumping ahead to the idea of a funeral. He'd heard about those. Sounded so sad and scary. Would they have to go? Would they have to see Grampa dead? He was relieved when Gar got up the nerve to ask and Dad said no, of course they didn't have to go some church thing.

But then it turned out they'd be having this special memorial service where everybody who liked to fish with Grampa would go out and put their boats in the river in December during steelhead season and float down it in a big long line.

So here he sat in the stern with Gar, bundled up in parkas and lifejackets. Mom held Grandma Betty's hands in the bow, being especially nice to her. In the middle, Dad gripped the oars, but mostly just to steer as they rode the strong winter surge downstream.

Woodsmoke drifted up towards the gray sky from cabins here and there along the banks, but Cody couldn't smell it. Instead, filling his nostrils was the stench of sloshed gasoline from the backup outboard motor. He stared woozily at the sludgy puddle in the bottom of the boat, still feeling carsick from the hairpin twists of the road from Corvallis over into the Alsea Valley. Somehow he always suspected it was the red dirt of the steep-cut road bank that made him want to throw up.

Four boats were ahead of them, and every once in awhile he'd turn around to count five or six following before a bend in the river blocked the view of even more. Looked like lots of people must have been friends with Grampa Dan, because look how many were willing to huddle in these boats on such a cold, miserable day for his send-off.

Facing forward again, Cody got a shock. His father was crying. Alarmed, he turned to Gar. Had he seen? Gar glanced sideways, gave a slight nod of his blue stocking cap at the strangeness of it. Dad crying. They'd never seen this before. Dad rowing and crying, his face all wet. Cody raised his eyebrows at Gar. Hadn't Dad usually been kind of mad at Grampa?

Gar was nine, old enough to understand things better, and looked wise as he gave Cody's questioning look a philosophical little shrug. Grownups. Who could know?

After that, Cody kept his eyes fixed on his own clenched fists. Only once, toward the end, did he dare raise his eyes and look at his father. Ah. Good. Not crying anymore. Dad's eyes met Cody's and he winked.

Cody mustered a small smile of relief. Winked back.

CHAPTER 32

"Wake up, buddy." Will flipped on the light and shook Cody's shoulder. "Time to get going."

Cody moaned and snuggled deeper into his bedding.

"Up and at 'em." Will grabbed the blankets and yanked.

"Dad!" Cody sat up, enraged.

"Hey, it's four-thirty. Bacon's cooking. Gotta get going if we're gonna make it to the launch by sun-up."

Cody gathered his comforter back around his bare shoulders. "Dad? I told you. I'm not going."

"What? Not go fishing? On the first day of trout season?"

Cody groaned.

"We always go," Will said.

"*You* go. You go with Doug."

"Cody, Doug died."

Cody twisted, tilted an instant, then let gravity take him face first into his pillow, which now muffled his voice. "That's who you *used* to go with, not me."

"Well, okay, yeah, so I guess I thought maybe this year'd be a good time to start a new tradition. Hey, I even got you a floppy hat like mine. Gotta start getting that thing broken in."

"Dad?" Cody pushed back up. "I've told you a million times: the Alsea Highway always makes me carsick. And I know you hate to hear me say this, but I just really don't like to fish."

"Aw, come on. How can a son of mine not like to fish?"

Cody regarded him through the curtains of his long black hair, not answering, letting Will's lame question hang there.

Yeah, he was probably sounding like his own dad. *How's a kid a mine think he can make it in college?* Are fathers always shocked when their sons aren't just like them?

"Remember when you first asked me about opening day?" Cody said. "I told you that then."

"You didn't say you absolutely wouldn't go."

"Oh, that is so not fair. You're mad 'cause I tried not to be a total asshole about it? And anyway, I'm hanging out with Tessa."

Tessa. Will sighed. "Okay. Well, I better go get that bacon before it burns. Go on back to sleep then."

Will stood at the stove, listening to the rain beat on the window, the bacon sizzling in the pan. The kid didn't like to fish. How could that be? All those trips when they were little? They were loving it. He forked over a strip. A father should take his sons fishing, Will always thought, and he'd made a point of doing it. But maybe it wouldn't have mattered what he'd gone out there and done with them, as long as he'd been paying them attention. As long as they were together.

Now they'd have their own ideas of how a guy ought to spend his free time.

Which was fine.

Which they were entitled to.

So, what the hell? Why did it bother him so much?

The thing was, he'd have sworn an oath on his best Eagle Claw fly rod that he hadn't been doing any imagining about the future at all. He would have claimed that ever since Shelley died he'd been so busy scrambling to stay ahead of the boys, one day at a time, he'd never considered what a relationship with a grown son might even be like.

Now he realized he *had* formed certain assumptions. What would you call that brand new fishing hat sitting there on the counter? Hadn't he nurtured a mental image of Cody wearing it, getting it grimy? Dirtying it into something to drive his future wife to joking despair? What a fool, recognizing these hoped-for visions only now as they faded.

And sure, he was always saying the boys could do whatever they wanted in life, but was he actually promising himself this meant whatever they wanted— even save the world like Gar hoped—as long as they didn't move too far from Corvallis?

Gar liked to fish, yeah, but neither of his sons were growing up to be his new fishing buddies. Already he hardly ever saw Gar, and when he did, the kid usually had that Hannah girl's delicately tattooed arms twined around him. Cody was turning into a handsome heartbreaker himself, and had launched his love life with great flair, meeting this Tessa at his gay support group, where they found each other engagingly empathetic, supportive and—most important for the budding relationship—ragingly heterosexual.

Note to self, Will thought. Give Cody the condom talk.

He cracked eggs into the grease. Salted and peppered them. Yep, these sons would find their own women, flail around with their own schemes. Probably have kids of their own, too.

Hey, maybe *they'd* want to go fishing. With Grampa Will. He'd take them. Girls too if they came up with some spunky ones who didn't take after Shelley too much. Maybe Gar and Cody would humor him once in awhile, go camping with him or something. Yeah, with the grandkids.

But however all that played out, Gar and Cody were not going to be the people to help him figure out what on earth to do every weekend for the rest of his lousy life.

He sighed. He could still go fishing on his own today. He'd hitched up the boat last night. Had the gear all packed, too. He'd even remembered to bring home Doug's lucky sinker and put it in his creel. His own battered hat sat right beside Cody's new one. He and Doug had always sworn there was absolutely nothing on earth they'd rather be doing than sitting in that boat on the Alsea on the opening day of trout season. Whether they caught anything or not, with plenty of beer and the right grub, it'd always be fun.

But now, somehow, doing it alone didn't sound so great.

So, if fishing today was out, what then? The constant rain had turned the yard into a jungle of grass and weeds, but even if it stopped raining long enough to dash out there and start yanking, it was the last thing he felt like doing.

The first year or two after the accident, he'd tended Shelley's flower beds on autopilot, craving the connection with her, feeling like she was watching everything he did and wanting her approval. But in the end, fussy flowerbeds were not his thing, and sometimes now, when he was out there on his hands and knees with the clippers, he felt like he'd merely been left behind and assigned the job of caretaker. Caretaker of memories.

He especially hated working near that damned sundial. *Grow old along with me, the best is yet to be.* When they first moved in, he'd been eagle-eyed for places to draw the lines that would say this was *their* home now. The Trask home. He'd argued with Shelley. No way they had to keep the sundial just because Spark and Charlotte stuck it there. He and Shelley were young! Why should they have to be reminded of getting old? Go get one of those cement deer, he'd suggested, but of course Shelley wouldn't budge. Her Grammie wanted the sundial there and that was that.

He remembered himself so young and full of it, doing his damnedest to figure out what being the man of the house was going to mean when you'd married into the Garland clan. Married into the clan, accepted help on the down payment, and moved into Spark Garland's house.

Now the sundial was forever mocking him from the bed of lilies-of-the-valley, depressing him for a different reason.

Stupid kid. He'd thought a sundial was worth fighting over.

He'd wanted them never to get old.

And then Shelley hadn't.

He poured his coffee back in the pot, plated the bacon and eggs and ate leaning against the counter. Finished in short order, he shuffled back and fell into bed, the bed that was always going to be the one he'd shared with Shelley. Was this queen-size? He'd never paid any attention. All he cared was that when he crawled in, she was there. Now he fell asleep thinking of Bridget, who would right this minute still be snuggled in a nest of fluffy comforters in that big brass bed he'd helped her set up.

Him here, her there. What kind of sense did that make? None.

Waking later to the gray light, he decided: today was the day. Time to pull up a plan from his own File of Dreams Deferred. Something that had been darting around in the back of his mind like a fawn in the forest shadows, an idea that hadn't wanted to hold still long enough to be seen and acknowledged: He was sick of rattling around this place. What, was he supposed to keep up a campus-close hideaway forever just to facilitate his sons' love lives?

Inside of an hour, he was down at his office, writing up a full asking price offer for the Hopestill Creek property. Having quietly sabotaged promotion of the property at every turn—he'd taken the prettiest pictures off the listing site—he could, in fairness, offer no less.

When summer arrived, there'd be another Sierra the Heiress, and the next one might not wimp out. The surprising relief he'd felt when that girl went slinking back to California without making an offer had served as a warning. Sooner or later somebody besides him was bound to see Hopestill Creek as the special place it was and have the smarts to go for it. And then he'd be kicking himself.

Unless it was Bridget. She'd love that place if she could settle down and take an open-minded look at it, stop focusing on the scary and annoying aspects of trying to buy property like she had that crazy day out at the Spring Lane place. In that case, he wouldn't mind turning it over to her.

But what if he just built a house in that meadow for himself? He'd have lots of plain walls for his paintings, and when he threw open the front door, there'd be nothing but daisies, lupine, Douglas iris, and wild roses that would do their own thing. Just soak up the rain, bloom in the sun and demand nothing from him.

Better than being *here* alone, the caretaker of this house, the left-behind guardian of the spirit of Spark Garland. Wouldn't Spark himself approve of Will getting out? Didn't he always talk about getting on with it, sinking in roots where a tree—or a person—could thrive?

Spark Garland's spirit wasn't here anyway.

It was out there beyond the ridges layering back to the horizon, healthy green fir trees of every age, pointing heavenward.

CHAPTER 33

"**H**op in," Robin said, holding the pickup truck door so Mattie could take his usual place, riding shotgun. Good old Mattie the Mutt. Jane thought he was a mix of Atolian Shepherd or maybe Great Pyranese. Whatever. Robin privately, fondly referred to him as her "Greater American Yellow Dog."

He wagged his tail, excited. Poor boy, he thought they were going for a walk.

She took the tight curve on Whiteside Drive, stomach churning, as she headed up towards her dad's house. She'd be so glad to get this over with.

Ever since that appalling foundation meeting, life with Jane had been unbearable. Yes, they'd been hashing this out for years, Jane throwing around words like dysfunctional and enabling, Robin stubbornly defensive. They were the Garlands. They were Family with a capital F. Yes, Jane said once, a capital F family firmly entrenched in the tradition of White Men Rule the World. Robin argued. Always agreed, her cousin John was a total asshole, and it was really painful, the way the balance had shifted with the loss of Robin's mother and sister, but hadn't her dad always supported her?

But now Jane was talking about the need for somebody to draw some lines, for God's sake, and if nobody else would, maybe it'd have to be her. Because she wasn't sure she could stand the idea of continuing to be with Robin anymore if it meant dealing with these people. The meeting had been the last straw. It was particularly painful to watch Robin, she said, put in the position of covering for Ed and his secret new love while everybody got sniffly over Alice. But when Robin pointed out how happy she was for her father about this and took up her usual refrain, how much she respected him and how lucky she felt that he'd never seemed to mind that she was gay, Jane's touchiest button finally got pushed and she said it straight.

"So he didn't kick you out because you're a lesbian. And you're grateful for that. You're so *sickeningly* grateful. And oh, right, he's so grateful that you're such a great daughter he can count on. But does all this gratitude give him a pass on everything else? You're supposed to have his back but he doesn't have yours? He should have defended you at that meeting when your stupid cousin went on that rant, but he just sat there. Do you actually not see that?"

Jane was sounding alarmingly decided. Finally and suddenly, the timing for making a change seemed good because, well: Julie Pomeroy. No way could Robin have said what she had to say today while Ed was watching Alice die of cancer. Or after, while he was grieving her. But now, he had Julie.

And she had Jane, somebody loving her enough to finally deliver a swift, judicious kick.

Robin never had to come out to her mother, Alice claiming she first began suspecting when she saw how reluctantly her little girl would wear a dress, her intuition telling her Robin was only agreeing to a hand-smocked pinafore to please her mother.

Over the years, Robin had often reread the handmade card Alice had mailed her at the apartment she'd rented after college. It featured a poem called *Wild Geese* by somebody named Mary Oliver. With that line about letting the soft animal of your body love what it loves, Robin thought her mom was trying to say it was okay about crushing on other women. But later, it was the first line that always jumped out at her. *You do not have to be good.* She wondered if Alice had seen this in her, this heart-hurting effort to please, as if she were apologizing for not turning out to be the daughter everyone expected. Maybe her mother understood her way better than she ever realized. Maybe she'd only been trying to say this: *Give it up already. You're fine.*

You do not have to be good.

What a concept.

Mattie by her side, Robin strode up to her father's front door, trying to look calmer than she felt, maybe fake her brain out with body confidence. "Don't get too excited," she told the dog. He wasn't going to like this or understand it any better than her dad had when she'd called and said she wanted to come over for a talk, and no, not to take the dog out. Because since when did she ever show up without a hike on the agenda?

The thing is, she just didn't know how this would go. She and Jane had debated and tried to refine the lines she planned to deliver, but this was all so far from any conversation she'd ever had with her father, she couldn't even imagine how he might respond. If it was bad, she didn't like the idea of being halfway out Woods Creek when he blew up, fell apart or whatever.

He opened the door, bent and patted Mattie. "Hey, boy." He straightened and smiled. "I thought we weren't doing a walk."

"Right, we're not." She would not explain that she felt safer, having her dog along. This time it wasn't about warding off cougars, it was just...well, Mattie's warm presence always made her feel better about everything.

"Come in, then," he said. "Coffee?"

She shook her head. Her stomach couldn't take it right now.

"A drink?" They weren't above an afternoon beer.

But Robin shook her head as Mattie bounded back to the truck. *You guys are making a mistake!*

"No, come on, boy, we're going inside."

Ed motioned her into the living room. Robin smelled furniture polish and wondered if her dad had deliberately, defensively scheduled Robin's requested meeting for right after his cleaning lady's morning, just to ward off any suggestion he was having trouble holding it together. Well, he might be relieved to be spared an assisted-living lecture, but he probably wasn't going to appreciate the issue she planned to lay before him any better.

They dropped into identical, hunched-over postures, sitting at right angles, heads lowered. Mattie worked his way in. Robin noticed her knee was bouncing. Mattie felt it too and looked back and forth between Robin and Ed.

"Dad, this is really hard and I'm sorry, but I think I'm done. I don't want to be part of Garland Forests if it means being part of Uncle Pete's show."

"What?"

Robin hesitated. "I think you heard me."

Ed looked baffled. "But Pete's show? What are you talking about?"

"Okay, I don't want to be part of Garland Forests anymore if Pete's in charge."

"Pete's not in charge. He and I are co-owners."

"Maybe technically, but it doesn't matter. What I'm saying is, I don't want to work with him and John anymore."

Ed's expression remained one of stubborn puzzlement.

Their relationship had always been so nice and easy, hadn't it? But in this moment, Robin realized it had only seemed this way because they were always keeping it to business or sports or even politics. They never sat around and traded personal stuff. Feelings. And now that she had somebody in her life to whom she really *could* lay bare her innermost thoughts, the lack of real communication with her father was right there in her face.

"I guess that foundation meeting was pretty hard on you," Ed said. "You and Jane. Sorry about that."

She concentrated on stroking Mattie. "You should have stuck up for me."

"Didn't I?"

"Uh…" She glanced out the big front picture window, back at him. "No?" Was he just remembering the words he'd been *thinking* of saying?

"Well, Will did." Said almost cheerfully, as if clearly this son-in-law of his would get him off the hook.

She paused. "Yeah…?"

"I was proud of him."

Robin narrowed her eyes at her father.

Mattie scooted out and went to the door. *It's time to go now, right?*

"So, like I said. I really don't think I can do this anymore."

"But isn't this a little extreme?" Ed said. "On your part, I mean? Because John's always been this way."

"Not arguing that."

"It's just how he is. We all agree."

"Yeah, and I have now officially had it with how he is. And it's not just that one meeting. Or even just him. It's everything. Like I said, it's Pete, too. The stuff he's been saying at these public hearings about the foundation grants. That's not me. That's not us, right? I'm sorry, Dad, but your brother is out there in the world talking like a right wing nut job."

Ed looked pained. "Yeah. S'pose so."

"And Phil. Come on, he never even tries to hide how much Jane and I disgust him. You think we enjoy that?"

"Oh, you shouldn't pay any attention to him."

Right. So simple. Why hadn't she thought of that?

"Look," she said. "Can't we find a way to split up the foundation trust? We are so at odds with them over the things we want to support. I don't want to be at that conference table with any of them. Not even one day a year. It's just stupid to sit there arguing."

"Yeah, I know, but we're working on it. A way to separate it all into two individual entities."

"We? Like Pete thinks it's a good idea, too?"

"Well, I haven't actually brought it up to him."

"Oh, Dad—"

"But I'm planning to."

"Dad, you've been talking about this for years. Ever since Spark died. They do the mills and we manage the timber tracts. But, the thing is, I don't see you actually *doing* it. Unless there's stuff I'm missing? Things you haven't told me?"

"Well, it's hard. It just doesn't feel good, breaking up a family."

"But we're not. We're trying to divide up a business."

"A *family* business."

Family. Family family family. So sick of it. What did family mean to Pete and Ardis, anyway? Just that everybody was bound to support *them*.

"So," Robin said, "are Pete and Ardis being supportive about Julie?"

He hesitated. "Still waiting for the right time to tell them."

"Dad. You promised if I wouldn't out you at the meeting you'd go ahead."

"Well, how was that going to look, you and Greg with your memorial? I'm supposed to announce I've got a new woman right there and then?"

"Oh, come on. You know perfectly well that's not the point. Nobody was trying to make you do that. But you promised if we just got through that…"

"Listen, you have no idea how complicated this is. This family's just got so much history with Julie Pomeroy. You can't begin to know."

"Not if nobody tells me. If you're talking about how she was engaged to Uncle John when he died, I did hear that somewhere along the line."

"There's more than that. It's—"

"Dad, why are you so careful with Pete? More careful than you are with me?"

"Because he's family. He's my brother. I'm kind of surprised at you, Robin. Of everybody, I thought you were the one who really valued that."

Like she hadn't been hashing this over for years, the concept of family dynamics. How it worked; how it *didn't* work. She was now down to one grateful but physically distant brother, a clueless father, and the side of the family who had no use for her. Where was the mythical family protection for her in that?

"Pete's had so much on his shoulders," Ed said, "and he's worked hard trying to hold us all together. In the end, isn't family the most important thing?"

Robin couldn't look her father straight in the eye. "Dad?" She chose to focus on stroking Mattie's dear yellow head. "I'm family too, right?"

"Well, of course you are. What kind of a question is that?"

She put her hands on her thighs, pushed to standing. "Maybe one you ought to think about?"

"Robin—"

"Look, I know I don't get to call the shots for you. But I do get to make the rules for myself, and I've decided. I'm not doing this anymore. I've been putting up with John Garland my whole life and I'm done."

"So what are you saying here? You're just resigning?"

"Uh huh. Unless you break off with them. You either give up running the business in support of the Garland family façade or you give up me. Your choice."

"Well, I have to say, I'm a little—"

"And I don't care what you put in your will."

She walked out with Mattie, flinging a farewell hand over her shoulder, conscious she was shaking. She didn't dare look back, afraid of whatever expression might be on her father's face. She loved him too much. She hated to hurt him and didn't need to actually see the evidence she had. Didn't care for his disapproval either.

She was going home to Jane now.

Damned if she'd show up reporting she'd caved.

CHAPTER 34

Will was standing in the buffet line for the Oregon Small Woodlands annual luncheon when George Henderson innocently dropped his bombshell. Across the long, narrow table from each other, the two of them were tonging out servings of tossed salad from the same big bowl.

"How about that father-in-law of yours?" George said with a chuckle, shaking his head. "Gotta hand it to the guy."

Will looked at him.

"About the wedding?"

Will's eyes widened. Wedding?

"I mean, isn't that something?" George edged along to the stainless-steel tray of chicken pot pie squares. "Ran into him out at Timber Supply the other day and it was like he couldn't wait to tell me. And you know the last time I saw him, in the Fall I guess it was, he just looked like a guy ready to call the whole thing quits."

"Oh, yeah." That rang a bell anyway. Will stared at the salad dressings. Behind him, people were waiting. He was supposed to make a decision here. He slopped something white on his lettuce.

"I know he'd kill me if he heard me using this word," George said, meeting Will at the end of the table, "but he was kinda cute, you know? Like he was excited, but kind of apologizing too, worried what I'd think because of Alice and all. But I just told him I thought it was great. I'm happy for him."

"Well, sure," Will nodded, like he'd had the exact same reaction to the news.

The news that Ed hadn't bothered to give him, damn it anyway! What the hell, Ed? Here he was, sent to this meeting to get up and give, one more time, an after-lunch talk about the history of Garland Forests, and his father-in-law hadn't even had the good grace to clue him in. This was family news. Shouldn't he have heard it before the owner of Henderson Tree Farms, for God's sake? Embarrassing as hell. Will gazed, unseeing, across the room of round tables. Had all these people already heard about this? He was making a point of veering away from George when Brad Kennedy, the group's representative at the state capitol, flagged him down, pointing to a seat saved for him up front.

Will threaded his way between the tables, faking friendly greetings to the members, mostly retirement-age guys in jeans and vests, accompanied by their wives. A few families dragged along their kids or grandkids, trying to get them interested, one of the on-going threads of discussion being how to pass the management of your timber parcel to a new generation. The Garlands were forever being called upon to dish up talks with titles such as "Inheriting Green," "Your Forest Legacy," or "Growth for the Generations."

Family tree farms—that's what this bunch was all about. In Benton County, Garland Forests dominated all, and with 80,000 acres of timberland, they risked looking like one of the giant timber companies the environmentalists loved to hate. Thus the imperative to have a Garland Forests representative at every one of these meetings, guarding their status as an honest-to-God family tree farm.

Today it was Will Trask's turn; it had been on his calendar for months. But never had he felt his awkward position as a Garland in-law so keenly. An employee might not have cared or taken it personally, but shouldn't a real family member know the family business (people getting married!) ahead of everybody else in town?

Will took his place at the table and started forking up food, swallowing it down to his churning stomach. He buttered his roll, tried to join in the chit-chat.

Was the market for wood chips dying forever, what with the closing of Publishers Paper Mill in Albany?

Should they be hedging their bets with this global warming thing? Would Plum Creek increase their production of Coastal Redwood plugs or would people have to keep driving down to California nurseries to pick them up?

Booming Shanghai had approved wood-framed construction in its newest building codes and Canada had wasted no time upping their shipments of logs to China. Shouldn't the Northwest get in on this too?

Will did his best to pay attention and help them out, grateful they valued his opinion, glad at least nobody was bringing up the Garland Grant tuition brouhaha. To this crowd, the name Garland meant timber and how to grow it, not grants and how to get them.

Will spaced out when Brad Kennedy got up and gave an update on various legislative issues in Salem, and he was still mentally distant when they began the door-prize drawings for rolls of hot pink flagging tape, write-in-the-rain notebooks, and hats bearing the advertising logos of various local suppliers of industry related goods and services—Terra Tech, Trout Mountain, Hudson Logging.

Ed getting married. And Alice hadn't been gone a year. Will had no idea who it could even be. Suddenly he remembered Ed's fancy little Christmas tree. Guess that could have been a hint something was up. Okay, so he'd been too caught up in his own problems to remember to ask Robin or anybody what they'd heard. Still, wasn't leaving him completely out of the loop a pretty harsh punishment for not coming up with the sort of pushy questions he hadn't appreciated having directed at himself? *So Ed, are you dating yet?*

"Will." Brad elbowed him. "I think you won."

"What?" Will looked at his ticket. "Oh." He pushed up from the table and went to the front. A prize?

"A bottle of Lurking Turkey wine!" it was announced. "Locally grown and bottled!"

Perfect, Will thought, holding it recklessly aloft and blurting, "Hey, can I drink this before I give my talk?"

Which earned him a hearty guffaw. Such a fun guy. They had no idea how sincerely he meant it.

A few minutes later he was directing somebody to cue up the PowerPoint show.

"The first John Garland never graduated from high school," Will began as he had dozens of times before, "but he valued education highly and sent his son Spark to Oregon State College in the 1920s."

Didn't everybody already know this? Didn't everybody already know the whole damned story of Garland Forests?

As he yet again rehashed the details, he thought how much more interesting it would be if he could have popped open that Lurking Turkey, knocked it back, and started spewing the story of what was really going on among the Garlands right now, behind closed doors.

But then, obviously, he wasn't the guy to tell that story. Hell, he didn't even *know* that story.

CHAPTER 35

"Will. What on earth?" No surprise to open her front door and find him standing there, but she'd grown used to his various shades of sheepishness, not whatever this was.

He thrust a bottle at her. "Help me drink this." Pushed past without waiting for an invitation, shrugged out of his jacket and threw it on the sofa.

Smoldering rage?

She read the label. "Lurking Turkey?" She wanted to laugh, didn't dare.

"Oh, Bridget. Jesus Christ. Ed's getting married."

"Ed Garland?"

He turned back to face her. "And don't tell me you already knew."

"I won't. I mean, I didn't." Snagging his jacket, she took it to the pegged rack by the back kitchen door, calling over her shoulder, "So that's a good thing, isn't it?" She opened her cupboard and reached for a couple of wine glasses. "Who is it, that Julie Pomeroy?"

"See? You even know who it is and I don't. Who the hell is Julie Pomeroy?"

"An old family friend, I think. Some patient of mine told me she'd seen Ed getting a swine flu shot with her or something. But nobody's told me anything official."

"I'm just his dumb son-in-law or ex-son-in-law or whatever. Why tell me?"

"Oh Will, come on."

She opened the wine and poured generous glasses. No sniffing. No swirling. She took a sip. Will just started knocking his back, refusing to sit, leaving the kitchen to pace the dining room. Over his plaid flannel shirt he was wearing that Filson vest she liked. Moleskin. Probably soft.

"I don't know which bothers me more," he said, circling the table, "that Ed never saw fit to clue me in or that the whole thing's happening in the first place. I just wonder how everybody's going to take it, being so soon after Alice."

"Well, I think it's wonderful. You saw how he was. He came in to my office about his shoulder last summer and honestly, he was so depressed, I was trying to get him to go talk to somebody. So to me this is like a miracle. And it's not like they've got all the time in the world. Shouldn't we be happy for them?"

"I guess," he said, but the last thing he looked was happy. He went out to the living room and dropped onto the sofa.

She took a breath. "So, do you want dinner?"

"Of course I want dinner. You know I do. I always do. I can't fool you."

Well. Could this count as progress?

"And it's time, right?" He glanced at his watch. "I've waited long enough? Because actually what I felt like doing was coming straight here from lunch to tell you all this and start right in drinking. So, see? I'm really making an effort to act more civilized. You'll notice the bottle was *not* open."

"Okay." She looked at his boots, stuck with grassy bits. "So where've you been?"

"Oh, up at that property I told you about. Just trying to get my head clear."

"Yeah, I can see you're all calmed down."

He had to laugh. "Yeah, well." He blew out a big breath. "So, what's for dinner?"

"Well, let's see…" Actually, Will had been showing up so regularly, she'd boldly laid in enough groceries to save him from always having to run out for steaks. "How does chicken fajitas sound?"

"Fine."

Bridget went back into the kitchen, and the first thing she did was light a candle for the table. She didn't have to ask Will to come into the kitchen while she cooked. He was already following her. Good sign.

She kept his wine glass full while they ate and when they'd emptied the Lurking Turkey she started pouring Elk Cove. She dished out seconds on the fajitas and sat with her elbows on the table watching him, listening, nodding in agreement with everything he said, persuading him to relax. He looked especially good to her tonight. Was it the candlelight? She was thinking she'd never known a handsomer man in her life than Will Trask. Those brown eyes. Ruddy, outdoorsy skin. He had his plaid sleeves rolled up, and his forearms on the table were so strong looking, the veins standing out, pulsing with life.

She poured herself more wine too. This idiocy between the two of them had gone on long enough. No more dancing around.

"I liked that *Avatar* movie," he said at one point when they'd pretty much finished the meal. "That blue girl reminded me of you. How she wouldn't take any shit. And when they got on that big bird and flew around. I don't know, that was just—"

"Yeah." She'd liked that part too. "Sorry I don't have a big bird to fly you around on."

He gave her a lazy, appraising grin.

Encouraged, she lowered her voice. "But I might have a couple other things we could try."

Uh oh. Grin gone. His eyes widened. This is where he'd have jumped up, she thought, if she hadn't already plied him with so much wine.

"Now take it easy," she said, as he slowly pushed up from the table.

"Uh…" He took an unsteady step back, bumped the wall with the coat rack.

She leaned back in the booth, threw her right arm over the seatback. "You know you're really kind of a tease, Will Trask."

"What."

She looked up at him through the tendrils falling over her eyes. "You put your arm around me at that movie."

"Yeah?"

"No fair."

"That was different," he said. "That was public."

"Oh, right. Public's safe. No worries what happens next."

Bingo. He flicked on the light, turned around and started pawing ineffectually for his jacket.

"Oh, no you don't. You're not going anywhere."

"The hell I'm not."

"Honey, you're too drunk to drive."

He turned from the coats, eyes flickering surprise.

"Yeah, that's right. I called you honey. You want to make something of it?"

He seemed frozen in place.

She stood up. Whoa. She was drunk too. But as she moved slowly, unsteadily toward him, something deep in her brain was urging her on. She reached behind him to flip the light off again and backed him against the coat rack until his head was against her plaid wool scarf. She put her hands on his chest. Yeah, that vest felt so nice. Then she worked her hands under it to feel the flannel. Soft, but beneath it, those muscles, so firm.

"There now." She moved her hands to his shoulders.

The sound of her voice seemed to wake him up and he shrugged her off, circling away.

"Look at me, the way I come running over here. Every Goddamned time something happens, the first thing I'm always thinking is *Oh, I'll go tell Bridget.*"

"What's wrong with that?"

"It's pathetic."

"Not to me." She edged up to him again. "I like it. When I open that front door, there's just nobody in the world I'd rather see standing there than you."

His eyes registered this, but still he backed away, and when he glanced behind and saw that only two steps had trapped him at the counter, something so close to panic flared his nostrils that Bridget might have found it comic if she weren't feeling so dead serious about where this was heading. He braced the heels of his hands against the counter and tried to arch back from her.

She didn't care. She pressed up to him, ignoring his resistance, worked her arms around him.

"You can show up at my front door anytime," she murmured into his chest. "Or my back door too. I'll always be happy to let you in."

"Oh, will you stop it?" he pleaded. "It drives me crazy when you talk that way."

She laughed softly.

"Hey."

"I can't help it. You're so cute when you're confused."

"But when you say those things…"

"Okay, okay. I'll shut up."

But she didn't let him go. She'd had it with giving him time to come around. Sick to death of giving him so many chances to slip through her hands with his escape-artist tricks. And now—oh, God—he was actually lifting his arms and gently settling them down around her shoulders. He was curving over her. She shut her eyes. Sweet Jesus. She'd wanted these arms of his around her for so long. This was finally happening. Right now. She couldn't believe she'd at last managed to steal close enough to breath him in, the smells of forest, the fir needles washed by clean rain. When he shifted just the slightest, she still held tight.

"Don't," she said. "Just…just stay."

For now. Forever.

"It's healthy," she whispered. "Hugging releases the feel-good hormones."

Wrapped in his arms she felt…protected. That thing women these days weren't supposed to need or want but, admit it, *she* sure did. Wanted to give it back too. Because look, he needed her too. She could tell by his ragged breath, and the sense she had he was at some tipping point.

Finally she risked breaking the silence.

"This doesn't feel so bad, does it?"

He looked down at her. "You promised you weren't going to talk."

She widened her eyes innocently. "I lied."

He laughed a little helplessly.

"But you feel good now, right?"

"Uh…yeah."

"So, see, I think that means something."

"Like what? The hormone thing's working?"

She took a breath. She had to be so careful. "Have you ever thought it might mean maybe you could love me?"

After a beat, "No."

"No?" She pulled back and looked at him. "That's your answer? Then you're a liar too. I think you already *do* love me."

"Oh, Bridget, the last thing you need's—"

"Shh!" She pressed her cheek against him. "Your turn to shut up. I know what I need."

"But—"

"Just let me take care of you." She nuzzled his chest.

He sighed as he settled his cheek down on the top of her head in surrender. And oh, God, would anything ever again feel as good as this moment? And just what would it take now to unleash everything she suspected he'd been holding inside for such a long time? She got her hands under his shirt and ran her hands up and down his back. He could lie or he could tell the truth. He could hold back or he could pretend whatever he wanted. What he couldn't do was boss his heart into line. She could hear it pounding to burst. Couldn't hide any of his body's other betrayals, either. The hard yearning below his belt buckle.

That's for me, she thought. Right here, right now. Not for somebody long gone. Mine if I can claim it.

So just how far do I have to go here to set off this trigger of his?

Steady, don't bolt on me, boy. She slipped the fingers of her ringless left hand down under the back band of his Carhartts.

He groaned.

Down a little further. One hand's worth just wasn't going to do it, though. She had to get all the rest of him.

He seized a fistful of her hair, holding it aside to drop his mouth on her neck. The burn of it zapped straight down hot to the place where she was already molten. Rebracing her shaking knees, she slowly, carefully pulled her right arm out from around him and hooked her finger in the loop of his belt where it threaded through the brass buckle.

Looking up, she locked her eyes on his.

And gave that leather strap a tug.

Okay, that did it.

CHAPTER 36

The Pacific Northwest provides the opportunity for a variety of accidents in which people may die, many involving the risky posing for photographs against the backdrop of spectacular scenery. Vacationers, thrilled into an excited carelessness, edge too close to the volcano rim, the waterfall, the ocean cliff.

Loggers get pinned by trees. Fishermen drown in rushing rivers. Hunters shoot each other. People go missing in the woods and die of hypothermia.

Every great once-in-awhile, some poor beach-bound soul goes driving blissfully down the Sunset Highway and has the appallingly unfortunate timing to pass just as, after a life of three hundred years, an old-growth Doug fir at that instant gives it up and crashes across the pavement, crushing the car.

Will lost Shelley, though, to that most common of highway accidents occurring anywhere. Driving home from their anniversary weekend at Black Butte, a car coming around the curve crossed the center line and smashed into them. That's all there was to it.

Except...Oh, what if Shelley hadn't been driving? Maybe he could have steered clear. Or at least have been the one to take the hit. But she'd said the mountain curves made her carsick and she felt better in the driver's seat. How could he turn her down on that one? Still, he should have insisted she keep the shoulder seatbelt on instead of slipping her left arm over it, complaining she was so short it rubbed annoyingly across her neck. She would have nagged him if the tables were turned. Insisted on the red shirt when he went hunting. Always risked a big fight, just to keep him safe. So he *should* have. Should have refused to let her drive unless she wore the seat belt right. But then, whoever imagines they'll have an accident? Whoever worries the airbag won't deploy?

Somehow an ambulance showed up and they rushed her to Salem Memorial. Once people made it alive to the hospital, they usually survived, right? She looked fine; nothing was messed up on the outside, but clearly she was hurting. How bad could it be, though, if the drunk in the other car came through it well enough to be left trying to walk a straight line for a state trooper? As they wheeled Shelley into surgery, he'd phoned Ed and Alice, asking them to please go over to the house to be with the boys.

Everything was under control, he assured them.

He sat in the intensive care waiting room for two hours before a doctor in stained scrubs came out. Will stood up.

"Sit down, son."

Son. Something in this word, in the man's tone, hurtled Will forward toward some black, blood-draining abyss. Son. Too much pity, too much of what sounded almost like affection in the way this stranger said the word to mistake it for anything but what it was—a prelude to the most horrible news.

"Your wife's gravely injured."

Will stood up again. "No, where is she? My wife wasn't even bleeding." As if maybe they'd got his wife mixed up with somebody else's.

The doctor regarded him with great compassion. "Internally. The force of the lapbelt cut right across her middle."

"Oh, Jesus."

Gently the doctor pressed him back down into his chair. "I'm going to be straight with you. You need to prepare yourself. This is the worst injury of this type I've ever gotten off the table alive. And I was a medic in Vietnam."

A numbness.

"We're doing everything we can. Dr. Steiner's still in there, but it's going to be…" He shook his head. Then he sighed and swept his gaze around the empty waiting room. "Is there somebody you can phone to come be with you?"

The floor rose and smacked him. People had him on a cart. Cold rubber disks were taped to his chest. A machine was rolled in and began to beep.

This couldn't be happening. This must be a nightmare.

This was the nightmare he'd keep right on having.

"Where's my wife?" He pushed someone's hands away.

"Shh, hold still now. Don't try to talk."

"But where's my wife?"

CHAPTER 37

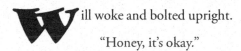ill woke and bolted upright.

"Honey, it's okay."

He felt arms around him. "Oh, my God." He pulled away, scrambled off the bed. "Where's my wife?"

Where *was* he? It was dark. He was buck naked. His head throbbed.

"Will. Sweetie, you were having a bad dream."

He turned. Bridget? Bridget Garland kneeling in a pile of sheets and comforters. He looked around. Her brass bed. Her bedroom. She crawled over to him, swung her bare legs off the bed, threw her arms around him again.

"You conked out, just like that, and after awhile I could see you were having a nightmare so I thought I ought to wake you up."

He stepped back.

"But everything's okay." She looked all soft and concerned. "It was just a dream."

"No. No, it was—" He jerked away. "I gotta go home."

She sat back on the bed, clutching the comforter, her voice small. "I wish you wouldn't."

"I'm sorry." He found his Carhartts on the floor and pulled them on. "I'm sorry for everything."

"But, why do you have to go?"

He had to think. Couldn't. Why did he?

"Cody," he said. "Cody'll wonder where I am."

She glanced at the bedside clock. "It's only ten-thirty. It's Saturday night and he's a sixteen-year-old boy. He's probably not even *at* home."

"Yes, he is."

Bridget's tenderness turned pouty. "Whatever. You realize he's not even the reason you're leaving."

He turned back on her. "If you think you know so much better than me why I do what I do, why are you even asking? Why don't you just tell me?"

"Oh, Will." She dropped her head, curls falling forward. "It was so good. Why can't something just be good?"

That brought him up short. It had been good. Way beyond just good, actually. And after so long…But then the bad part all came crashing back.

"So you think this was just fine and I ought to feel proud of myself?" He started following the trail of his clothes out of the bedroom, grabbing up each item back to the kitchen.

She slid off the bed with a bounce and was right behind him.

They'd never turned out the dining and living room lights but it was dark in the kitchen, the little candle on the table having guttered out. He flipped on a switch and the light fired pain straight through his eyes to his brain. He found his shirt, flung on the counter, one sleeve wet from the sink.

"We just knock back a bottle of wine—two bottles—and jump into bed? Just get drunk and—" He turned back and, "Oh, God."

She'd followed him without stopping to dress; now she was just standing there naked, so gorgeous, cheeks flushed, eyes flashing, hair loose and wild over her shoulders.

"Speak for yourself," Bridget said. "Your Lurking Turkey didn't make me do anything I haven't wanted to do for a long time."

The shock of her angry beauty paralyzed him. He'd been imagining her naked body, wanting to see her. Now here she was.

"A long time, Will. Like years. Like when Shelley was still around."

He couldn't hear her. He couldn't move. He could only stare.

"Oh, for Pete's sake." She whirled for the bedroom, yelling over her shoulder, "I hate arguing naked if the other person has their clothes on!"

What. Like this happened a lot? When she came out in a flannel shirt she was buttoning, he tried to explain what he'd figured out. "I really shouldn't drink at all when I'm around you, Bridget, because see? I told you this would happen. I told you sex would ruin everything."

"You never told me that."

"Yes I did."

"No, you didn't."

"Well it's what I've been telling myself." He sat down in the booth and shoved his feet in his boots, accidently knocking off a dried-up plate of dinner scraps. "Crap." He started picking up the smelly, food-plastered shards.

"Forget that!" Bridget ordered.

"All right, whatever, I'm sorry. Jeez. I don't want to be breaking your stuff."

"Goddammit, Will, it's a plate. I'd let you break every dish in the cupboard if it'd keep you here."

"Oh, don't." He smashed his ears to keep out her words. "Don't don't don't."

"What."

"It's not about plates, right? Oh, God, everything's ruined."

"What's ruined? The only thing wrong is you're running away again. Are you even listening to me? Aren't you the one who said good hearing was such an important survival skill? Well, NOW HEAR THIS. I want you to stay with me. *Please* stay with me. You don't have to stay all night. Just for once don't… run away. I'm *not* sorry this happened. I love you, can't you see that? Jesus, I think I've been half in love with you since Kona Village."

"Maybe I just need more time," he said.

"Time!" Her eyes blazed. Her tiny dangle earrings trembled with fury. "Like it's unlimited. Like it's fine to just waste it. News for you: Ed and Julie aren't the only ones who don't have all the time in the world. None of us do."

"Bridget, I'm sorry. Really. God, I hate having you mad at me. Please don't be mad."

"Well, I *am* mad," she said, breathing hard, but slowing it down, like she was trying to get control. "Okay, lemme try again. Between the two of us, I seem to be the one who's clear on what she wants. I want *you.*"

"You don't know that," he said, turning away, finally snagging his jacket off the peg like he should have done several hours ago.

"Oh, yes I do. And I don't have to check out every other guy in the world first. And naturally, being human, it would be nice for me if you wanted me back, right? And guess what? I think you do."

What could he say? Hadn't he pretty well just proved her totally on target with that one?

"So to me, if you won't let yourself love me, whatever your excuses and explanations are, it's just a sad, sorry waste. And it's selfish! Because who are you doing this for if it's not about your own noble picture of yourself you want to have? Is it for Ed? He doesn't care what you do. Is it for Shelley? Because if you're just going to keep that up forever well then yeah, maybe you should just get out of here. Because for sure I can't compete with the memory of a dead woman."

"Hey!" That stung. "I don't need reminding she's dead, okay?"

"No, but you do need reminding you're not."

"See, maybe that's the part you don't get, Bridget. You've never had anybody die on you so you don't know how dead you feel yourself. You're always asking me what I'm afraid of. Think about it. Isn't it pretty obvious? Maybe if you'd been through what I have you'd get how I might be just a little bit reluctant to risk going through it again."

"Oh. Swell. So if I could just promise to stay alive forever, you might consider sticking around?"

"Jeez, Bridge. That's kind of harsh, isn't it?"

"Well, what good's it do you to have everybody acting like it's perfectly fine and normal and mentally healthy for you to just grieve your life away? And anyway, after a point, what makes you think you're so special about this? Every single person who loves another human being risks losing them, right? If you're afraid of loving and losing and you think you're gonna save yourself by avoiding the loving, that's just ridiculous. All you're gonna wind up with is the losing."

"Oh, Bridget. To me, Shelley was just—"

"I know, I know." Bridget started crying. "Shelley was perfect."

"Bridget, I—"

He couldn't stand seeing her cry. He'd almost edged his way out the door but now he could only go back and put his arms around her and let her cry against him for awhile. What a mess.

"Okay," she said after a moment, breaking off with the torrents, backing away, holding up her hands. "If you're having trouble with this, think of it like one of your real estate deals. You know how you write up those offers— it's good for forty-eight hours or whatever, take it or leave it? The offer's not good indefinitely, right? Both sides have to know it's a gamble to stall, because something better might come along for the other party. Well, that's how it is for me, Will. I love you. I do. I've wanted to love you for the longest time. If you even knew…Yeah, I know I'm not Shelley. But she's just not one of your options anymore, is she? So that's my offer. But I've already wasted too much time married to the wrong guy and I'm not willing to waste life away like you apparently are, so don't think you can just…just *brood* about this for a couple of years or something and when you finally smarten up I'll be sitting around waiting like a goddamn faithful puppy!"

Will stared. She really did take his breath away. Here he thought he was comforting her out of a crying jag and turns out she's just taking a break, sobbing on his chest long enough to think of what all she ought to holler at him next.

"So, just like that," he said, "I'm suppose to—?"

"Oh for God's sake, just go, Will. You're right. You're hopeless." She grabbed the front door knob, yanked it open and stood aside. "Just leave. If this is how you're gonna be, honestly, I can't take it."

He stepped out onto the porch and on second thought turned back. Maybe if they could just—

"And don't ever come back!"

The door slammed in his face.

He stood there a moment, catching the flicker of light through a dropped curtain across the street.

Wait a minute. He turned back and stared at the green door.

What was that she said several hollerings ago? Something about ever since Kona Village?

CHAPTER 38

Sad business, Bridget thought, when a solitary trip to check out the new Trader Joe's had to count for a weekend outing.

She picked up a plastic basket, turned to the bouquets by the door and plucked out the brightest bunch. Sensible people probably took theirs on the way out, but she wanted something to hang onto as she walked the aisles. Something cheerful to camouflage her despair. People with flowers looked like they had something pleasant planned, and somebody they were planning it with.

She found the wine in the back corner, but not her usual Elk Cove. No connoisseur, she chose wine by the appeal of the label, and now opted for a pretty ocean scene. Better than the one with the demented goat.

WHAT'S FOR DINNER? A big sign read.

Who knew? Who cared?

Will hadn't called. No need to stock up on groceries for two anymore. He hadn't come around at all since the night it all blew up, and as the rainy days dragged on, it was beginning to seem unlikely he ever would again.

What was this, high school? She felt abandoned. No fair! To let her get a taste of him only to disappear. She'd been in a bad way before; now it was ten times worse. Her knees wanted to do that helpless collapsing thing every time she thought about it. She kept seeing his face, and that soft, surrendering expression, that inexpressible, private sweetness he would never show outside of a bedroom. Looked like love to her. At the time, anyway. Now, with every day that passed, the plaguing doubts engulfed her.

Well, you idiot, she thought, staring at the breakfast cereal offerings. Did you really think showing your banshee side in a big yelling fit was going to be just the ticket for bringing him back real soon? That's what John had always called her when she lost her bottled up temper. A banshee.

And there'd been a hell of a lot bottled up in her where Will Trask was concerned. Always so much she wanted to say but couldn't. So much it flipped him out to hear.

Okay, so other than the screaming, where'd she gone wrong? In stupidly overestimating the power of sex itself? Maybe she'd deluded herself into imagining that she, as The Good Witch, could perform some sort of magic. Lay it all down, heart, body and soul, right there across her big brass bed, and the pure physical force of what she felt for him would break the spell of Shelley. Hit him like a lightning bolt, open his eyes to the truth, that anything but the two of them planning for a future together was just a huge, wheel-spinning waste of time and a futile struggle against the forces of destiny.

Ha! Pretty damned close to the adolescently deranged thinking of a love-struck sixteen-year-old. If Charlotte came to her—not that she would—saying she was plotting to get laid by some kid because then he was sure to stick around, Bridget couldn't have jumped in fast enough with the warning: *Oh, no you don't. Not smart. Not smart at all.*

So why couldn't she have advised herself better? *Back off, play it cool, be hard to get.*

Except, what had playing hard to get gotten her so far? First time around, John Garland, the Alpha male, who seemed incapable of valuing her except when he couldn't have her.

And how were you supposed to play hard to get with a guy you wanted like she wanted Will? A guy so determined to punish himself with holding back and being alone? Maybe he had some kind of post-traumatic-stress-disorder thing going and—wow—hadn't she been a great relief delivery system, shrieking him out the door, telling him never to come back?

Maybe she should just pick up the phone. Might work if she made it a favor begged. *Hey honey, could you come over and throw me across the bed again like you did?*

Right.

Oh, it just made her sick, literally, thinking what they could have had together if he weren't so hopelessly hung up. Life is a gift and he was wasting it. Yes, she no doubt came off like a banshee, but God knows he'd given her months for all those words to fill up her head and coalesce into what she hoped would be a convincing speech. And seriously, she didn't regret a single syllable. If he didn't get it, that was his problem.

But it was still her loss.

Okay, okay. Get with the shopping program here. Sighing, she moved on down the aisle. Oh, nice. Steel cut oatmeal. In such a cute old-fashioned can. She stooped to grab one from the bottom shelf and when she stood, turned and came face to face with her sister-in-law.

"Company for dinner?" Cindy said, sounding tired.

Bridget tossed and caught the oatmeal can. "Only if the Three Bears drop by for porridge."

Ignoring the lame joke, Cindy nodded at the contents of Bridget's basket. "I meant that."

Bridget looked down. Ah, flowers. And wine.

"Nope," she said. "Just for me." What was supposed to make her feel worse, the suggestion she might be orchestrating some intimate little dinner party for two, or this evidence of drinking alone. The self-indulgence of flowers. Cindy probably wouldn't approve of either.

But surprisingly Cindy said, "Well, good for you." And then added, "I guess."

Bridget dropped the defenses that usually went up against her sister-in-law. Cindy looked so worn down. And she was letting her roots grow out. Bridget didn't think she'd ever seen gray in Cindy's hair before.

"Cindy, are you okay?"

"Well, no, I'm not. How could I be?"

Bridget waited, letting Cindy decide for herself whether she wanted to go into confessional mode.

She did.

"The stuff in the paper about the foundation's been bad enough," Cindy started, "and then Dad's just so upset to hear about Ed getting married. Like it's some kind of betrayal. I said 'Dad, why are you making this is all about *you?*'"

Bridget pressed her lips together. Maybe because, in a way, Ed marrying Julie *was* all about Pete.

Ed had called Bridget last week, sounding like a little kid in his eagerness to share his good news. Could you beat that? Julie Pomeroy having been his lost brother's fiancé all those years ago? But clearly he was calling just as much because he appreciated the way Bridget always listened. Man, oh, man, he needed somebody to hear what a can of worms this had opened with Pete. Bridget had murmured sympathetic responses, understanding the emotional complexity of this but not wanting to let on that she was privy to the part Ed still wasn't choosing to reveal, that it had been Pete himself who'd pulled the trigger, Pete who'd had this guilt dogging him his entire life.

"And then I have to deal with my mother," Cindy was going on, oblivious to any clues Bridget's expression might have betrayed. "She's so angry about the wedding date they've picked and—" She stopped abruptly, fishing her vibrating cell phone from her jacket pocket. "Oh. Funny. It's Charlotte."

Bridget blinked. A pang of dismay. "*My* Charlotte?"

"Uh huh."

"She calls you?"

"And texts, too," Cindy said. "All the time."

Bridget stared longingly at Cindy's cell. Charlotte, the baby she carried, bore without drugs, and nursed two full years under difficult circumstances, had not contacted her all the dark rainy winter, not by any of the many methods available to modern teenagers. Nor had she bothered to answer any of Bridget's own attempts to reach out.

"Aren't you going to take it?" Bridget asked, hating the plaintive note in her voice. The requested Christmas meet-up at New Morning Bakery, the last time she'd seen Charlotte, had consisted of forty-five torturous minutes of her daughter resolutely refusing to maintain eye contact.

"I'll call her back in a minute," Cindy said. "We do this all the time." She punched in a delaying text, then noticed Bridget's forlorn expression. "Look, I'm sorry, but maybe you kind of brought this on yourself? I don't think you quite realize what your decision to get a divorce has meant to her. She's definitely been feeling the need for someone she could talk to."

Ouch.

"You know what really disturbed her? Seeing you at the movies with Will Trask."

"What! She was there? At *Avatar*?"

"That's right."

"I never saw her."

"Well, of course not. She didn't want you to. She just was so mortified by the whole thing."

"Oh, for God's sake."

"Didn't surprise me." Cindy's mouth went sideways. "That guy's always been so flirty with you."

"Will?"

"Well, yeah."

Hm. Not the worst thing to hear.

Cindy was squinting at her appraisingly. "Has Charlotte really not talked to you about this? I encouraged her. Told her I thought she ought to let you know how she felt about it. You're sure she never did?"

Really. As if Bridget might think just a bit harder and suddenly recall that yes, of course, Charlotte had been in touch. And while she was remembering, she might conveniently recall that actually, she and Charlotte had a standing lunch date, where they fondly traded the latest news of their lives and sought each other's most intimate insights.

"Sometimes I wonder whether you have any sense of gratitude, Bridget. I don't mean to our family or anything like that. I mean to the universe. You have your own career and you have a daughter. You know how much I wanted a baby? And now you have this poor, mixed up, beautiful girl and you don't even communicate with her."

"Jesus. Is that how it looks? Is that what she's saying, that I won't talk to her?"

"Well, hey there, Cindy." A woman in gym clothes with a cart had paused beside them. "Long time, no see."

Cindy instinctively dropped the angst; Bridget likewise. They were instantly just cheerful women, all chatting and happy to see each other. When this friend looked from Cindy to Bridget like she expected to be introduced, Cindy obliged. *Move along,* Bridget was thinking with a forced smile. *Nothing to see here...*

The minute those yoga pants rounded the aisle end, Bridget picked right back up, but now with a lowered voice. "Look, Cindy, I am *not* one of those people ready to do a big spiel about the resilience of children and how they bounce back from a divorce. Nobody hates it more than me that I didn't give my daughter two parents who love each other and stay together for her. The reason I haven't chased her down on campus to hash all this over is that it's really *hard*. There's so much I can't even say to her. Things I'm just hoping she'll understand somewhere down the road when we can talk about it."

"Oh, but see, there's where you're making a big mistake. You should be talking about it now."

Bridget closed her eyes, shook her head. "Seems like the number one rule of civil divorce is to not bad-mouth the other parent to the child."

"Well, of course, but—"

"You're not supposed to weaponize all the sordid details."

Cindy looked blank.

At first Bridget thought her ex-sister-in-law wasn't familiar with the term *weaponize*. Then she realized. "Oh my God." She looked down at the terra cotta painted cement floor, then up. "Ardis never told you."

"Told me what?"

"The reason I'm leaving him."

"Said you'd decided this wasn't the life you wanted."

"Yeah. Dumb me, trying to be nice and soften the whole thing. Should have figured she'd seize on that for her main talking point. What I told her is that John has had six full-blown affairs that I know of and I can't even count the casual—you know—one night stands."

Cindy's mouth fell open.

"I told her he gave me gonorrhea and I'd already stuck around and given him way too many chances after that to bring home something penicillin couldn't cure. More chances than a woman with any brains or self-respect would. Especially a woman with a daughter watching."

Cindy's poor shocked face segued through a series of emotions and finally settled on something resembling disgust.

"Does my dad know this?"

"More or less. But you know how people can be—sometimes they have trouble hearing things they don't want to hear."

"This is just...I swear..."

And now Bridget was afraid Cindy was going to start crying, right there in the cereal aisle.

"Can you imagine, Bridget, if it had been me who'd pulled this? If I'd been tramping around town and Phil caught me and wanted out? You think they'd have blamed it all on Phil like they're blaming this on you?"

"Probably not."

"They have always favored him, Bridget. Honestly. From day one."

"Yeah, I got that. Long time ago."

"Well, it's not fair!"

"Nope." But where were they supposed to plead their cases? "I'm sorry, Cindy."

"It's not your fault."

"Well, I'm sorry you're stuck with John for a brother."

Cindy sniffed.

"You got a raw deal. You did."

For this poor woman, Bridget suddenly felt an overwhelming sadness. They were both of them facing lonely lives, it seemed, but Cindy's looked worse, locked into her role as a Garland.

No lonely like trapped-in-a-family lonely.

CHAPTER 39

D riving down to the title office, Will was a wreck. Couldn't think about anything but what went down at Bridget's. That finger in the belt buckle thing while she just stared him down. Not a question, more like a warning: no stopping, no turning back and Christ, she didn't want him to. Amazing how he'd known the way back through that hall to the bedroom, like maybe he'd imagined hauling her in there so many times it was no trick at all, even drunk. He kept seeing her bare arms over her head, grabbing the bed's brass bars, the look on her face. And her mouth. Open. Like she was just—hungry for him. He never knew a woman could be that way. And that part where she was on top? And her hair was all falling down on him and it was all kind of lit up from the lights left on in the diningroom. And not a single pretty please required from him in any of this. He kept thinking how she'd looked at him, her eyes all glowy. She was even crying. Not upset but like she was happy, like it just meant so much to her. And when she reached up and—

BLEEEP! Will slammed the brakes. Ohmygod.

The irate teenaged driver who'd nearly T-boned him gave him a look: *You fucking idiot!* Disgustedly waved him through. *If you're gonna run a red light, you better keep running!*

Will cleared the intersection, pulled over, stopped and sat there breathing hard, heart pounding. Way too close. And he'd never had an accident in his life, not even a fender-bender. Not with himself at the wheel. Now he'd just about pulled a GAME OVER.

He probably ought to be arrested and locked up until he got over whatever love/hate spell The Good Witch of Benton County had cast over him.

After a few more deep breaths, he pulled out again. Okay, big deal. So he almost got killed. Why take himself so seriously? The only plans messed up would be those of the sellers of the Hopestill Creek property, waiting in Texas for the word he'd showed up with his cashier's check for the closing.

He parked and went into Willamette Valley Title, nodded as he passed the receptionist he saw all the time, headed on automatic pilot for the desk of the escrow officer.

"It's just me," he said to Tina Barlow. "We can skip all the ceremonial shit."

She pouted, halfway flirty. "You don't want an Willamette Valley Title mug?"

He smiled and rolled his eyes. "Just the papers'll be fine, thanks." He took the rubber band off his wallet, pulled out the cashier's check and tossed it on the table along with his driver's license. Signed the notary book, initialed and signed each page as fast as Tina could push them toward him with those ringed and flashily-fingernailed hands. No need to make it take all day just because it involved more money than a new car.

Inside an hour he was parking at the Hopestill Creek property gate, fishing his can of spray marker from the jumble of stuff behind the seat. The place needed thinning. He was forever explaining it to people, how any woods could be improved with a judicious cut. He'd already alerted Wade Hudson he'd be needing his crew in here for a day or two. Couple of truck loads of good logs. Maybe more.

He parked at the gate and started walking down the timber-lined corridor, admiring again the trees the California girl had wanted to call old-growth. Even if they weren't, technically, they were still impressive.

He held up his spray gun and marked a big L on one of the handsome giants. L for "leave." Although recently he'd heard some young guy from that Trout Mountain bunch call it L for "legacy." Kid just got out of OSU Forestry, so maybe that's what they were calling it these days. Well, legacy was a good word. No problem with that. Main thing was, he didn't want Wade goofing and taking any of these, and for Wade, L would be real clear: Leave this tree alone.

But, damn. When he stepped back to check this first marking, he felt an odd wave of dismay. An ugly swatch of turquoise paint did not improve the looks of this Doug fir. *His* Doug fir. One he intended to let grow just as long as it wanted to. He looked up and down the road. Didn't want any of these cut, actually. But why deface them with this blue junk? Maybe he'd just tell Wade to leave all these and he'd use orange flagging tape on the ones around the meadow he wanted logged.

But when he got down there, a funny thing happened. Damned if he could find a single tree he wanted cut. All too pretty to mess up. Why haul the trucks in here and drag the logs across the daisies, only to barely break even after he settled with Wade, what with the price the mills were paying for logs these days?

The market had spoken. Hey, his *heart* had spoken. Let them all be legacy trees. Leave them alone. He'd move out here and just watch them grow. Be a hermit. Insist on removal from everybody's worry list. Just sit out here on his funky front porch and commune with the critters. Talk to the trees like some idiot hippie. Wasn't it pretty clear he wasn't fit to hang around with people anyway? He always did feel better alone in the woods.

Trouble was, after about five minutes of standing there telling himself this, he saw it for what it was: a load of crap. The alone part, that is. He didn't want to be alone. He wanted to be with Bridget.

He got in his truck, drove back to Corvallis. He should have stopped at his office. An earthquake in Chile had knocked out all their mills down there. A huge hole in the lumber market had opened up and just before this damned thing with Bridget, he'd been planning to feed about two million board feet of his clients' good hemlock into that market. If he was any kind of decent timber manager he'd be sitting in his office right this minute making the calls that would nail down those sales.

But oh no, instead he did what he'd been doing day after day recently, whirling around in this hair-on-fire state. First he'd drive by Bridget's Kings

Road office, check that her green Subaru was parked in the lot. Why? No clue. No plan. Reassured she wasn't at her house, he'd drive over there and park at the curb, pull from his wallet the little picture of her he'd cut from the family portrait. By now the corners were soft with handling and for the first time he thought he could understand why some of these stupid star types made sex tapes somebody'd steal and post on the internet. Because if it wasn't ever going to happen again, he sure wished he had a tape of everything he'd done with Bridget that night. Each thing she said, each look. He was still just stunned. It wasn't like she'd had a bunch of those tarty tricks guys hinted about or anything. She was just…Well, she *liked* it. Liked everything he did. A lot. A woman could be like that? A wife-type woman?

One day when he should have been phoning people about shipping logs to Chile, he'd sat in his office and tried to write her an email saying how sorry he was for the big scene that night. Explain how he'd always have that freak-out dream, but to have it and then wake up in her bed was just…Well, he couldn't help how he acted, that's all, the way it triggered him. Re-reading, though, he hated how whiny he sounded. PTSD happened to guys traumatized by combat. You weren't supposed to fall apart forever over a car accident, right? Three more versions until he judged he had a solid paragraph, only to find he couldn't hit send. Because—think about it—that would just start the torture of waiting, and what if she never answered?

Now he sat in his truck, looking at her yard. The lush lawn was a foot high. Everyone's was, with nothing but rain and never a clear day to get out and fight it back. Would she be mad if he offered to come over and mow it? Was she supposed to be leaving that to the landlady?

He got out of his truck and climbed the wooden steps to her front porch. Somehow he just wanted to stand there at the green door where he'd been the last time he'd seen her. Yep, brought it all back, the last words she'd lashed at him. *And don't ever come back!*

He glanced around, feeling, like Bridget said, that he was on a stage. He knocked, just for show, in case the landlady was watching. But then, when he thought he heard a noise inside, he got scared. What if somehow Bridget was home after all? Then he kicked himself. What a wuss. And crazy, too. Her car wasn't in the driveway. Clearly she wasn't home. Appalling, the way Bridget Garland had completely unhinged him.

"What do you think you're doing here?"

Will startled.

"Seriously," John Garland said, standing there in a blazer, a raincoat over his arm. "What are you doing?"

Will had to laugh. "Honestly? Beats the hell out of me."

"Well I wonder who we should ask then. 'Cause it looks to me like you're stalking my wife."

"Your wife." Will came down the steps.

"Well, she is still. On paper, anyway."

"So what's that paper worth about now?"

"That's what we're waiting for the lawyers to tell us, looks like. In terms of my own plans, I just need to keep in mind it's not officially over. She's done this before, you know."

"She has not," Will said. "She's told me all about it."

"Okay, maybe she hasn't left physically, but emotionally she's pulled this on me dozens of times. She could come crawling back yet."

Will shook his head. "Not happening."

"You're sure."

"Yep. Your *wife* is the most decisive woman I've ever met, and she made up her mind about you a long time ago. You're history, pal."

"No. I will never be just history to her. We have a daughter together. So I might have to be the mature one and leave the door open a little longer, so to speak. I know the family would like to see us get back together."

Ludicrous? Brother. Will smiled. "Not happening. And if you really don't give a rip, why are you lurking around her house?"

"Why are *you?*"

"Well, obviously I *do* give a rip, as it turns out."

"Ah! Well then, in the spirit of male camaraderie, may I give you some advice? I'm sure you think that temper of hers is kind of cute, but up close, every day? Trust me, you would not want to go there."

"Hey, you're the one who made her mad all the time. If I had Bridget, I wouldn't go pulling all that shit. I mean, come on. Anybody ever point out you don't set the bar very high for treating a woman halfway decent?"

"Think what you want," John said. "You really have no idea what a bitch she can be."

"She says what she thinks. I'll give her that."

"Like I said, she's a bitch." John glanced at Will's flexing fists. "Gonna pop me one? Isn't that how you logger boys like to settle things?"

"Well now that you mention it, we do kind of favor decking a guy who talks trash about the women we admire."

"Oh, you admire her. Guess I better watch myself then. You really know how to put the fear in a man."

"Don't worry, I'm a Corvallis guy myself now. We don't punch each other in the street. Unless we're frat boys. Oh, right, that would be you. But you know, I couldn't bring myself to hit even a frat boy if he's all duded up in a suit."

John glanced down as if to reconfirm his attire. "Channel nine wanted me to do a little acceptance speech in front of the courthouse."

"Oh, that's right. Jeez, I forgot. Congrats on fooling enough people to elect you to whatever that is."

"State rep." John shrugged. "But it's just the primaries."

"Whatever. I wouldn't think of messing you up right here in spitting distance of that very courthouse. Also Bridget has a strict policy against getting dramatic where her landlady can catch the whole thing, okay?"

John held up his hands. "Fine, fine. I was just kidding. I know you've worked really hard at…stepping up a rung. Mannerswise, I mean."

What a piece of work.

"So," John said. "Since we're still technically family, I guess I should pass this news to you. As of yesterday, I'm engaged."

"Engaged!"

"That's right."

"Oh, I get it. That's why you came by here, to tell Bridget? Man, that's choice. Presumably your fiancé won't mind you holding out a little longer, hoping Bridget'll come crawling, like you put it?"

"I never said I was hoping. And you know I'd have to think long and hard about whether I'd even be willing to take her back."

"Oh, bullshit, John. She's told me all the stories. You'd take her back in a heartbeat and then get busy dumping on her all over again."

"No, you're wrong there."

"Huh. Well, no use arguing. 'Cause nobody's giving you that chance to decide." Will jingled his keys. "So who's the lucky lady?"

John lifted his chin. "Liza Madison? You must have heard of her. Rather prominent real estate agent. Very successful."

Will's eyes bugged out. "You're shitting me! Liza Madison? You're gonna marry Liza Madison?"

"Your manners really haven't improved that much, have they? Usually offering congratulations is considered preferable to 'You're shitting me.'"

"But, but…Oh, my God!" Will reeled, laughing. "Oh, yeah, I know her." He had to wipe away tears. He held up his hands. "Hey, we gotta stop right here." He pulled his truck keys from his pocket, turned and trotted backwards down Bridget's front walk. "Loved this little chat but I gotta get outta here before I say stuff I might regret."

"What are you talking about? Come back here."

"No, really," Will laughed. "Help me out here, pal. I'm trying to take the high road and be a gentleman."

"I'll have to ask Liza about you," John called after him.

"Yeah, you do that." Will was still laughing. "Seriously, congratulations. Just makes my day, thinking of the two of you together!"

CHAPTER 40

"Morning," Ed called, hunching against the rain, starting around to the pick-up's passenger door to help Spark.

"I can do it." Spark waved his son back to his place behind the steering wheel and, with a bit of a struggle, managed to wrench the door loose and creak it open.

"So, howya doin, Dad?"

"Oh, good enough for an old guy, I guess." Spark thrust his cane behind the seat, grasped the hand hold over the door and tried to get his leg up into the truck. "Damn."

"Okay, hang on there." Ed got back out and came around to help after all.

"Don't get old, Ed," Spark said as he submitted to his son's boost.

Ed clicked from the side of his mouth. "Beats the alternative, right?"

"Oh, sure, sure." Course it irked him to have to let his kids help get him around, but he sure didn't hanker to sit inside at his Stoneybrook apartment or even at the office he still kept at Garland Forests. If he had to swallow a little pride for the chance to get out and check on the trees, well, he guessed that was a worthwhile trade-off. And he'd hate to miss the kids' Tree Planting Day. Seeing them out there always did him good.

Ed switched the windshield wipers to high. "Perfect weather, huh?"

Spark squinted at the rain-blasted glass. "Oh, yeah."

"But really. You been doing okay, Dad? Feeling good?"

"Oh, yeah, sure." Spark always felt his boys didn't quite believe his reassurances. Like maybe they'd expected him to drop dead right after Charlotte and were a little suspicious that he hadn't. Like maybe they thought he didn't miss their mother as much as he should.

Well, of course he missed her. He wondered if they had any idea what the two of them had gone through together. Gone through and kept going.

He sure hoped none of them would ever find their marriages tested with the loss of a child like they had with John. Didn't matter how old, your child never stops being your child. And as Charlotte had always struggled to explain in justifying her endless tears at the time, she wasn't just mourning the loss of her firstborn, it was the loss of his entire future, the children he would have had with that precious Julie Pomeroy. She seemed to make it even harder on herself, Spark thought, nursing her guilt at suspecting she was grieving harder because John, her firstborn, had been her favorite. Surely it was wrong for a mother to have a favorite child, even if it had always been her heart's own secret until she cried it out to him that one dark night.

For himself, it seemed he worked so hard at not appearing to blame Pete for the accident that he never dared spend one moment thinking whether he actually did or not. His solemn priority had always been to protect Charlotte from what would only make it worse, the knowledge of one son pulling the trigger on the other. Maybe, he sometimes thought, he'd told himself the story of the stray bullet so often, he'd years ago left the truth behind and started believing his own fiction.

But they'd survived this and lived a good life, he thought, so of course he missed her. She was like half of him, and you don't climb in bed with somebody for over sixty-five years and not notice when suddenly you're all by yourself. The thing was, though, he didn't want to be dead any sooner than he had to. As long as he didn't feel too bad, he thought he'd kind of prefer to go on being alive, if that didn't bother anybody too much. He wanted to stick around and see how these kids did, watch every tree he'd planted grow just as tall as it could before he checked out.

Not to mention all the business he had to take care of—making sure all the Garland Forests paperwork was in order, the mill and every last section of forest accounted for, ready to be passed down right. Heck of a challenge, trying to make sure these kids and grandkids had the idea how to handle everything when he was gone. It worried him a little, trying to picture Pete and Ed sharing the reins, but he just couldn't begin to think how to divide the business fairly between the two of them. Seemed like whatever he did, Pete would find a way to feel he'd been cut short, getting the punishment he'd been expecting his whole life.

Better to let them fight it out after he was gone, Spark thought, leave him completely out of it. The only personally controlling thing he put in his will was setting aside enough dough to send them all over to Kona Village together. That seemed like a good thing for the family.

He thought Charlotte would agree.

He would never tell the kids this—they'd be putting him on those mental drugs or locking him up in the looney bin—but sometimes what he did was, he'd just talk to Charlotte about all of it. He'd just pretend she was there, in the other easy chair, staring into a log fire with him, even if actually it was just a blank TV screen now. It worked out pretty good as long as he remembered to not look over at the empty chair.

They always chose a close-in site for the kids' tree planting, so it wasn't long before Ed was helping him out of the truck, handing him his cane. The rain had let up on the barren hillside, and kids in colorful jackets were stomping around, dragging shovels and tree bags.

Spark looked up, rocked back in awe. "I can *see* them!"

"Yeah?" Ed didn't sound like he quite understood.

"I mean, the surgery. Well, that's amazing. I can see every single tree top on the ridge, just like I used to."

For years the doctors had been wanting to operate on his cataracts, but he'd always put them off. The idea of them sticking sharp tools in his eyes unnerved him, and what if they botched it? Wouldn't be much help to poor Charlotte blind. He'd surprised everyone, including himself, when, a few months after she passed, he suddenly thought, oh what the heck? Why not let the doctors give it a try?

And now he could see.

"Well, I can't get over that," he repeated. "Guess I should have done it sooner."

Ed waved away the regret. "It's great you did it now. Didn't you always tell us not to look back, to look forward?"

Spark laughed. "Did I say that? Kid, I'm so old now, I couldn't tell you what all I said. Or what I meant to say and didn't." Spark sniffed the air, catching the scent of wood smoke. Somebody had a slash fire going. "The boys torch those piles over on Woods Creek?" He still liked to keep a handle on every bit of Garland Forests business that went on.

"Oh, yeah, that's all wrapped up."

"Good, then."

Ed set up a couple of canvas camp chairs and poured cups of steaming coffee from a thermos. Then, in companionable silence, they watched the junior crews work.

"You know," Spark said after awhile. "I got one gripe."

"Yeah? What's that?"

"Life's too short. Frosts me I won't be around to see these trees get big."

Ed cracked a smile. "Maybe we shoulda gone into strawberries."

"Huh." Spark didn't feel like joking. "And the time goes by too darned fast."

Side by side, they were both looking up at the young planters on the hillside.

Ed cleared his throat. "Well, you've made a good run of it, Dad."

"I think so." Spark cranked his head toward his son. "But you don't have to say it like it's over." He looked back up to the ridge top. "Way I figure, I'm not done 'til I'm done."

Ed nudged his father's shoulder with his own.

"Say," Spark jerked his chin. "Is that Will Trask up there?"

Ed followed his father's gaze. "Yep."

"Hot dog, he's a good guy, isn't he?"

"Oh, yeah, Dad. The best."

"Well, you guys hang onto him, you hear me?"

Because frankly, sometimes Spark worried. It was a tough idea to get across, and he wasn't sure he'd ever actually put it into words to anyone but Charlotte, that time he'd tried to say how glad he was he'd married her. But it seemed like it applied to other things too. Looking back over his years and the points where a decision needed to be made, where you went one way or turned the other, he thought now that if a person wanted to get anywhere, if you wanted to have any fun or make your mark in the short time God gave you on this earth, it sure did help if you could know a good thing when you saw it.

And then have the smarts to latch on for dear life.

CHAPTER 41

D riving out to Kings Valley, Will thought Ed had a lot of nerve asking him to meet for a consult when he hadn't even been in touch about the wedding. Not that Will was still totally out of the loop, planning-wise. The ceremony at Castle Glen was being thrown together with all haste, and Will had been getting his directives from somebody named Beth, Julie Pomeroy's daughter.

The heavy green Garland Forests gate was open when he reached the acreage, so he drove in over the bridge and back and forth up the steep switchback to the top of the ridge. There he found Ed, leaning against his pickup, arms crossed over his chest, looking across at the forty-year-old trees crowning the nearest crest. When Will got out of his truck, Ed came toward him, put out his hand to shake. Which seemed a little formal, Will thought. But they hadn't seen each other in awhile.

"Thanks for coming," Ed said.

"No problem."

"Your opinion always means a lot to me. On the trees and—well, it means a lot."

Will waited. It was Ed who'd called this meeting. His agenda. But when he couldn't seem to get on with it, Will figured he'd better speak up.

"I hear congratulations are in order."

Ed's head snapped toward him. "Oh, so you heard?"

Will laughed. "Well Ed, it *is* pretty much the talk of the town."

"Really? Hm." Ed smiled a little sheepishly. "Well, sorry I didn't manage to let you know myself. You should have heard it from me."

"Yeah, but that's all right." And really, it was. Will had bigger things to stew over now.

"Well, I hope you're okay with the whole thing."

"Me?"

"Well, yeah. I mean, there were a couple of people on this deal where I had a harder time telling, and you were one of them. Wasn't sure how you'd feel about seeing me go falling for somebody else so fast. After you've been so...loyal."

"Loyal." Will snorted. "That's putting a nice spin on it."

"You know what I'm saying."

"Yeah. Okay."

They started along the graveled road toward the four-year plantation Ed wanted to discuss, but when they turned the corner to where the light came flooding in from the west over the young trees, Ed took a seat on the half-log bench they'd placed there. Will took the cue and joined him.

"I don't like to talk in offices," Ed said. "I'd rather be looking out over our trees."

"Same here."

There they sat, taking time to breathe in the fresh forest air. Nothing better. The purple Douglas irises were at their peak, blooming all over the road banks.

"So here's the deal," Ed said finally. "Robin came around and did the put-up-or-shut-up thing on the business of breaking up Garland Forests and getting out of working with Pete."

"Did she."

"Yeah. Laid it right out there. It was her or Pete. My choice. My daughter or my brother. And maybe it wasn't quite cricket of her, but later she came around and tried to sweeten the deal with you."

"*Me?*"

"Yep. Said she thought if you didn't have to deal with Pete and John and Phil, you might be more willing to come on board with us."

Whoa.

"I know you've always wanted to keep a little distance from Garland Forests and do your own thing. Always admired you for it, too. And I know you've never gotten along with John. But if he's out of the picture, think you might reconsider? Robin and I have talked about it. When we re-structure everything, we could really use your expertise. We'd like to cut you in as a full partner."

"Ed! I never thought—"

"You know, with your boys' shares to look out for and all…"

"Well, yeah." Will could hardly take this in. "So what exactly would my position be?"

"Property acquisition. Marketing anything we decide to sell. Consultation. Robin won't be able to manage everything on her own. So just a lot more of the kind of stuff you're already doing for us anyway."

Will shook his head in wonderment at the turn this had taken. "Well, gee, Ed. Okay if I take a little time to think this over?"

"Sure. How about you let me know when I get home from my honeymoon?" Will's father-in-law threw back his head and grinned up at the trees. "My honeymoon!" He shook his head. "Old codger like me. Can you believe it?"

"Uh, codger's not the word the women are throwing around, Ed."

"Oh, yeah?"

"Yeah. Julie Pomeroy's daughter called you a prince."

"Ha! Well, I only got one thing to say to that."

Will waited.

Ed winked. "Hot dog!" He slapped his thighs and stood up. "Oh, and I also do have a little real estate business to discuss with you."

"Real estate?"

Ed nodded. "Your boys said you were making plans to move. And I've got a bride who would just love to get in there and get that flower garden of yours back up to speed."

"Seriously? Nice. I'll leave her the tools."

Ed started down the road. "You're gonna be pleased with the leaders on this four-year-old section."

"Good, huh?"

Ed nodded. "Twelve, eighteen inches. I have to admit I wasn't too keen on your idea of skipping the pre-plant spraying, but I can't argue with the growth rate we're getting."

"Hey, I appreciate your willingness to give it a shot. You know how I feel about that stuff."

And then they walked down to check out the plush and promising fir tips, two men in unspoken agreement that whatever astonishing events unfolded in their personal lives, they meant to hold fast this priority: to keep a close and loving eye on these growing trees.

CHAPTER 42

At the curb by McNary Hall, Charlotte slipped out of the backseat of her father's car, said goodbye to the others, shut the door with less than the slam she felt like giving it. A year ago, upset like this, she'd have walked away without looking back. Now she thought better of it. Apparently she'd have to learn to get along with these people. But when she turned with a well-intentioned goodbye salute, the car was already pulling away.

Nice. So her father was going to marry this Liza Madison. And Charlotte hadn't even known they were dating. Such a special touch, Dad, springing the news in a public place, a restaurant, with Liza and her nine-year-old daughter right there watching her reaction.

And could he have been any more insulting to Charlotte and her mother? Hooking up with somebody the exact opposite of Bridget? Probably Liza Madison's skinny butt that got him noticing and comparing Charlotte's new stress-induced muffin top in the first place.

Well, what did she care? She was nineteen. She was going to have her own life now, right? Except, no getting around it, her new life was apparently going to include a witchy little stepmother and stepsister. ("Ondrea, you pronounce my name, not Andrea.")

In the dorm lobby, she phoned her cousin Gar.

"One question," she said when he answered. "What was the name of the woman you scared away from your dad a couple years back?"

"Uh, Liza Something? A real estate agent."

"Little and skinny?"

"Yep."

"Shit. Just what I was afraid of."

"What."

"Hey, thanks for saving your dad, Gar. Now she's got her claws in mine."

"So?" Brit prompted when Charlotte opened the dorm room door.

Charlotte shrugged, for once completely uninterested in giving her roommate a blow by blow of the brunch with her dad she'd announced upon leaving.

Instead, she experienced a strange and unfamiliar urge: She wanted to talk to her mom. She opened her phone. Bridget had been texting her with more urgency lately, insisting they really did need to talk. Now, suddenly, Charlotte agreed. Who better to commiserate with on the subject of what a total asshole John Garland could be?

Yes, Charlotte had an idea her father hadn't played straight with her mother. She'd overheard enough of their fights to get the gist of it. And then that time she'd actually seen her dad with some other woman. Oh, sure, it was a school function—that thing in Portland where the reps from Yale and other East Coast colleges had come to give their pitches—perfectly legit and he wasn't actually *with* this other Corvallis person. But it had totally creeped Charlotte out, the way he gravitated to her. Not an opening overture. Worse, in a way. From the woman's chummy response, more like something was already going on. And she was somebody else's mother, for God's sake. Charlotte had always done her best to dismiss this and other such episodes. Now, though, in light of the way things had turned out, it was starting to seem pretty clear why her mom finally got fed up.

"But if you know your dad's a cheater," her roommate had said when she confessed this a couple of months ago, "how come you've always blamed your mom about the divorce?"

Good question. So weird, how she sort of needed it to be her mother's fault. If not, it was just too scary. If a woman could be a good wife and mother and her husband still messed around on her, well, what hope was there? Why would you ever want to have anything at all to do with the male sex? Sometimes she wished she could sit down and have a chat on the subject with Chelsea Clinton.

For once Charlotte did not text her mother—she phoned. And loved the immediacy of Bridget answering on the first ring and telling her yes, she was home. She would love it if Charlotte just got on her bike and pedaled right over.

Like a lot of other local kids going to Oregon State, Charlotte had been trying hard to pretend she was away from home, but it was actually just six blocks to her mother's rental, and before she knew it, she was sitting in Bridget's breakfast nook, drinking peppermint tea and pouring out the story of her father's engagement.

Which, Charlotte thought, Bridget was receiving with an air of unnatural calm. Of course she'd already heard about it, but it was more than that. She seemed preoccupied, sitting there snapping a loose piece of wicker on the market basket she had beside her, as if Charlotte were telling her a story about people she didn't even know and not her father, the husband who wasn't even officially an ex and yet was somehow engaged to another woman.

"I thought you'd be more upset," Charlotte said.

Bridget gave it a mini-shrug, as if that's all it was worth to her. "Charlotte," she said, "you know how I've been texting you that we needed to talk? I do have something that I—"

"Okay, okay. So I'm here and we're talking, right? I guess it's good you're not flipping out about Dad, but I am, and the thing is, Mom, I do not, like, want to *live* with them, you know? Course Dad says I can have this suite thing in his new house. You heard about that? This gazillion room house on the golf course he's buying?"

Bridget nodded. She'd heard. And didn't seem too interested in that, either. "Well," she said, "you're probably going to be pretty much on your own now, right? Weren't you hoping to get an apartment for next year anyway?"

"Yeah, I guess."

"And obviously you haven't wanted to take me up on it, but you know you've got a room here."

"Yeah, thanks."

"And even if I move, there'll always be a place for you."

"I know, but I hope you don't feel too insulted I don't want to live with my mother."

"Not at all, honey. A mother hovering over you would totally cramp your style."

Hm. Bridget actually got this. Charlotte had expected a plaintive argument.

"When all this hit with your father," Bridget said, "and it got grim in the winter, I have to admit it crossed my mind to run back home to *my* mom's."

"Really? So why didn't you?"

Bridget laughed. "Well for one thing—and this'll probably shock your socks off—your grandmother has a boyfriend!"

"What!"

"But that was just the immediate reason not to go."

"I don't believe it! Everybody has a boyfriend but me! Even my grandmother! How lame is that?"

"But see, she didn't stumble into this relationship with me living there, did she? A mom and a grown daughter living together might be easy and safe, but safe doesn't really move things forward if you have hopes for any other plans at all. So, here's the deal, I'll always be your mother. I'll always have a room for you if you're desperate. But you've got a life to live."

Wow. Charlotte marveled at her mother's wisdom. The way she was always texting and trying to get in touch, Charlotte had imagined she was just so miserable and lonely, she'd love nothing better than to have Charlotte choose her over her father and come move into that room she'd set aside, be her new best friend.

"You poor thing," Bridget said now. "You've just had so much thrown at you, haven't you?"

Charlotte did feel pretty bad for herself, and she appreciated her mother's sensitivity.

"So that's why this is so hard for me," Bridget said. "What I have to tell you." Her mother's gaze shifted away, then back. "Oh, Charlotte."

"What." At buzz of alarm. That pained look on her mom's face. "Mom, you're scaring me."

"Okay. Well…" Bridget looked her full on. "Honey, I'm pregnant."

Pregnant? Her mother? "Oh, my God."

OMG if there ever was an OMG!

"Wait. Does Dad know?" Her mind was whirling. "You better tell him, Mom, right away, you know, before he goes ahead with this other. 'Cause doesn't this mean you'll have to change your mind about the divorce?"

Her mother's soft gaze was unwavering.

What? Charlotte thought. What part was her mother not understanding?

"Honey," Bridget said, "your dad's not the father."

Charlotte stared. What? But that would mean her mother'd been having sex with somebody besides her father. And then, of course.

"Will."

Her mother nodded, wincing.

"Oh, Mom. So was this an accident or what?" Charlotte shook her head as if she were the mother here and totally exasperated. "I can't believe this, after all your lectures about unplanned pregnancies and condoms and everything."

Still that guilty, cringing expression. "I guess I'm the worst role model ever, aren't I?"

Charlotte looked at the ceiling.

"And it's not like I have any great excuses," her mother said. "I guess I thought I was past the point of being able to get pregnant that easy and then, you know, the way things have been with Will ever since your Aunt Shelley, and with me leaving your dad, well, the two of us weren't exactly people walking around with condoms at the ready, were we?"

"Well, apparently not." Charlotte was quietly congratulating herself that although she had yet to reach this crossroad and demonstrate the ability to make the right and safe decision herself, at least she hadn't blown it yet, either.

"But, Charlotte? I do have this to say for myself. I'm in love with Will. This wasn't just…you know, like I've always said I hoped you'd be in love with whoever your first turned out to be."

"Yeah, yeah."

"And anybody after that, too. I mean, I realize I've totally lost my credibility in terms of handing out advice, but I still stick by what I've always said. Please, sweetie, do not go being somebody's booty call, okay?"

Charlotte couldn't help smiling at her mother's use of this term. "Gotcha, Mom." Wow, it was like her mother had turned into a different person. Fallen off the parental pedestal. Who knew she could be a person who could go crazy with love and forget to think straight? She was not just Mom, she was actually a person having a life. An interesting life.

"So what are you going to do?" Charlotte said. "I mean, have you considered all your options?"

"Well, of course, but I've given it a lot of thought and it's decided. I'm having it."

Charlotte sighed. What a dilemma. But there were things her mother really did need to know.

"Mom, Dad hates Will Trask. Says he stalks you. Like his truck is at your house every weekend."

"Was," Bridget said regretfully. "Not is. And now okay, honey, here's the thing. Nobody knows about this. Well, except Grandma. California Grandma. And really, by rights the first should have been Will."

"Oh, my God. You haven't told him?"

"Hey, I'm scared, okay? Gimme a break."

And now the ramifications of this just kept rolling up like ocean waves, one after another. What would Gar say? He and Charlotte were in the same boat. This baby would be a half sib for each of them. Wait until she told him. But no, she couldn't. It was a secret. So unfair. It was actually all Gar's fault. These clueless parents of theirs probably never would have got together in the first place if he hadn't suggested that movie date.

"Dad's going to have a fit," Charlotte pointed out to her mother in what she thought was a very practical and mature tone of voice.

"That will be so sad," Bridget whispered, the corner of her mouth twitching. Then, from this studiously downcast pose, she looked up, and their eyes locked.

Amused agreement: *Tough.*

"I've actually been more worried about you," Bridget said after a moment. "I feel bad for the way this probably just seems like one more crazy thing for you to deal with."

"It's okay, Mom," Charlotte said, enjoying the opportunity to show she was capable of being magnanimous.

"But you really have to promise not to tell a soul, okay? Not until I get up the nerve to tell Will. He was so freaked out to be the last to hear about Uncle Ed getting married, and me being pregnant, well, he really deserves to be first on this, doesn't he?"

Charlotte nodded.

"And absolutely no Facebook posting!"

"Mo-om!" How insulting. Except, to be honest, it had just that second flashed across her mind what an outrageously attention-grabbing post this would make.

"But even though I guess Will should have heard first," Bridget said, "I'm refusing to feel too guilty that I've gone ahead and confided in a couple of women ahead of him. My mother..." Her voice broke. "And my daughter."

Charlotte bit her lip, then surprised herself by getting up, going around the table and throwing herself down at her mother's lap for a hug. Wasn't this whole thing just amazing, she thought, her head resting on Bridget's thigh. All this drama. All these people in her family with these...relationships. And most of them, Charlotte suddenly saw, had very little to do with her. Her mother, her grandmother, Uncle Ed. They were all just...living their lives, playing out their stories.

And here's what struck Charlotte as a brand new idea: Each clearly saw themselves as the star of their own show.

Well, and really, who's to say they weren't?

CHAPTER 43

Handled *that* pretty well, Bridget thought, sauntering along the riverfront walkway, threading the crowds with her wicker basket, checking out the various Farmers Market stalls.

And it hadn't been easy, trying to couch this amazing news to Charlotte as a cautionary tale—*Viewer discretion advised: kids, don't try this stunt at home*—hoping to model the way a less than perfect adult attempts to calmly, responsibly handle the consequences of her own highly questionable actions.

Had she considered the alternatives, her daughter had asked, so sober, so mature?

Oh, of *course*, dear.

Ha ha, nope! Now she couldn't help smiling. If she'd played it right Charlotte probably still didn't have a clue. Bridget was walking around with Will Trask's baby on board and she was thrilled.

But she would save that story. To gush about it now would hardly seem sensitive, given how her poor daughter was being so thoroughly battered by the doings of the older generation. The story of Bridget's delight would be better told someday when Charlotte was pregnant herself for the first time.

Still, Bridget felt entitled to her private happiness. She knew what she was getting into. She was not a teenager, assuming her own mother would help with the baby and blithely insisting she would not only finish high school, but would probably go on to Princeton as well. No, she'd been down this road before.

She knew a baby would take over her life. She had already cut back on her PT bookings so she could rest. No more pinot gris. Only the best, healthiest food for the body growing the best, healthiest baby. And after the baby came, she planned to sit around and nurse that kid just as long as the two of them wanted.

She'd take the time to thoroughly enjoy the whole thing. She'd make a proper baby quilt. And people were knitting again. She'd get her mother to teach her. And she'd sew that Folkwear pattern she'd bought when she first found out she was pregnant with Charlotte but never had time to make—the Prairie Dress.

Bridget eyed all the beautiful, locally-grown produce. Wasn't it wonderful this stuff was available? Because she had to eat right. She was having a baby. And not just any baby. Hers would surely be the most loved and wanted baby ever to arrive on the planet.

In front of the strawberries (Vitamin C! So red! So sweet-smelling!) her phone buzzed. A text message from Charlotte:

TOLD HIM YET?

She snapped it shut, looked to the sky. Wonderful. This mother/daughter bond renewed just in time to provide a witness to her procrastination. It had only been—what?—two hours since Charlotte herself got the news.

She moved along the walkway, trading folding green for leafy greens, piling the fresh stuff in her basket. At one point she looked up and saw strolling toward her on the walk a woman with a baby bump, knit shirt stretched tight, the new look—tops that clung instead of billowed. Tops that said *Yep, I'm PG. Take a good look.*

She sat on a bench, basket on her knees. She'd probably show faster than she had the first time around. If she didn't tell Will pretty soon, she'd have to go into hiding. Wouldn't that be choice, cut off from the world, her only contact Charlotte's hourly texts: TOLD HIM YET?

Well, of course she was scared. Who wouldn't be? Will was hardly known for taking shocking news well. Who wouldn't want to put off what might be the meltdown of all time?

She'd been lectured by that divorce lawyer of hers so much, she could easily imagine his get-your-ducks-in-a-row advice. *No question of this William Trask being the father? A DNA test would confirm it? Then tell him. He's responsible. Tell him to start setting up the support payments. He's connected with the Garlands? Try for a trust fund too.*

But that didn't feel right.

Oh, Will. She could just see him beating himself up for blowing it with the birth control. How was he supposed to talk to Gar and Cody about condoms now? What sort of example was he setting?

"Hey, Bridget."

She turned and focused.

The mother of one of Charlotte's friends, who cocked her head. "Are you okay?"

"Oh, sure." Bridget stood up and managed some inane chatter before moving on, but she was thinking maybe coming down here hadn't been such a good idea. The whole town seemed to be here. She was bound to run into more people she knew, have to fake her way through more forced conversations that had nothing to do with this amazing secret she could not talk about yet.

What was that whole crowd of soccer moms going to say when she started busting out of her Not Your Daughter's Jeans. *Not your daughter's jeans indeed*, she thought wickedly. Good thing the daughter in this case was behaving herself better than the mom.

And wouldn't everybody be appalled at her willingness to launch in with diapers again? All on her own? In fact, making a mental list of everyone she knew, she could not think of a single person who would be instantly thrilled for her. Nobody who would say, "Wow! That's so great, Bridget! The most amazing thing since the Virgin Mary got the news."

Well, to be fair, that hadn't actually been her very first thought either.

But it had definitely been her second!

And in spite of what anybody else might say, she was as sure about this being a good thing as she was sure English ivy was bad.

Childless women her age tortured themselves through infertility treatments. They agonized over the statistics of sperm banks for the right donor of the semen which would impregnate them. They bought eggs from women in Eastern Europe to be carried by women in India to make a baby to be raised in America. They got on their knees before clueless pregnant girls and begged *Please oh please let me be the mother of your baby and by the way could I buy you a condo?* They flew to Asia and paced in Beijing hotel rooms, humbly, desperately trying to comply with red tape in order to get back on the plane with that precious bundle. Sometimes they even had their hearts crushed when the adopted child to whom they'd lovingly bonded was torn right out of their arms, returned to a highly conflicted biological parent.

But nobody could take this baby away from her. It was hers. And obviously meant to be. What were the odds? Astonishing! But the more she thought about that night—and she thought about it constantly—the more she felt that a power beyond her had been directing everything. She and Will were part of the natural world, and the primitive, animal part of her brain that had known she was ovulating had also fired her up with determination to do something about it. *Look out. Here comes one of your last eggs. Get that guy! Get him in that big brass bed of yours.*

Poor Will. Darling Will. He hadn't stood a chance. And for this he should be sued for a trust fund?

Nations were at war, as usual. Powerful men seemed determined to keep cheating on their wives, announcing the grim news to the women of the world: *You cannot count on men.* In the Gulf of Mexico, every day now oil was hemorrhaging sickeningly into the water, washing onto the helpless shore, poisoning the plants, killing the animals and the fish. It was no trick for anyone who didn't want to bother with a baby to put forth the argument that Planet Earth was not a fit place for even one more. Or to self-righteously suggest that others shouldn't be having them either.

But to Bridget Garland, here in Corvallis, Oregon, things didn't look so bad. The world was green. Literally. Every flower and tree, every bird and animal, everything wanted to live—grow, thrive and reproduce. You could see the evidence all around you. She was just a little part of the big plan, her body already flooded with the powerful maternal hormones that told her if she lost this baby now, she'd be devastated.

Will Trask could get with the program or not; she was the pregnant one.

She was the mother, and she was having this baby.

Now, down the esplanade, she caught sight of Ed Garland buying flowers with a woman who must surely be this Julie Pomeroy.

Tears sprang to Bridget's eyes. Okay, probably hormones but still, the amazing change in Ed. She had always liked that guy. Now she wanted to trot up, meet Julie and gush about their upcoming marriage. But she didn't dare. These were two people who probably *would* be happy for her. People currently deep into believing that life was good and events ultimately unfold exactly as they should. Knowing this, she'd want to blurt out her own good news.

And she couldn't.

Not yet.

Besides, as she watched them, looking so happy in that little bubble of bliss they were so companionably occupying, she felt an awful stab of envy. *I don't begrudge them this,* she wanted to promise any potentially judgmental forces of the universe. It just hurt, that's all, watching somebody enjoying exactly what you wanted but couldn't seem to get.

Julie Pomeroy had managed to render Ed Garland completely smitten only months after the loss of his wife of fifty years. And you could ask anyone, Ed and Alice had one of the town's most enviable marriages.

So why couldn't *she* make that happen?

Why couldn't she be enough to make Will Trask awaken from his everlasting mourning, come back alive and love her?

CHAPTER 44

On Ed's wedding day, Will sat by himself at the end of the second row of white chairs placed on the lawn at Castle Glen. On his own, he would have scooted in at the last minute, minimizing the time he had to be stuffed into a suit, but he'd had to come early, bringing Cody to help Gar set up the equipment for the video Ed and Julie had been promised.

His boys were amazing, he thought, knowing how to do this. He, they'd informed him, would be stuck with the low-tech stuff.

Soap. He was to tag the getaway car.

A pretty little girl in a poofy pink dress approached him shyly from the side and held out a yellow rosebud buttonniere. "I'm supposed to give you this because you're a member of the family, right?"

"Well, I guess I am," Will said, taking it. "Thank you." He started pinning it on. "And let me see. Is your grammie's name Julie?"

The little girl beamed and nodded, then bounced and ran off.

A string quartet played music sounding so familiar, Will thought everybody with more culture could probably name it. He looked down to where Hope-still Creek meandered through the gardens, running out of the foothills on its way to join the Mary's River and then the Willamette. They were lucking out on the weather. It had been cool and overcast all morning, but now the clouds were breaking up.

He turned to watch people arriving, still somehow hoping for a glimpse of Bridget in spite of Ed's warning she wouldn't be coming. She'd been invited, but said she didn't want to risk stirring things up with Pete's side of the family on Ed's big day. Especially with Ardis complaining to anyone who'd listen about the unfortunate selection of the wedding date. So insensitive! Didn't people realize this would have been John and Bridget's twentieth anniversary?

Nope, Will thought when he heard. Nobody knows, Ardis. Nobody cares. Everybody was just thrilled to find a day when Castle Glen was available for a quick, joyful wedding that hadn't been in tedious, complicated planning for a year or two.

Will kept checking the arriving guests. Ah, Kit. Favorite family tree-sitter. She gave him a discreet little smirk. Also arriving were a handful of Ed's trusted Garland Forests employees. The people Will didn't recognize must have been Julie Pomeroy's kids, grandkids and friends.

He was grateful when Robin and Jane came and sat beside him, even though probably they were expected to sit in the front row. Robin was wearing her navy blue dress.

"Breaking out the usual formal wear?" he said.

"Look who's talking."

"Okay, okay." So she had one dress and he had one sport coat.

Robin shook her head. "Are you believing this?"

"Your dad getting married?"

"Yeah."

"Well, no. Can't say I am. But here we are, so I guess it's happening."

"Hey, did he talk to you? About coming on board?"

"Yep."

"We need you, Will. We already count on you for so much of this stuff anyway."

"Yeah, yeah."

"And that swap with the state on the Yaquina Falls property? That's going to be quite the project, doing the valuations on that."

"Really, Robin, you don't have to—"

"Well, I just want to say it, okay? That everybody agrees there's nobody better—"

"Robin, stop."

"But, I—"

"I'm in, okay? Of *course* I'm in."

Her mouth scrunched as if to stifle a happy whoop.

"The more I think about it," Will said, "the more I'm liking the idea of ditching the stuff that makes me crazy now. Go with you guys and I won't ever have to show a house again."

Robin glanced at Jane, who looked like she agreed this was excellent news, then settled back to face forward, content.

"Oh, catch this," Will muttered, as John and Liza made their entrance up the aisle.

Liza had a firm grip around John's upper arm and a defensive tilt to her chin, the little bag hung on her elbow requiring her left hand to be elevated in proper position for flashing her engagement ring featuring a diamond as big as a hazelnut.

"You heard, right?" Will whispered to Robin.

Robin nodded, eyes half closed. "Thank God, Will. Thank God we've got people like them willing to bravely stand up and protect the sanctity of marriage."

Will gave her hand a sympathetic squeeze, the hand with the gold band. Five or six years ago, she and Jane had run down to the courthouse and had a civil ceremony during the brief time Benton County had issued same-sex marriage licenses. Later, the state ruled the licenses invalid. Couldn't make them not act married though. Couldn't make them take off their rings. Will smiled past her at Jane.

John and Liza took their seats in the row ahead, next to the aisle. Liza's daughter, Andrea, followed closely, while Charlotte seemed to be making a point of hanging back, separating herself. The other three were all seated by the time she appeared, necessitating a rising and shifting down the row to vacate the aisle seat for her.

Funny, while John and Liza sat resolutely facing forward, ignoring him, it was Charlotte who now twisted around with a wistful gaze. He glanced away, looked back. What the heck? Bridget's daughter hadn't actually looked at him in years. Couldn't get him out of her dorm room fast enough that day last Fall. And now she was staring him down? Finally, not knowing what to make of the big soulful eyes, he gave her his best generic wink and shifted back uncomfortably into his seat.

The chairs were filled now. Up front, Ed and son Greg, as his Best Man, came out. Good. Will hated every second wearing this suit and he was all for getting this shindig started. Ed looked handsome, happy and a maybe a little dazed. Will wondered if he'd knocked back a stiff one for courage.

"Doesn't he look about twenty years younger than he did last summer?" Robin whispered.

Fresh music started up and Julie's daughter—she of the voice on the phone to Will—walked down the aisle as her mother's Matron of Honor. Now the Bride herself must have appeared in back because everybody was standing up and turning, getting misty at the sight of Julie Pomeroy on her son's arm, all glowy-looking in a long cream-colored dress.

'Til death do us part.

When people are young, Will thought, they say that at weddings and nobody pays any attention. Death's way out there in the future. Or at least that's the assumption. But Jesus, when the minister mentions death while the couple is in their mid-seventies, you can't help choking up. And the part about sticking together in sickness and in health? Damn. These two people better not die. Either of them. Not for a long time anyway.

However they used all this death-do-us-part stuff, though, however they worked it into the words they said to each other, nobody ever made promises *beyond* death. Nobody ever said *I'll be faithful to you until you die and then I'll mope over you the rest of my own life.*

Look at these two brave people up there, holding each other's hands, publicly stating what it seems everybody agrees, that it doesn't have to be over until it's over.

Will patted his breast pocket. No way he'd have thought to tuck in the handkerchief he suddenly needed. But what was that? He pulled out folded papers. Oh. Doug's funeral program. With the poem. Guess that was the last time he'd worn this jacket.

I tended my orchards,

Logged the hills and roamed the woods....

Nope. No reading that now. Today was about the future.

Now a woman to the side started singing, and people who had recovered from getting teary over the vows were struggling again for composure.

We are gathered here together

On this lovely summer's day

To celebrate your union

And send you on your way...

Less than a year ago, Will had pitied Ed because no one needed him. He'd figured that was it for the old guy. End of Story. Nobody ever *would* need him. Game Over. But now somebody loved him. He had a woman looking up at him. That's all it took. One person.

Surely there'll be trials along the way
And no one can be spared their share of pain
But though there will be hard times
We take delight in sunshine
Only when we've come to know
The lonely sound of rain...

Will thought about his own wedding. How young and clueless he and Shelley had been, no idea at all how their story would go. Well, whoever does? The whole thing was just a big crap shoot, really. Just going, well hey, whatever happens, how about we try going through it together?

And the one that you have chosen
Is generous and kind
Knows the wisdom of forgiveness
And the healing power of time
May they comfort and protect you
Give you shelter from the cold
And bring you all the joy your hearts can hold

Eyes down, Will saw Robin take Jane's hand. The entire audience shifted, in fact, with people reaching for each other. People who had somebody, that is.

The minister said he would read from Robert Browning, a poem that had special significance for the family.

"Grow old along with me, the best is yet to be."

Will leaned forward. The sundial.

"The last of life, for which the first was made.

Our times are in His hand who saith,

A whole I planned, youth shows but half;

Trust God: See all, nor be afraid."

Will sat stunned. How did this guy know? The guy who read it now, the guy who wrote it a long time ago. Wrote about being afraid.

Bridget. What *was* he afraid of? He could love her. Hell, he *did* love her. What else did you call it if you thought about somebody every minute. If you kept wishing it was your place to go over and check on her. Wanted to stick up for her against anybody who dissed her, punch out a guy who treated her like shit. And what if that person made you feel like it was okay to be alive and even happy again? And if you imagined something bad happening to that person, you just couldn't stand it? Didn't that mean you loved her? Didn't that mean you ought to man up, go over there, lay it on the line and try to make something good happen? And if you wimped out, too scared to take your chances, you'd be kicking yourself forever after for the dumb ass you were?

Bridget was right. Right about everything. Why play dead when he could be acting alive, doing the comfort and protect thing?

He looked up. The sky was completely clear now. Perfect real estate weather. His little patch of Eden up at Hopestill Creek would look gorgeous this afternoon, daisies waving in the breeze, sun shining on the meadow, backlighting the purple vetch, the blooming pink wood roses.

Bridget would love it. Hey, he could get out his witching sticks and start figuring out where the well should be. She'd get a kick out of that. He could sell her on building her house there. Their house. Maybe she'd even marry him. That's really what he wanted, wasn't it? At the next family wedding, to not be sitting there alone?

Maybe even *be* the next family wedding?

But get a grip. Don't be an idiot. It was enough, just trying to get up the nerve to ask for a fresh start with her. Hey, he'd plead if he had to. But go charging over there with some cockamamie ten-year-plan and he might piss her off worse than ever. She might still be hopping mad at him. So just calm down, he told himself. Just start with the property, just take her up there and see what she thinks of the place.

Showing a forest property—that was something he knew how to do.

Will stood drinking a glass of wine at the reception, lifting a toast for posterity as Gar aimed the video camera his way:

To Ed and Julie.

To the future.

When he watched this years later, he'd remember. This would mark the day he finally figured it out.

He glanced at his watch. He'd already put in a half hour doing the meet and greet. How long did you need to stick around to be polite? Was it too early to do the car soaping thing?

As he hesitated, Liza Madison minced up to him with a cold smile, flashing that ring in his face, looking back at John, who was a reluctant step or two behind her.

"I've already given him the good news," John mumbled, catching up.

Will grinned. "Yeah."

John shifted his weight. "Well, of course this will be just as soon as the... you know..." And here he looked at the lawn beneath his feet. "As soon as the divorce..."

Will winced theatrically, transferring his wine to his left hand. He held up his right palm, cutting John off with an insistent little wave. No need to go spoiling such a beautiful day with a lot of unpleasant legal talk.

"Seriously." He stuck out his hand to shake. "Congratulations, man. I mean it. Seeing how everything's turning out, I'm grateful to you." He had no animosity for anyone in this tender moment. Not even John and Liza. His affection extended to the whole world.

The newly-engaged power couple glanced at each other uncertainly.

Is he drunk? Liza mouthed to John.

"No way!" Will blurted. "See, if I were drunk, I wouldn't have noticed you saying that." He took another sip. "It's just that…Will you two lovebirds excuse me?" He looked past them, smiling on everyone milling around, on the universe in general. "I guess I'm just a softie, 'cause somehow all this—this beautiful ceremony—has made me realize I have something very important I need to go do." He lifted his nearly empty glass in another toast. "John? Liza? To *now.*

"To right now."

And passing Ed's car, he took out his soap sliver and scrawled, in letters as big as the back window would hold, this one word:

THANKS!

Bridget's car was there, but she didn't come to the front door, so Will walked up the driveway, ducked under the laundry line, and found her in one of the Adirondack chairs on the back porch, wrapped in a shawl.

Doing nothing.

Dozing, even. Strange. Not very Bridget-like. Beneath the flickering, leafy shadows he approached with the footfall of a man who knows how to silently tread the forest floor. Glancing around, he searched for the evidence of a tool, a book, something. Okay, on the small table beside her she had some knitting stuff—needles and a ball of yellow yarn.

She was sleeping with her head resting to the side, wisps of brown hair curling around her pink cheeks, buttons of a ruffled collar open, exposing her throat. Her parted lips made his breath catch. She looked so…vulnerable. For a moment he just watched her, one foot on the bottom step, a hand on the railing, mystified by the sudden instinct toward protectiveness stirring in him. Because, hey, this was a new one for him. This feeling. At least with her. Hadn't Bridget Garland always seemed like a woman who could totally take care of herself?

She looked so beautiful.

Wait. Was this where he was supposed to go kiss her awake? He took a breath. He was feeling determined, yes, but not quite brave enough for that.

Instead, he called softly, "Hey, Bridget."

She blinked awake, lifted her head.

"Hi." He smiled. "You okay?"

She took a deep sighing breath, waking up. Then she rustled upright, those gray eyes of hers widening at the sight of him.

Even though all the way here he'd practiced his opening pitch about the drive up to see the Hopestill Creek property, he now found he'd completely forgotten it.

"So what are you up to?" was all he could manage. Pretty much the same damn thing he said to her every other time he'd shown up these past months.

"Just sitting here." She looked down at her hands, which for once did not look dirty or encrusted with flour. No fingertips stained with paint. "Is that okay?"

She sounded cranky. Well, he *had* waked her up. But more likely, he figured, it was because she was still mad at him.

"Well, of course it's okay," he said, being so careful. He was determined not to blow things with her one more time. "Just that…I don't think I've ever seen you doing nothing, you know? You always have a project going."

"Ah." She flushed. "Well, actually, I *do*. Have a project going. A major project."

"Yeah?" He waited for her to throw off the shawl and lead him to a crate of hatched chicks, or something simmering on the stove. Maybe another room she'd decided to paint. But she looked too clean for any of that. And whatever she was trying to do with the yellow yarn, she hadn't gotten far enough to call the project major. He squinted. "What's that you're wearing, anyway?" Some kind of long pioneer thing, it looked like—tiny tan daisies all over it.

She pulled up her bare feet onto the chair, tucking the hem over her toes. "You've seen dresses before, right?"

"Ha! Not very often on you!" When she refused to join the joke, he took a breath, dropped back from the step and thumbed behind him in the direction of Castle Glen. "I was just at the wedding."

She nodded, her mouth going to one side. "The jacket and boutonniere did kind of clue me in."

"Oh." He frowned down at the yellow rosebud pinned to his lapel. "They made us wear these." He pulled out the pin, releasing the rose, handing it up the two steps to her. "Here. You have it."

She held it to her nose. "I knew today was the day." She tried to tuck the yellow bud into the knot of hair spilling out at the nape of her neck but, oddly, her hand seemed to be trembling. She gave up and tossed the boutonniere on the table.

"It was a nice wedding," he offered, sinking in the awkwardness of this. Then he brightened. "You probably wanna hear all the details."

She eyed him coolly. "Not really."

Sinking further. Brother. Could she make this any harder? Maybe he wasn't going to get anywhere at all with this little woods excursion plan of his. Maybe all that sentimental stuff at the wedding faked him out, got him feeling all mushy and made him forget that basically he was showing up at the house of a woman who was still mad as hell and hadn't the slightest use in the world for him. It didn't help that his wedding wine had worn off.

He sighed and jerked his chin toward the porch. "Mind if I join you?" It came out forlorn and sarcastic at the same time.

She waved at the vacant side of the porch, like what did she care.

He clomped up the steps and dragged the other chair close to hers. Placing it at an angle, he sat down and leaned forward, elbows on his knees.

"Guess you're still mad at me," he ventured.

No answer.

"Not going to say anything at all?"

"Well, Will!" She gripped the chair arms, dropped her feet to the porch boards and glared. "What am I supposed to think here? You haven't come around once since…you know." She sank back and curled into herself, wounded. "And now you show up all chipper, want to act like nothing happened?"

He took a big breath, closed his eyes. "I'm sorry, Bridge."

"Huh."

"Last time I saw you, you were yelling me out the door."

She bit her lip, looked up at him. "Oh, Will."

"You said, 'Don't ever come back.' No's suppose to mean no, right? And I'm sorry to say it, but did anybody ever tell you you can be kind of scary?"

"Oh, I know." She said this with great regret, as if no one wished more than she this weren't the case.

"Anyway, I just wondered if you wanted to go with me to take a look at that piece of property up on Hopestill Creek."

Her eyes flickered with what he took to be interest.

"Actually," he said, "I already bought it."

What—? Was she getting ready to cry?

"Will, I have to tell you something."

"Yeah?" He braced himself. "Okay."

"I know you hate it when people…when women…aren't direct, so I'll just say it. I don't know how you're going to feel about this, but I've thought about it a lot and I've made up my mind." She took a big breath and looked at him. "I'm going to be having your baby."

What? He was confused, flashing on a story she'd told him about somebody who'd lost her adopted baby, said how if she wanted a baby she'd steer clear of all that and head straight for the nearest sperm bank. She never told him she *did* want a baby, though. Now she wanted him to be the donor? Probably he ought to be flattered, but wouldn't that be a little weird for both of them?

"Gee," he said. "I guess I could help you out with that, but wouldn't an anonymous donor be better?"

She blinked, then startled him by laughing. "Maybe I'm still not being direct enough."

"Uh, apparently not."

"Okay, how's this? I'm pregnant. You're the father."

Will's heart stopped. She was looking at him, steady and direct. Not a joke. More like a dare. *Go ahead, believe it or not, this is for real.* His eyes dropped to where she'd carry a baby—if there was one. Nothing looked so different.

"I don't—I mean, how could— ?" She was telling him a baby was already started? His baby?

She had her arms wrapped over the baby place, looking down. She squinted over at him. "Your father didn't forget to give you the talk, did he?"

He just kept staring, stunned.

Her voice went husky. "And you haven't forgotten that night?"

Jesus. Now he had to look away, face on fire.

"Still," he said, "just that one time? I mean, even if it *was*—"

"Um, yeah." Now she was nodding and shaking her head at the same time, laughing and crying too. "Yeah. It was."

And for the briefest instant the memory united them.

Then it hit him. "Oh, man! How'm I gonna tell the boys?"

She burst into tears. "I knew you'd say that! I knew it, I knew it."

"Oh come on, now, don't cry." He leaned over and grabbed her hands. "You know I can't stand that. And I don't know what I'm supposed to be saying here. Gimme a break, Bridge, I'm in shock, okay? Doesn't a guy get a minute at least to...to...Well, I mean, you're sure about this? This isn't one of those *maybe* things where you haven't had the test or whatever?"

And in the infinitesimal fraction of time his question floated there between them, the time before she could even answer, he realized: "Maybe" would be a letdown. He was wanting her to say yes.

"It's for sure," she nodded, sniffling. "And...Oh, I just hope you're not too... Well, is it okay?"

"*Okay?* Bridget. Oh, my God. Come'ere." He pulled her over onto his lap and put his arms around her. Jesus. Hell of a thing. But hell of a *good* thing. Now he laughed out loud. It was crazy! Like he'd spun the arrow on a child's board game and it stopped on a future he hadn't even imagined could be part of the game: HAVE ANOTHER KID. Now they would start drawing from a whole new batch of "chance" cards. But what the hell? They'd be lucky. Look how lucky they'd already been. One time? Go figure.

He tightened his arms around her as she nestled close. She was so warm. So alive. So full of more life to come.

After a moment she lifted her head from his chest and looked solemnly into his eyes. "I'm not trying to make you marry me."

He laughed. He loved the way she always made him laugh. "Fair enough," he said. "But can I if I want to?"

Her face crumpled happily as she nodded and dropped her cheek back against his chest. And then her muffled voice rose up to him.

"Except I can't believe I just said I'd marry another guy in a suit."

"It's temporary! And I'm hating it, okay?"

"Okay."

"So I don't seem to have a diamond ring on me. But Ed slipped me this." He eased her off, got up and from his pocket fished the Bride's lacy garter, dangling it from his finger. "Doesn't this mean I'm supposed to be next or something?"

She grinned. "That'll work." She gathered up the hem of her dress, extended her leg, toe pointed.

Somebody needed him, he thought, kneeling and doing the honors, sliding the garter up over her calf. Two new people needed him. Gently replacing her skirt, he gathered her up again into the chair and put his face in her hair. Gratefully, he inhaled her sweetness. Don't look now, but wasn't this what he figured he'd never have again? A golden moment?

"Did you know this would have been our twentieth anniversary?" Bridget said. "John's and mine?"

"Yeah, Ardis seemed to think people ought to hear about that."

"Well, hey, I told you I'd be doing something better with myself by this time!"

They laughed as he rocked her.

I should be telling her something, he thought after awhile, but what? He wasn't one of those guys with the words. He doubted he could be convincing in promising stuff like, oh, she didn't have to worry, he'd always be there for her and all that. Guess he'd just have to stick around and prove it.

"Tell you what, Bridget," he finally said, "nobody's ever gonna say I don't know enough to close on a good deal when it comes my way."

That seemed to set her off crying again, but she waved to signal he didn't have to bother trying to stop her. This was just a last, happy burst, and before long, she was rubbing her cheeks dry, more like her old self, eager to talk, probably wanting to tell him out loud everything she'd been saying to him in her head since she realized exactly what was going to be coming at them.

"Will?"

"Yeah?"

"I'm really excited." Her red-rimmed eyes glowed, fixed on his. "I just know this is going to be a most excellent baby."

"Well, of course."

"Because it's your baby. And I've been thinking…It's kind of like starting a brand new family tree, isn't it? Also, trust me, I totally know how to do this."

He tightened his arms around her. Damn. This *was* a good thing. He'd be a fool not to hang onto it.

Hang on for dear life.

ACKNOWLEDGMENTS

THANKS–

For thoughtful critiques of various drafts: Rick Borsten, Molly Gloss, Theresa Nelson, Pam Smith Hill, Eleanor Bissell, Lynne Martin, Sally Brinker, Margaret Anderson, Nancy Ashby, Tim Verkler, Kathy Burke, Mary Crew, and Miles Crew.

For background and insights on hunting, fishing, forest management and water witching: David Brinker.

For educating me concerning Oregon divorce law: Tom Elliott.

For sharing stories of real estate, family, and for "just trying to make a difference": Clare Staton.

For continuing education on forest management in the form of tours and symposiums: Starker Forests.

For the sharing of their beautiful timberlands and lake: Thompson Timber. And to Gene Thompson, my uncle's long-time buddy, special thanks for the model train set up at Citizens Bank each Christmas.

For all the good they do, the Greenbelt Land Trust.

For continued loving support: Will Crew.

For permission to use the lyrics of his beloved wedding song: our local treasure, Neal Gladstone. We've been so lucky to have you in our small pond.

For the inspiration of their lives as timberland owners leaving philanthropic legacies:

T. J. Starker, Rex Clemmons, Charlie Ross, and Ralph Hull. I'm not sure all of them drove dirty trucks, but some of them did. We remember Charlie Ross in our fields at Wake Robin Farm, picking tomatoes in his high rubber roots, and Ralph Hull stopping by the fruit stand to buy raspberries for his millworkers at Hull-Oakes Lumber.

Special thanks to Madeline Rubin, for planting in my temporarily compromised brain the idea that I might once again be well enough to write, and showing faith that I would do so. To her I am forever grateful.

For information on the treatment of neuromuscular dysfunction as the basis of joint disorders and the inspiration of her practice, the memory of Margaret Bartlett PT. (1955-2019)

For Larry and Cathy Passmore (1948-2020) We go back years, and from the beginning I've followed with admiration their ambitious building and remodeling projects and been inspired by their rare ability to always assume the best of their fellow human beings. For specific help with this book, I owe them thanks for a lovely tour of the Owl's Nest.

To my mother, Marolyn Schumacher Welch Tarrant (1927-2020), my gratitude for a lifetime of freely shared confidences and stories, our own family's and everyone else's too. Her joke was that if she'd known I was going to remember her every word so accurately, she'd have been more careful with what she said. No problem. I got it all, the good and the bad, and only now that she's gone am I realizing how much of what I know of life in Corvallis had been coming from her. I miss the gossip.

And as always, unending thanks to my husband, Herb, my loving, faithful partner in facing together whatever comes our way.

ALSO BY LINDA CREW

CHILDREN OF THE RIVER

SOMEDAY I'LL LAUGH ABOUT THIS

NEKOMAH CREEK

NEKOMAK CREEK CHRISTMAS

ORDINARY MIRACLES

FIRE ON THE WIND

LONG TIME PASSING

BRIDES OF EDEN: A TRUE STORY IMAGINED

A HEART FOR ANY FATE: WESTWARD TO OREGON, 1845

ACCIDENTAL ADDICT: A TRUE STORY OF PAIN AND HEALING

WEDDING IN YANGSHUO: A MEMOIR OF LOVE, LANGUAGE,
AND THE JOURNEY OF A LIFETIME TO THE HEART OF CHINA